morningglories
volumeseven
honors

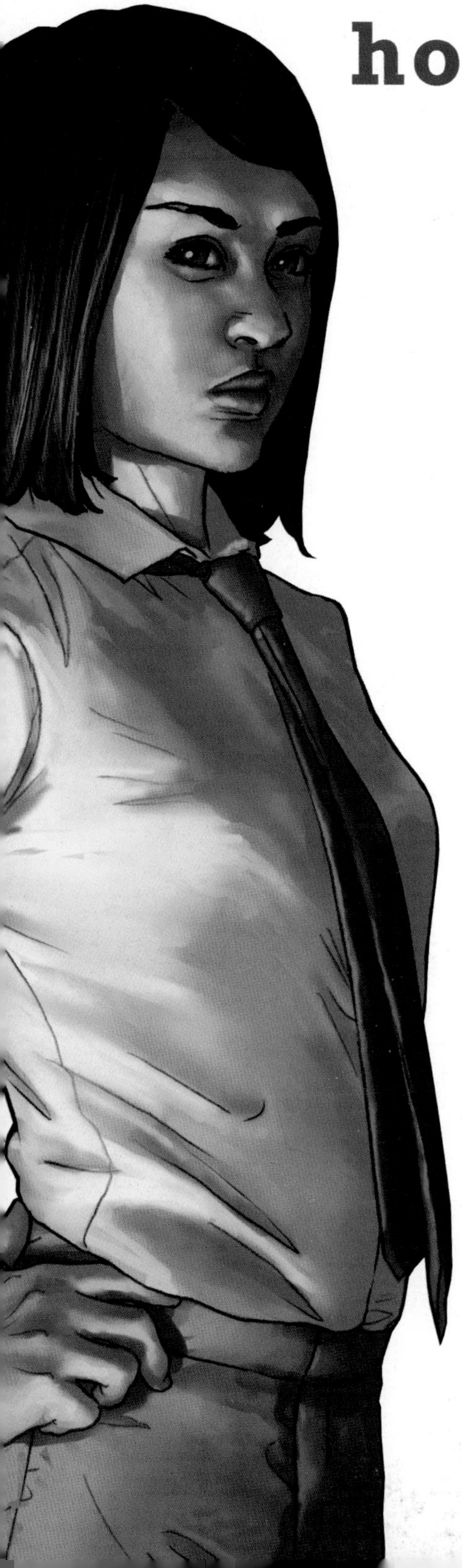

WORDS
NICK SPENCER

ART
JOE EISMA

RODIN ESQUEJO
COVERS

PAUL LITTLE
COLORS

JOHNNY LOWE - TIM DANIEL
LETTERS   DESIGN

IMAGE COMICS, INC.
Robert Kirkman – Chief Operating Officer
Erik Larsen – Chief Financial Officer
Todd McFarlane – President
Marc Silvestri – Chief Executive Officer
Jim Valentino – Vice-President

Eric Stephenson – Publisher
Ron Richards – Director of Business Development
Jennifer de Guzman – Director of Trade Book Sales
Kat Salazar – Director of PR & Marketing
Jeremy Sullivan – Director of Digital Sales
Emilio Bautista – Sales Assistant
Branwyn Bigglestone – Senior Accounts Manager
Emily Miller – Accounts Manager
Jessica Ambriz – Administrative Assistant
Tyler Shainline – Events Coordinator
David Brothers – Content Manager
Jonathan Chan – Production Manager
Drew Gill – Art Director
Meredith Wallace – Print Manager
Monica Garcia – Senior Production Artist
Jenna Savage – Production Artist
Addison Duke – Production Artist
Tricia Ramos – Production Assistant
IMAGECOMICS.COM

thirty**five**

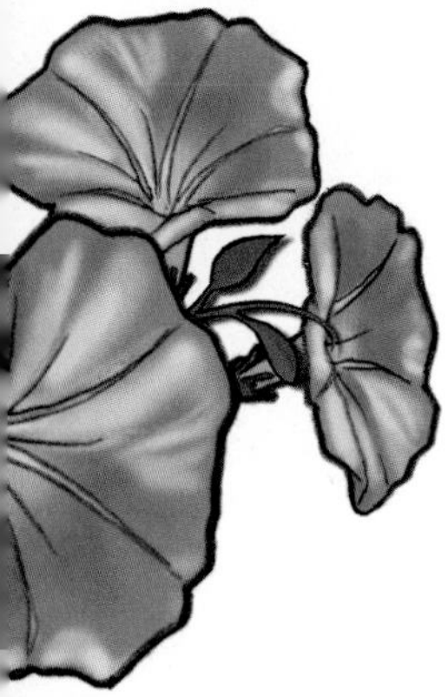

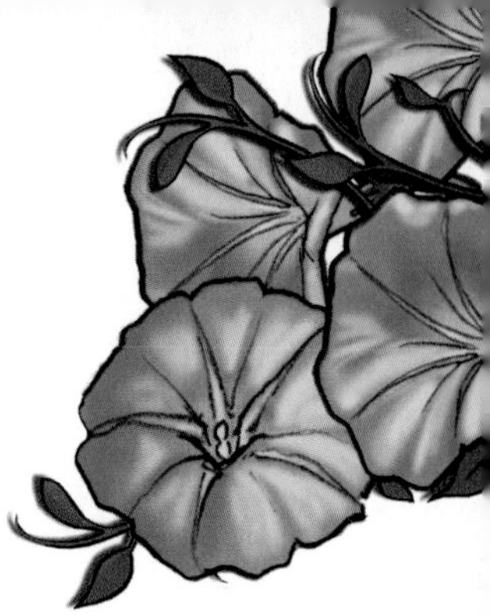

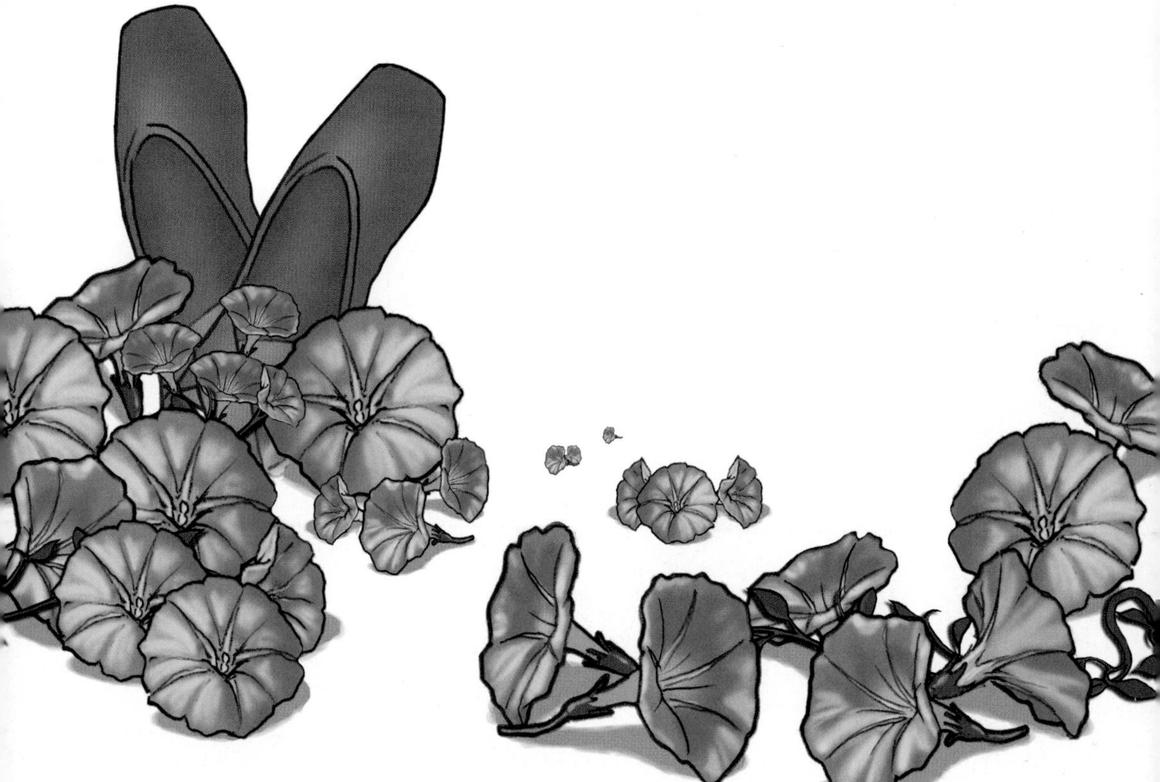

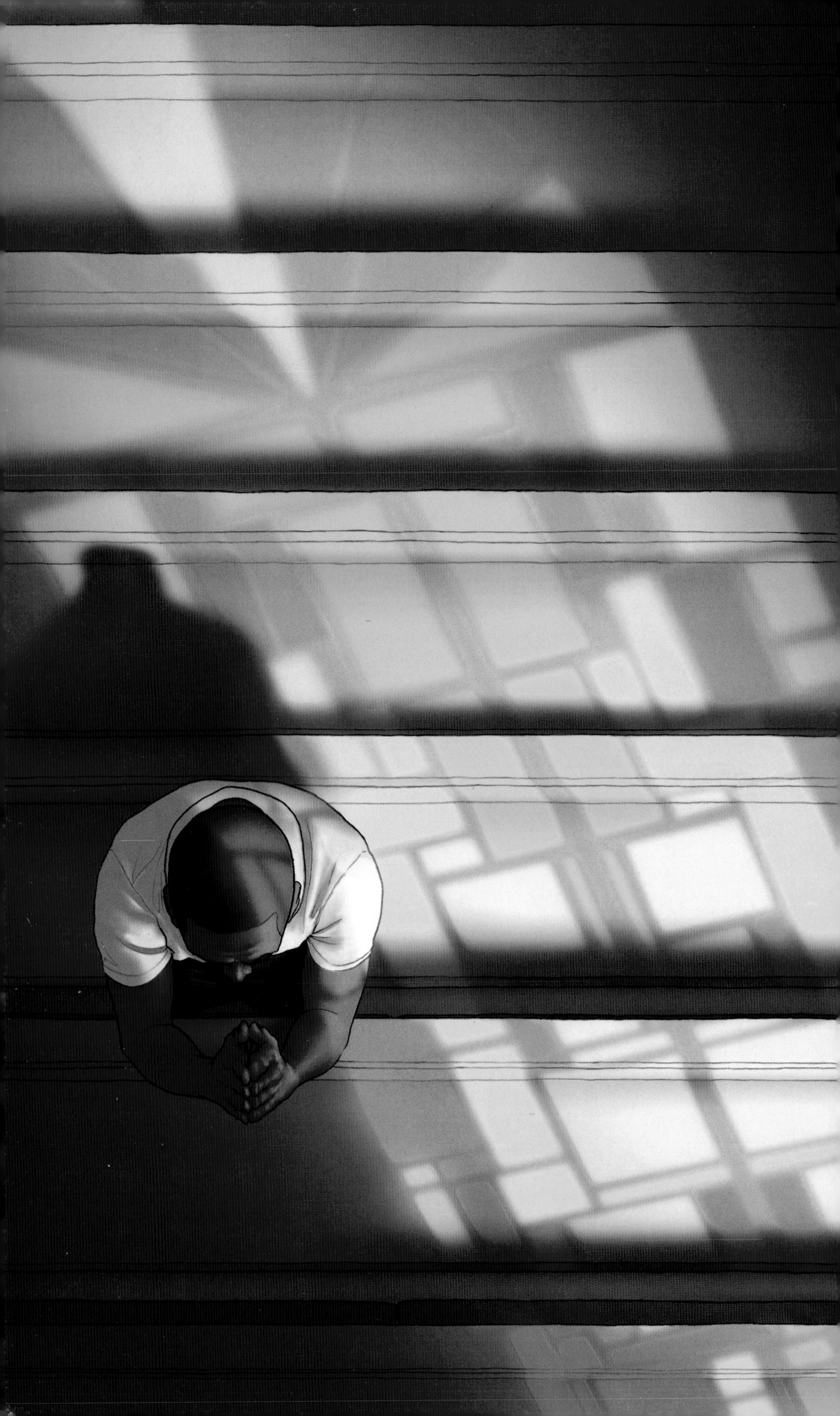

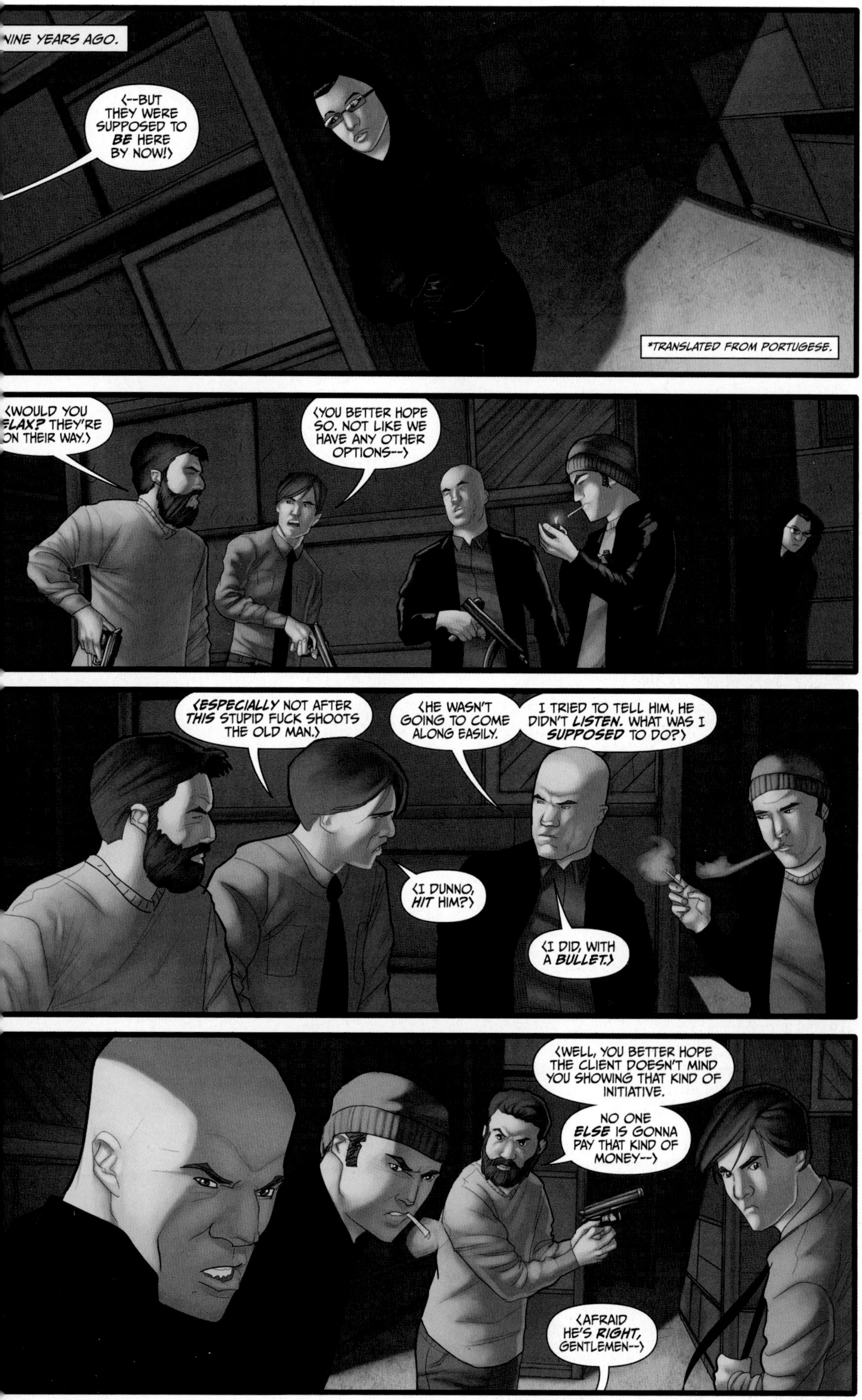
NINE YEARS AGO.
<--BUT THEY WERE SUPPOSED TO BE HERE BY NOW!>
*TRANSLATED FROM PORTUGESE.
<WOULD YOU RELAX? THEY'RE ON THEIR WAY.>
<YOU BETTER HOPE SO. NOT LIKE WE HAVE ANY OTHER OPTIONS-->
<ESPECIALLY NOT AFTER THIS STUPID FUCK SHOOTS THE OLD MAN.>
<HE WASN'T GOING TO COME ALONG EASILY.
I TRIED TO TELL HIM, HE DIDN'T LISTEN. WHAT WAS I SUPPOSED TO DO?>
<I DUNNO, HIT HIM?>
<I DID, WITH A BULLET.>
<WELL, YOU BETTER HOPE THE CLIENT DOESN'T MIND YOU SHOWING THAT KIND OF INITIATIVE.
NO ONE ELSE IS GONNA PAY THAT KIND OF MONEY-->
<AFRAID HE'S RIGHT, GENTLEMEN-->

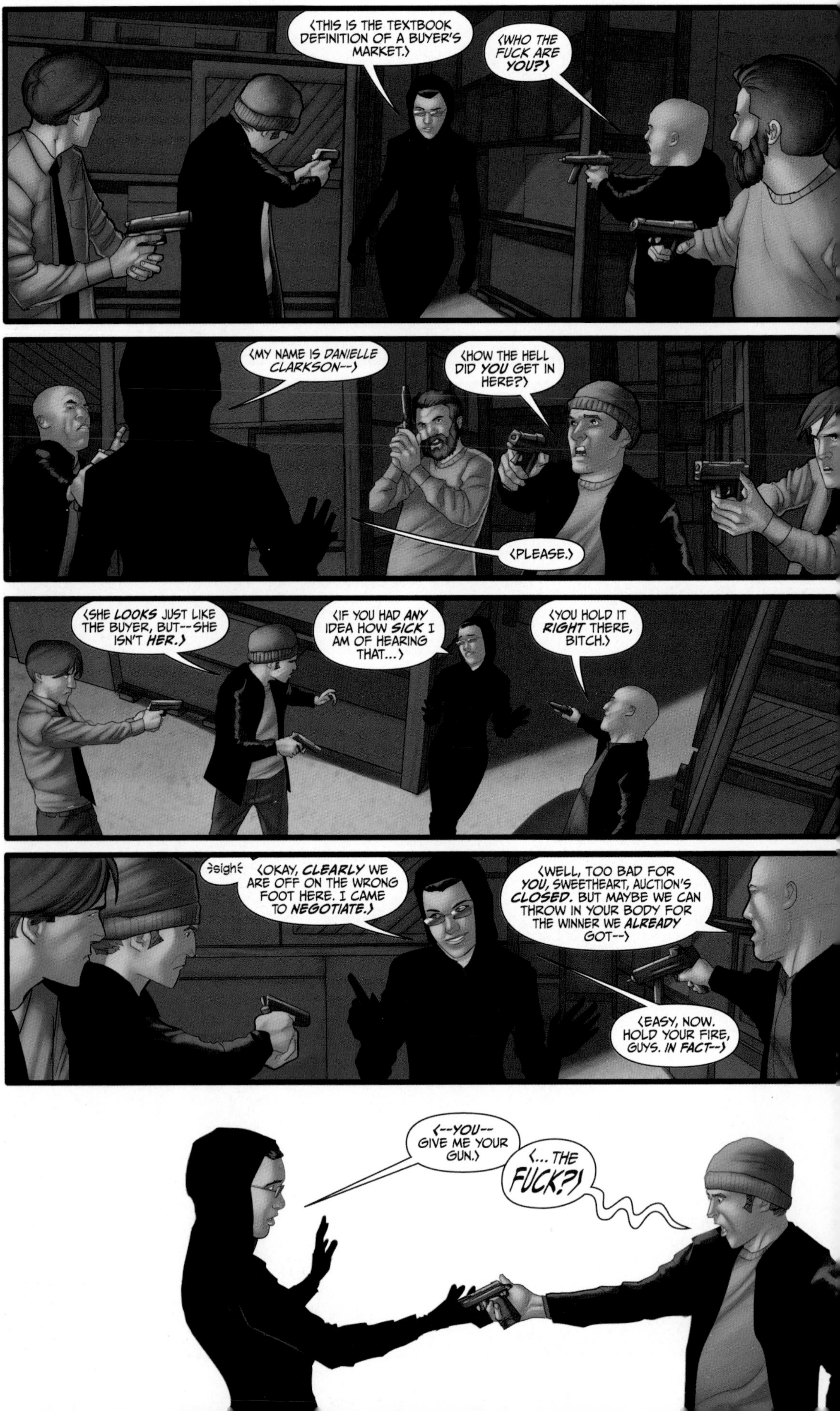

⟨THIS IS THE TEXTBOOK DEFINITION OF A BUYER'S MARKET.⟩
⟨WHO THE FUCK ARE YOU?⟩
⟨MY NAME IS DANIELLE CLARKSON--⟩
⟨HOW THE HELL DID YOU GET IN HERE?⟩
⟨PLEASE.⟩
⟨SHE LOOKS JUST LIKE THE BUYER, BUT--SHE ISN'T HER.⟩
⟨IF YOU HAD ANY IDEA HOW SICK I AM OF HEARING THAT...⟩
⟨YOU HOLD IT RIGHT THERE, BITCH.⟩
sigh
⟨OKAY, CLEARLY WE ARE OFF ON THE WRONG FOOT HERE. I CAME TO NEGOTIATE.⟩
⟨WELL, TOO BAD FOR YOU, SWEETHEART, AUCTION'S CLOSED. BUT MAYBE WE CAN THROW IN YOUR BODY FOR THE WINNER WE ALREADY GOT--⟩
⟨EASY, NOW. HOLD YOUR FIRE, GUYS. IN FACT--⟩
⟨--YOU-- GIVE ME YOUR GUN.⟩
⟨...THE FUCK?!⟩

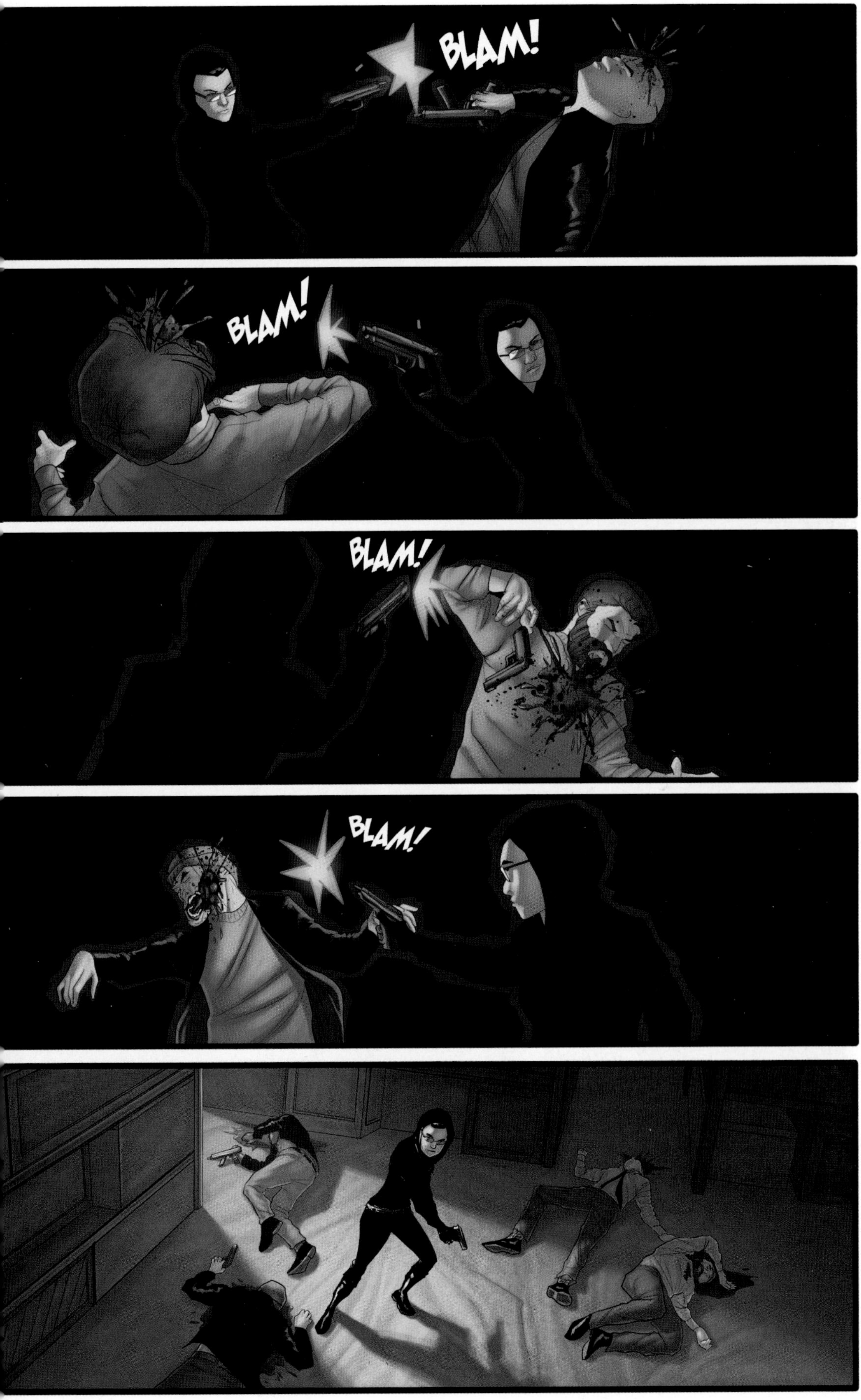
BLAM!
BLAM!
BLAM!
BLAM!

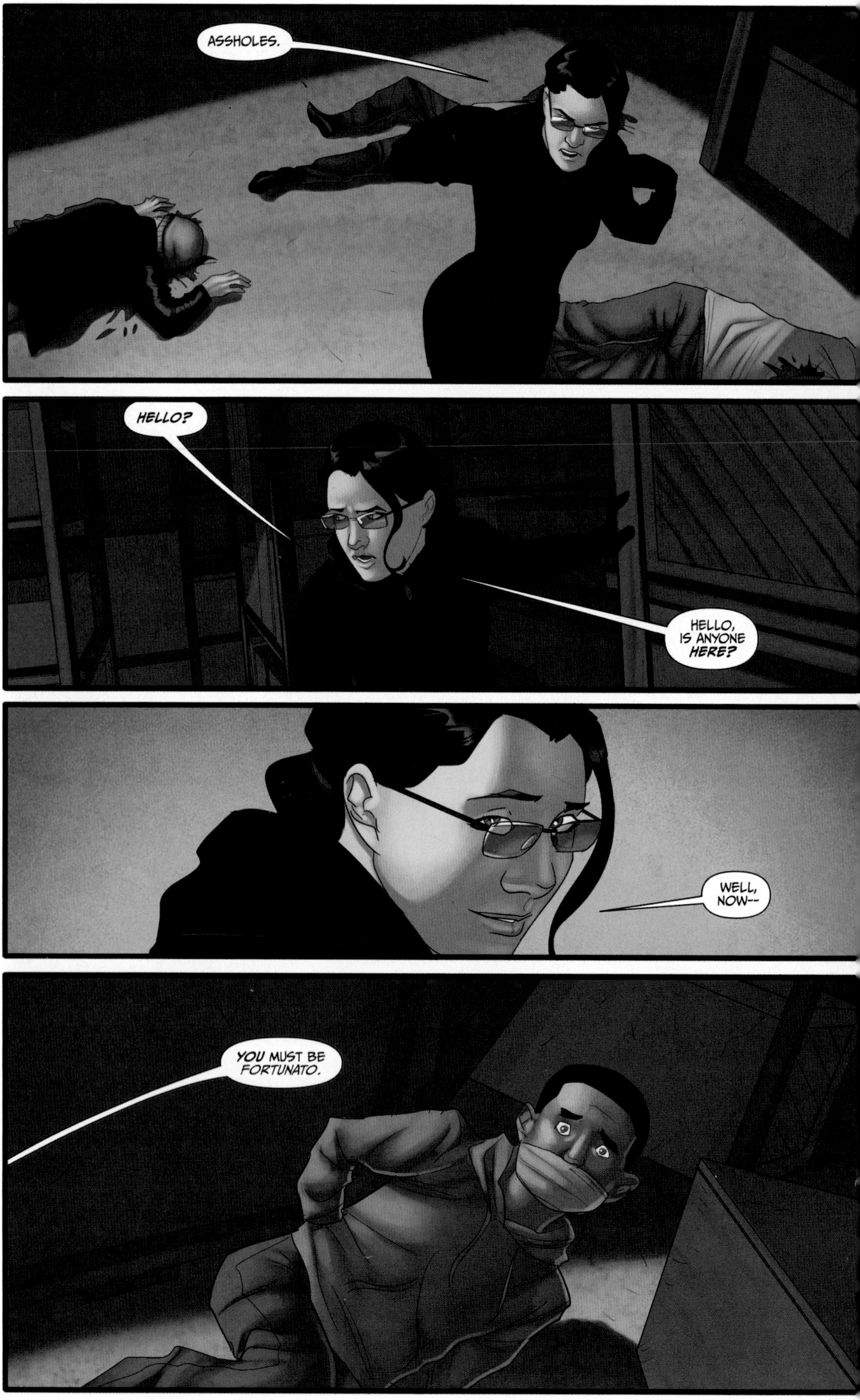
ASSHOLES.
HELLO?
HELLO, IS ANYONE HERE?
WELL, NOW--
YOU MUST BE FORTUNATO.

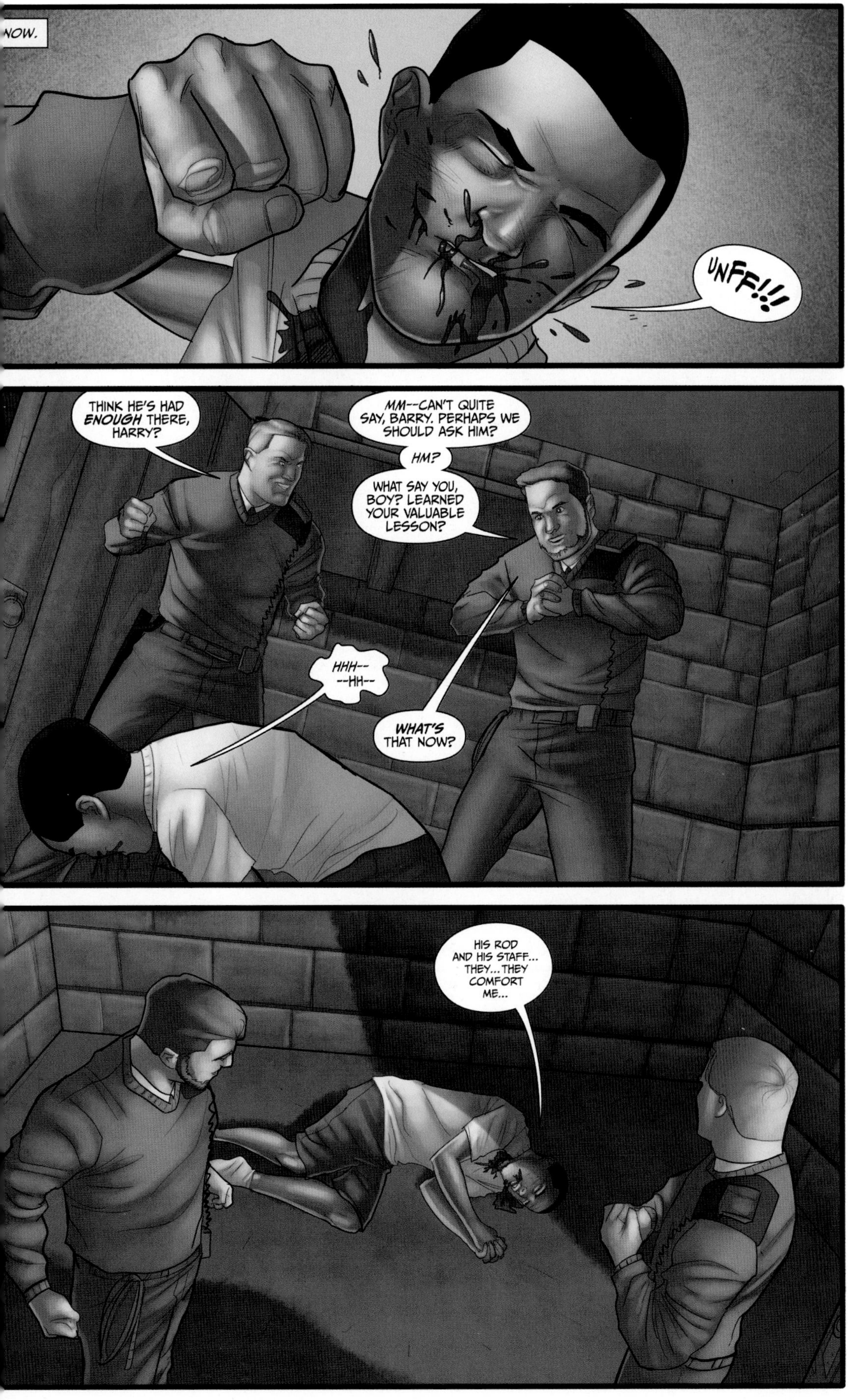
NOW.
UNFF!!!
THINK HE'S HAD ENOUGH THERE, HARRY?
MM--CAN'T QUITE SAY, BARRY. PERHAPS WE SHOULD ASK HIM?
HM?
WHAT SAY YOU, BOY? LEARNED YOUR VALUABLE LESSON?
HHH-- --HH--
WHAT'S THAT NOW?
HIS ROD AND HIS STAFF... THEY... THEY COMFORT ME...

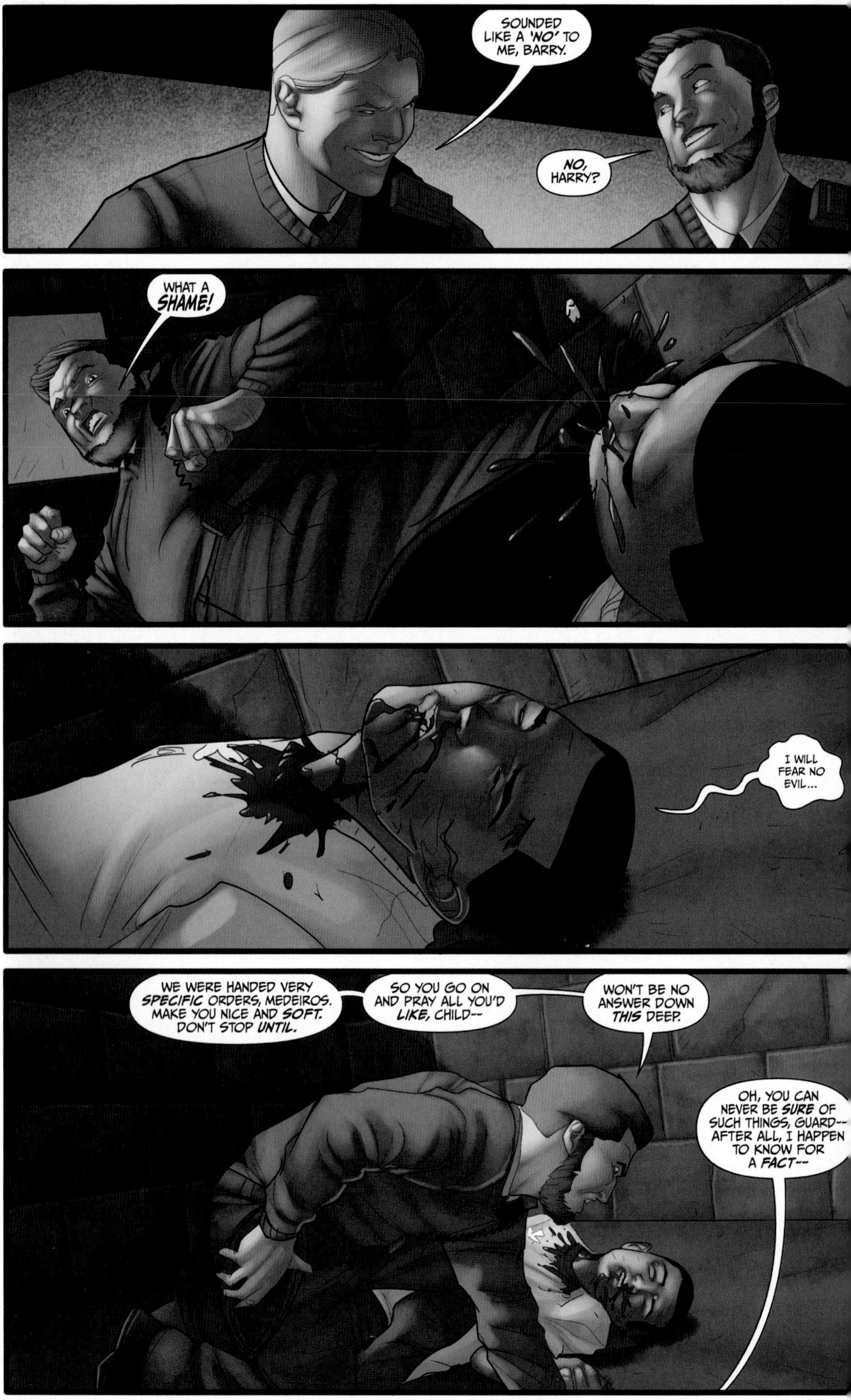

SOUNDED LIKE A 'NO' TO ME, BARRY.
NO, HARRY?
WHAT A SHAME!
I WILL FEAR NO EVIL...
WE WERE HANDED VERY SPECIFIC ORDERS, MEDEIROS. MAKE YOU NICE AND SOFT. DON'T STOP UNTIL.
SO YOU GO ON AND PRAY ALL YOU'D LIKE, CHILD--
WON'T BE NO ANSWER DOWN THIS DEEP.
OH, YOU CAN NEVER BE SURE OF SUCH THINGS, GUARD-- AFTER ALL, I HAPPEN TO KNOW FOR A FACT--

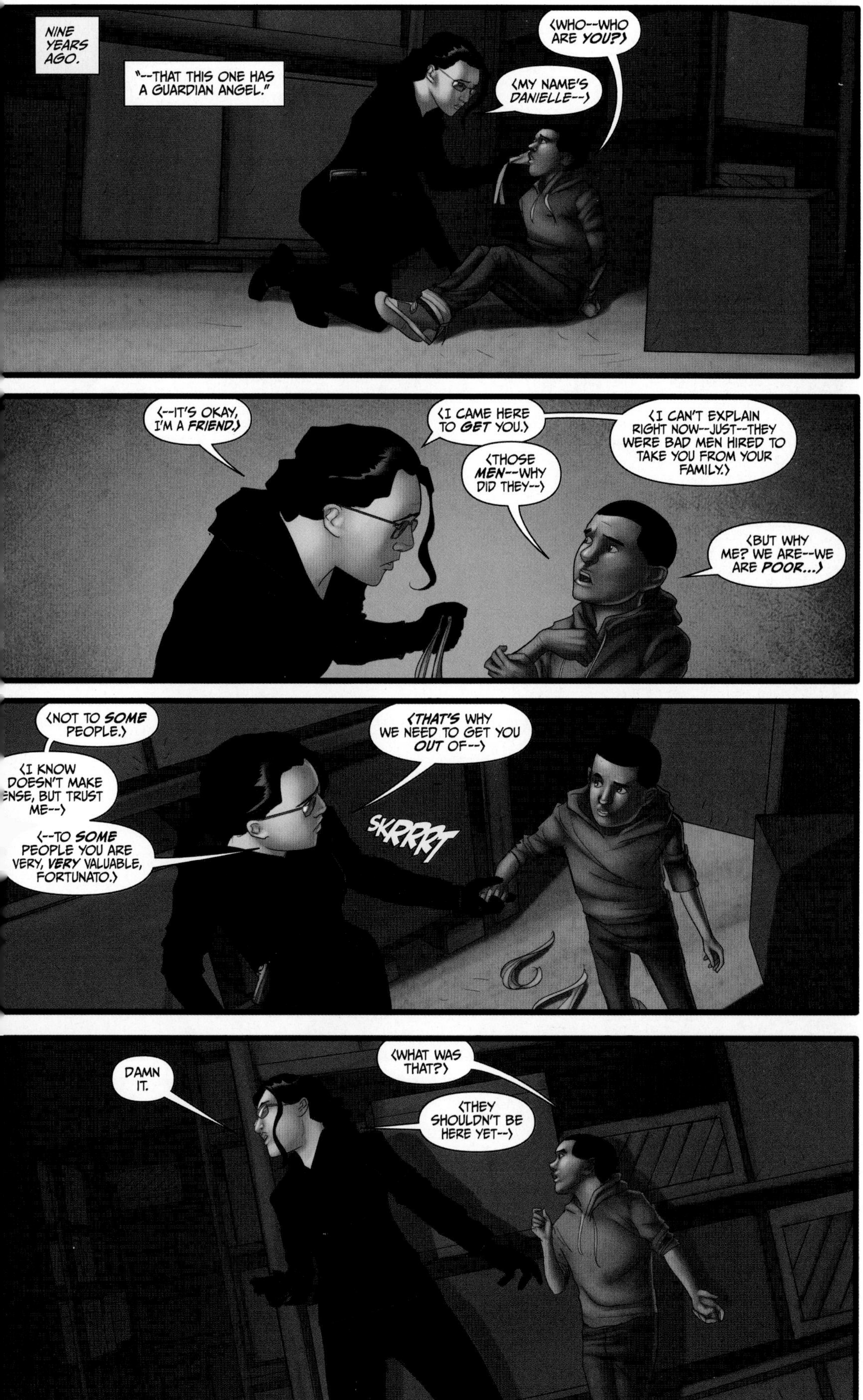
NINE YEARS AGO.
"--THAT THIS ONE HAS A GUARDIAN ANGEL."
‹WHO--WHO ARE YOU?›
‹MY NAME'S DANIELLE--›
‹--IT'S OKAY, I'M A FRIEND.›
‹I CAME HERE TO GET YOU.›
‹I CAN'T EXPLAIN RIGHT NOW--JUST--THEY WERE BAD MEN HIRED TO TAKE YOU FROM YOUR FAMILY.›
‹THOSE MEN--WHY DID THEY--›
‹BUT WHY ME? WE ARE--WE ARE POOR...›
‹NOT TO SOME PEOPLE.›
‹I KNOW DOESN'T MAKE ENSE, BUT TRUST ME--›
‹--TO SOME PEOPLE YOU ARE VERY, VERY VALUABLE, FORTUNATO.›
‹THAT'S WHY WE NEED TO GET YOU OUT OF--›
SKRRRT
DAMN IT.
‹WHAT WAS THAT?›
‹THEY SHOULDN'T BE HERE YET--›

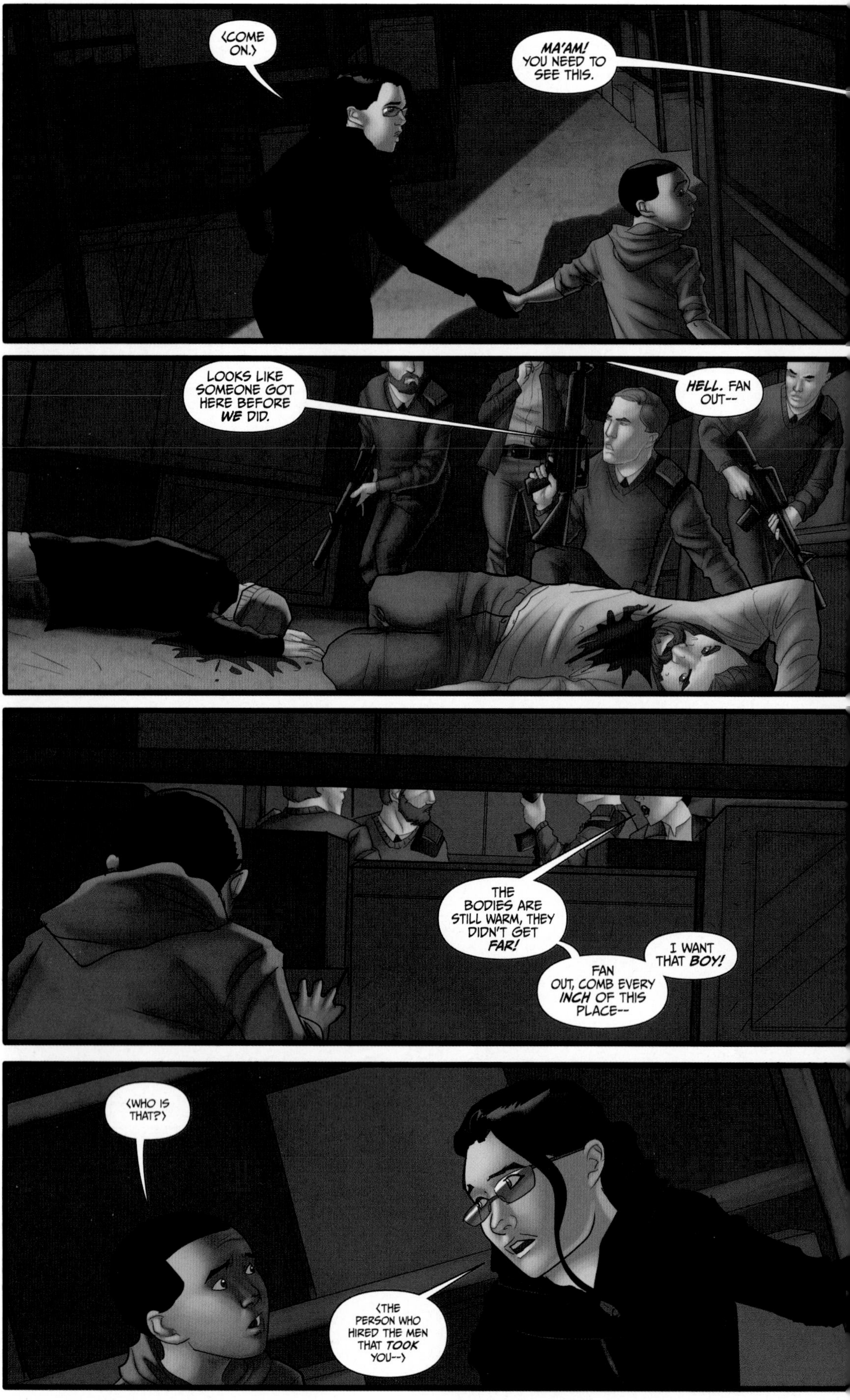
<COME ON.>
MA'AM! YOU NEED TO SEE THIS.
LOOKS LIKE SOMEONE GOT HERE BEFORE WE DID.
HELL. FAN OUT--
THE BODIES ARE STILL WARM, THEY DIDN'T GET FAR!
FAN OUT, COMB EVERY INCH OF THIS PLACE--
I WANT THAT BOY!
<WHO IS THAT?>
<THE PERSON WHO HIRED THE MEN THAT TOOK YOU-->

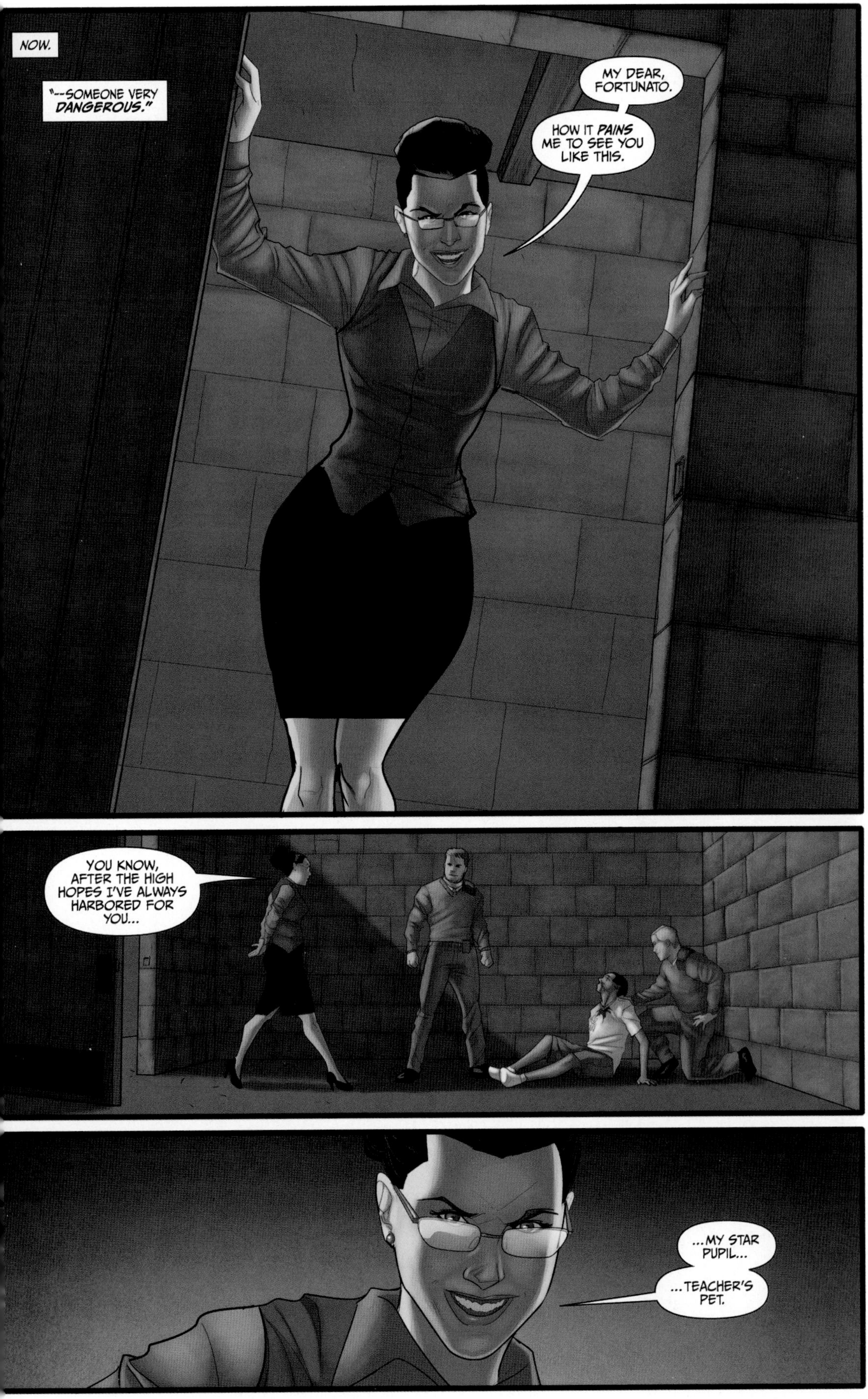
NOW.
"--SOMEONE VERY *DANGEROUS.*"
MY DEAR, FORTUNATO.
HOW IT *PAINS* ME TO SEE YOU LIKE THIS.
YOU KNOW, AFTER THE HIGH HOPES I'VE ALWAYS HARBORED FOR YOU...
...MY STAR PUPIL...
...TEACHER'S PET.

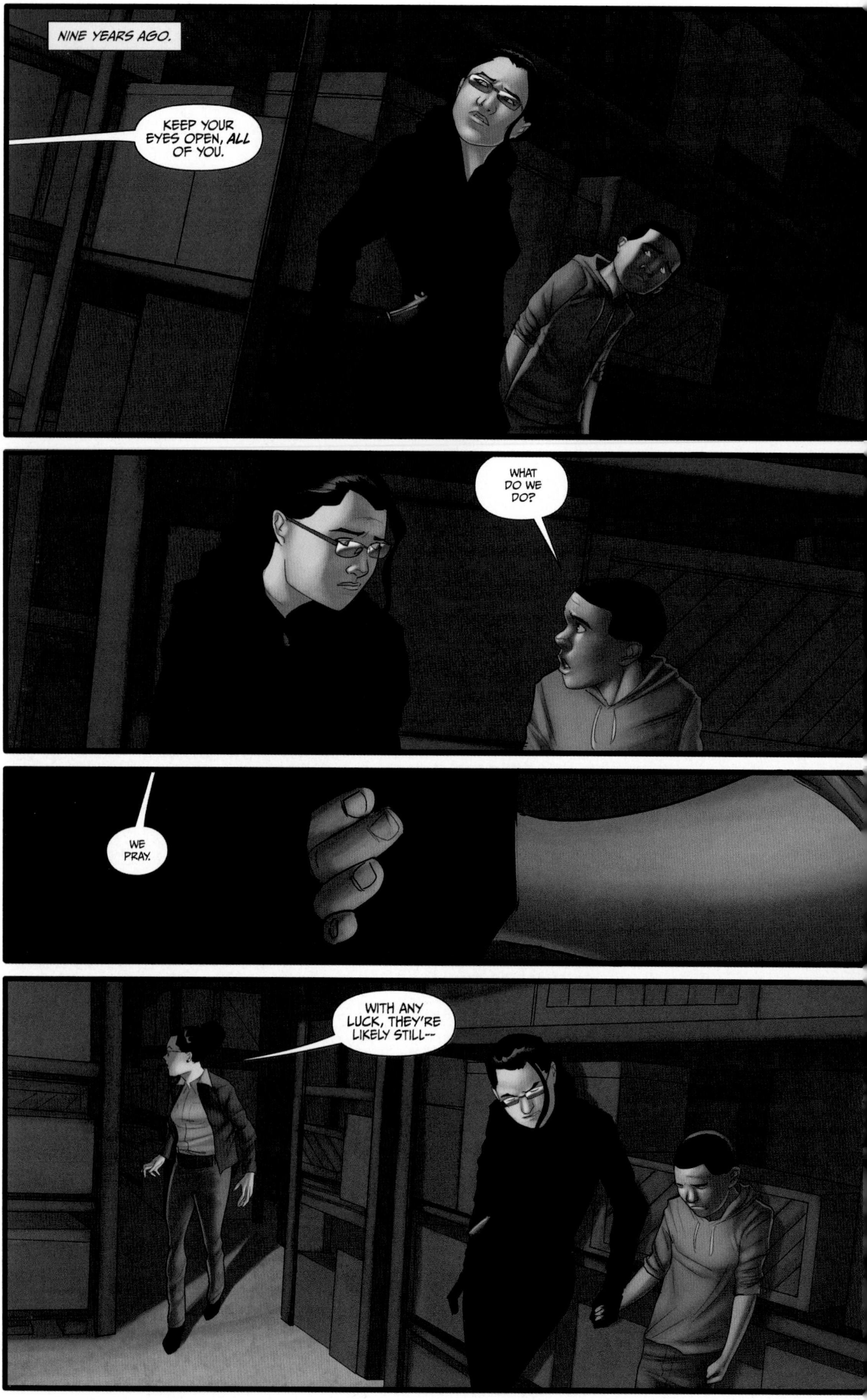
NINE YEARS AGO.
KEEP YOUR EYES OPEN, ALL OF YOU.
WHAT DO WE DO?
WE PRAY.
WITH ANY LUCK, THEY'RE LIKELY STILL--

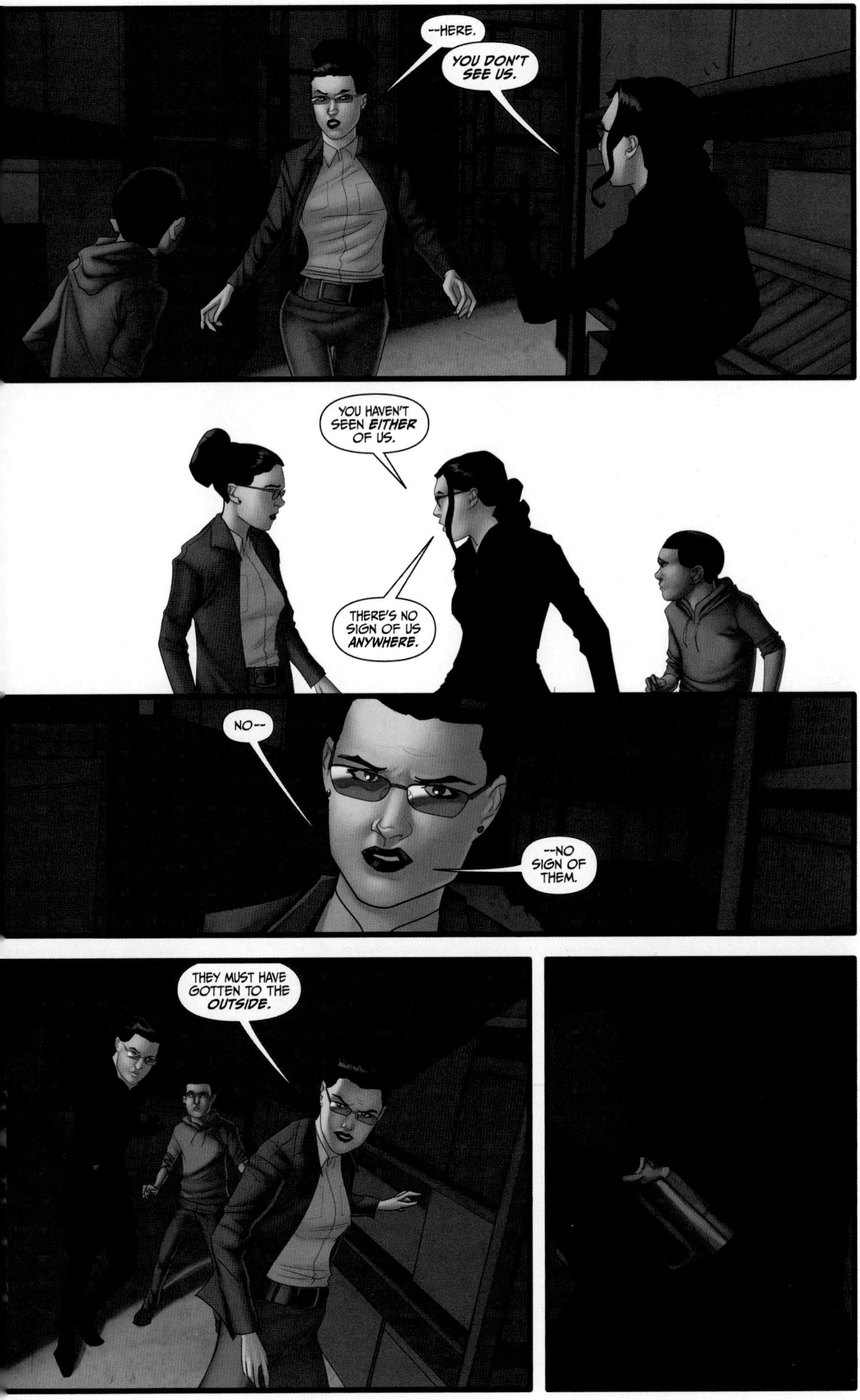
--HERE.
YOU DON'T SEE US.
YOU HAVEN'T SEEN EITHER OF US.
THERE'S NO SIGN OF US ANYWHERE.
NO--
--NO SIGN OF THEM.
THEY MUST HAVE GOTTEN TO THE OUTSIDE.

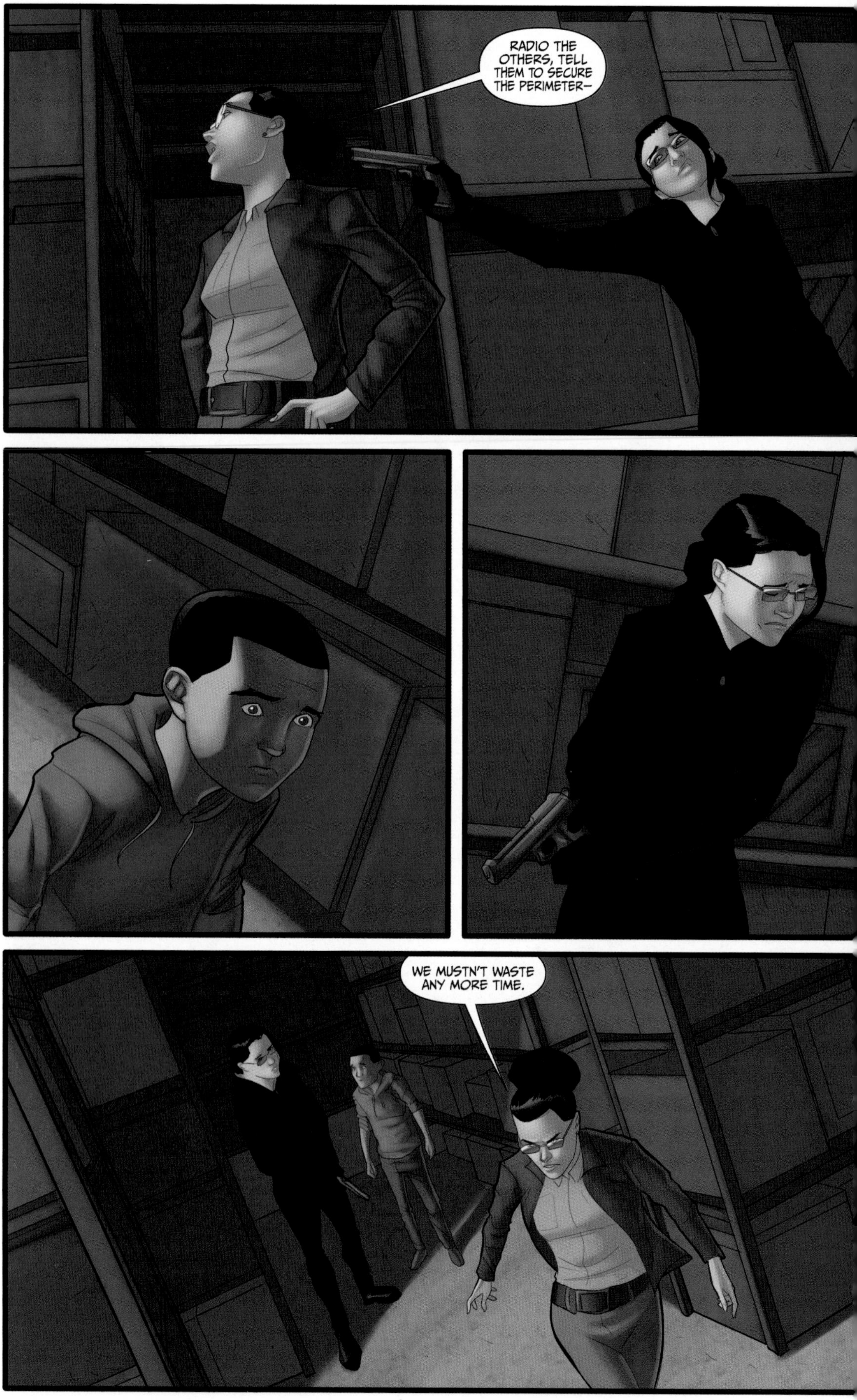
RADIO THE OTHERS, TELL THEM TO SECURE THE PERIMETER—
WE MUSTN'T WASTE ANY MORE TIME.

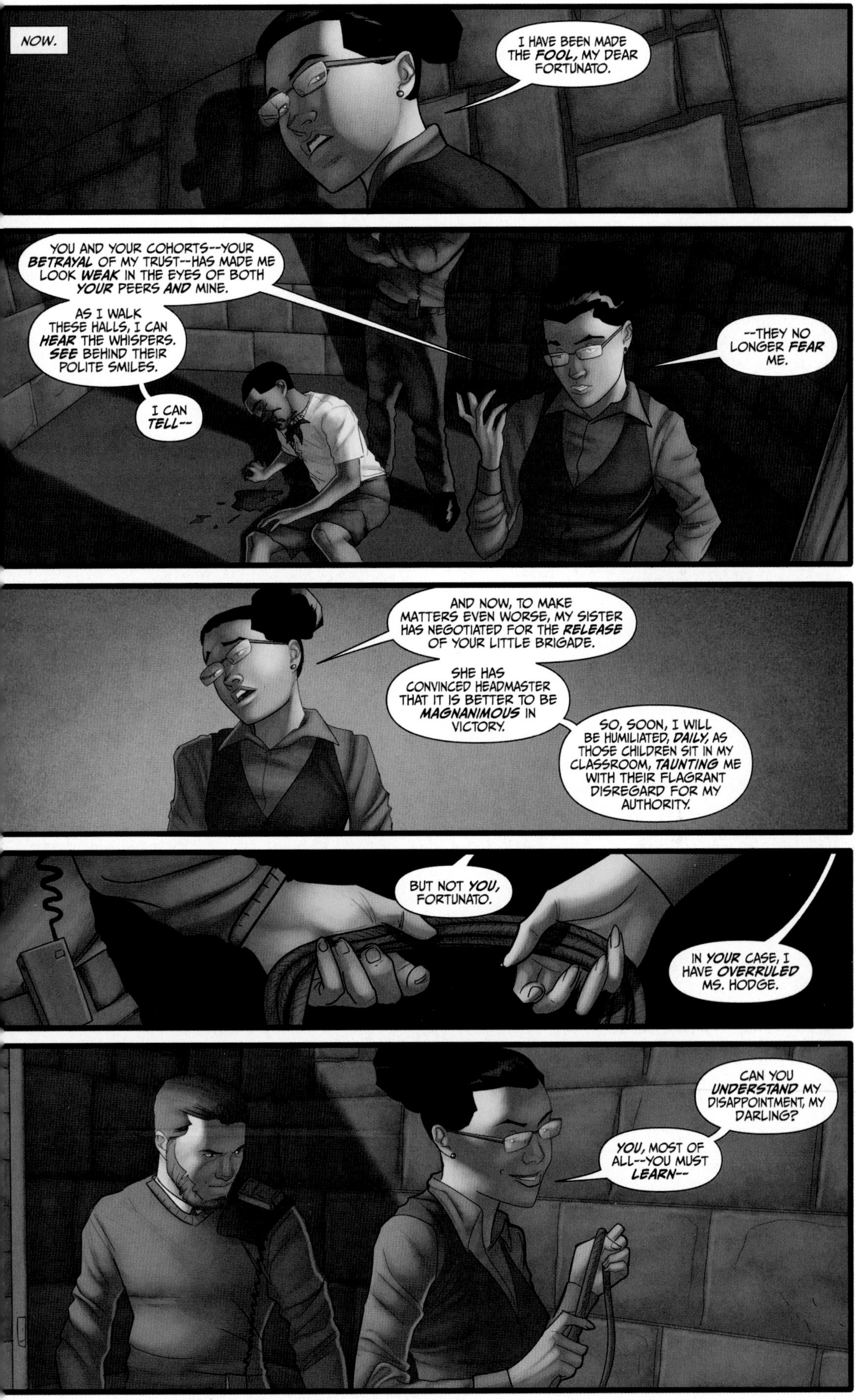
NOW.
I HAVE BEEN MADE THE FOOL, MY DEAR FORTUNATO.
YOU AND YOUR COHORTS--YOUR BETRAYAL OF MY TRUST--HAS MADE ME LOOK WEAK IN THE EYES OF BOTH YOUR PEERS AND MINE.
AS I WALK THESE HALLS, I CAN HEAR THE WHISPERS. SEE BEHIND THEIR POLITE SMILES.
I CAN TELL--
--THEY NO LONGER FEAR ME.
AND NOW, TO MAKE MATTERS EVEN WORSE, MY SISTER HAS NEGOTIATED FOR THE RELEASE OF YOUR LITTLE BRIGADE.
SHE HAS CONVINCED HEADMASTER THAT IT IS BETTER TO BE MAGNANIMOUS IN VICTORY.
SO, SOON, I WILL BE HUMILIATED, DAILY, AS THOSE CHILDREN SIT IN MY CLASSROOM, TAUNTING ME WITH THEIR FLAGRANT DISREGARD FOR MY AUTHORITY.
BUT NOT YOU, FORTUNATO.
IN YOUR CASE, I HAVE OVERRULED MS. HODGE.
CAN YOU UNDERSTAND MY DISAPPOINTMENT, MY DARLING?
YOU, MOST OF ALL--YOU MUST LEARN--

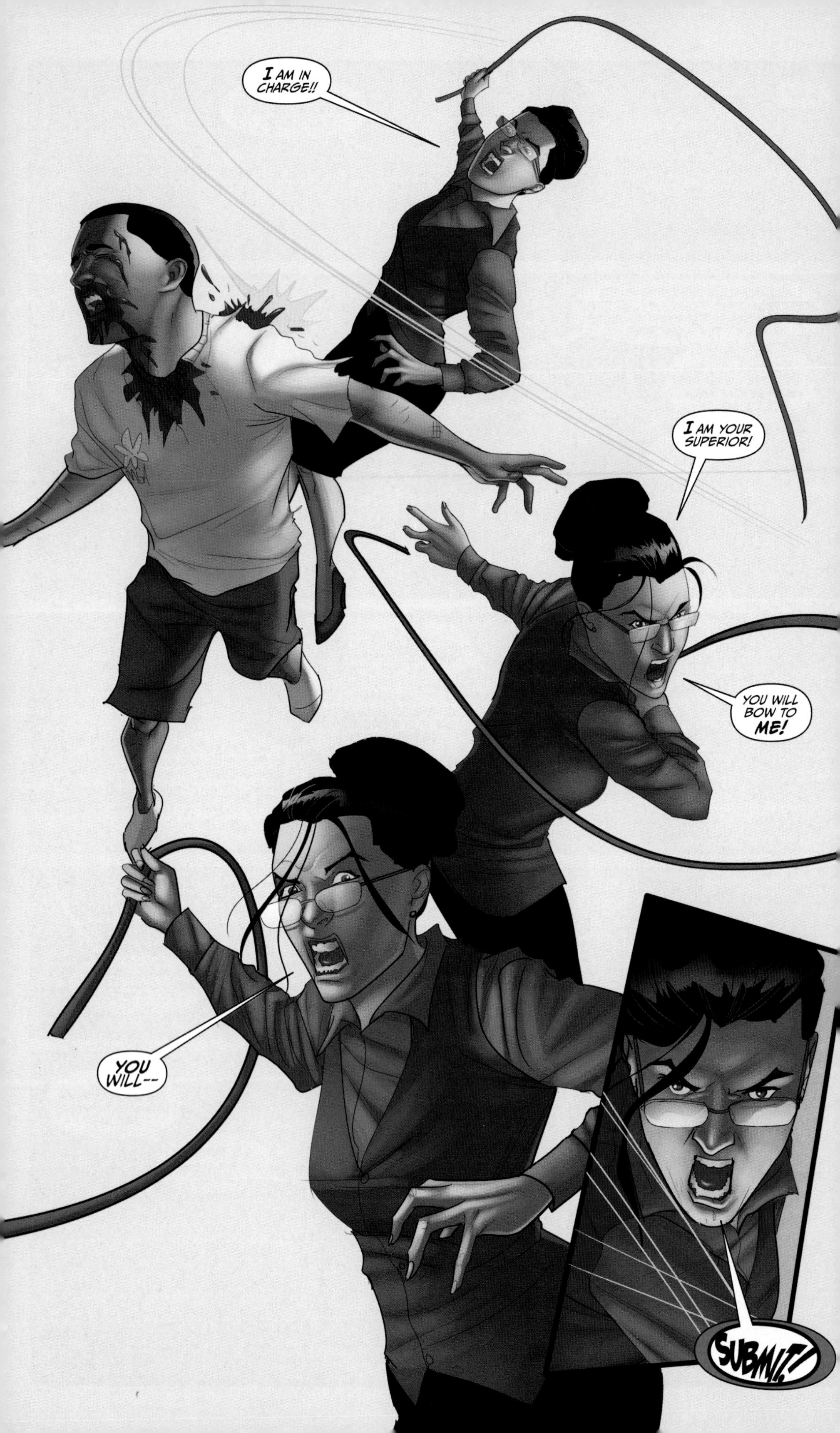
I AM IN CHARGE!!
I AM YOUR SUPERIOR!
YOU WILL BOW TO ME!
YOU WILL--
SUBMIT!

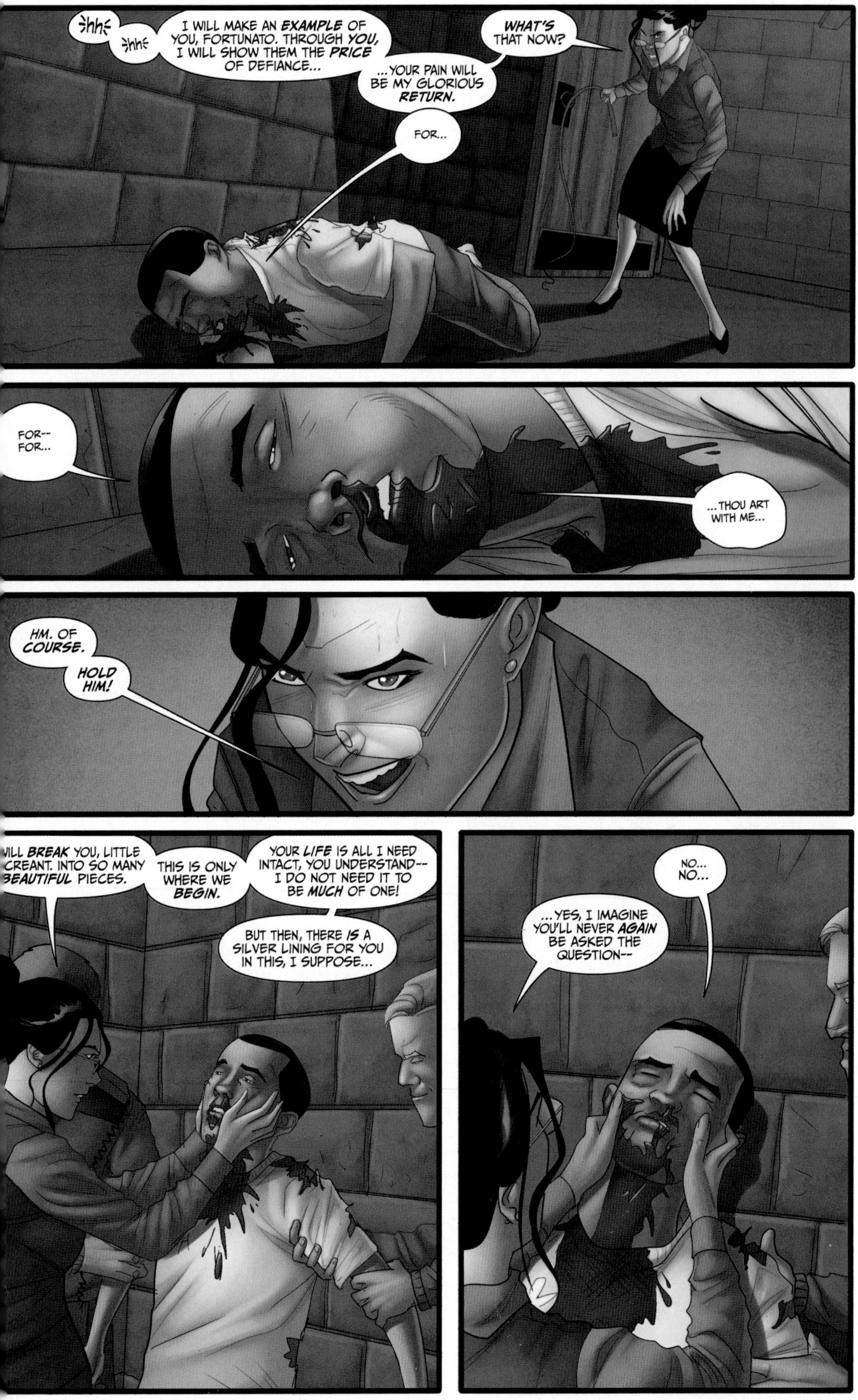

HHH
HHH
I WILL MAKE AN EXAMPLE OF YOU, FORTUNATO. THROUGH YOU, I WILL SHOW THEM THE PRICE OF DEFIANCE...
...YOUR PAIN WILL BE MY GLORIOUS RETURN.
WHAT'S THAT NOW?
FOR...
FOR-- FOR...
...THOU ART WITH ME...
HM. OF COURSE.
HOLD HIM!
WILL BREAK YOU, LITTLE CREANT. INTO SO MANY BEAUTIFUL PIECES.
THIS IS ONLY WHERE WE BEGIN.
YOUR LIFE IS ALL I NEED INTACT, YOU UNDERSTAND-- I DO NOT NEED IT TO BE MUCH OF ONE!
BUT THEN, THERE IS A SILVER LINING FOR YOU IN THIS, I SUPPOSE...
NO... NO...
...YES, I IMAGINE YOU'LL NEVER AGAIN BE ASKED THE QUESTION--

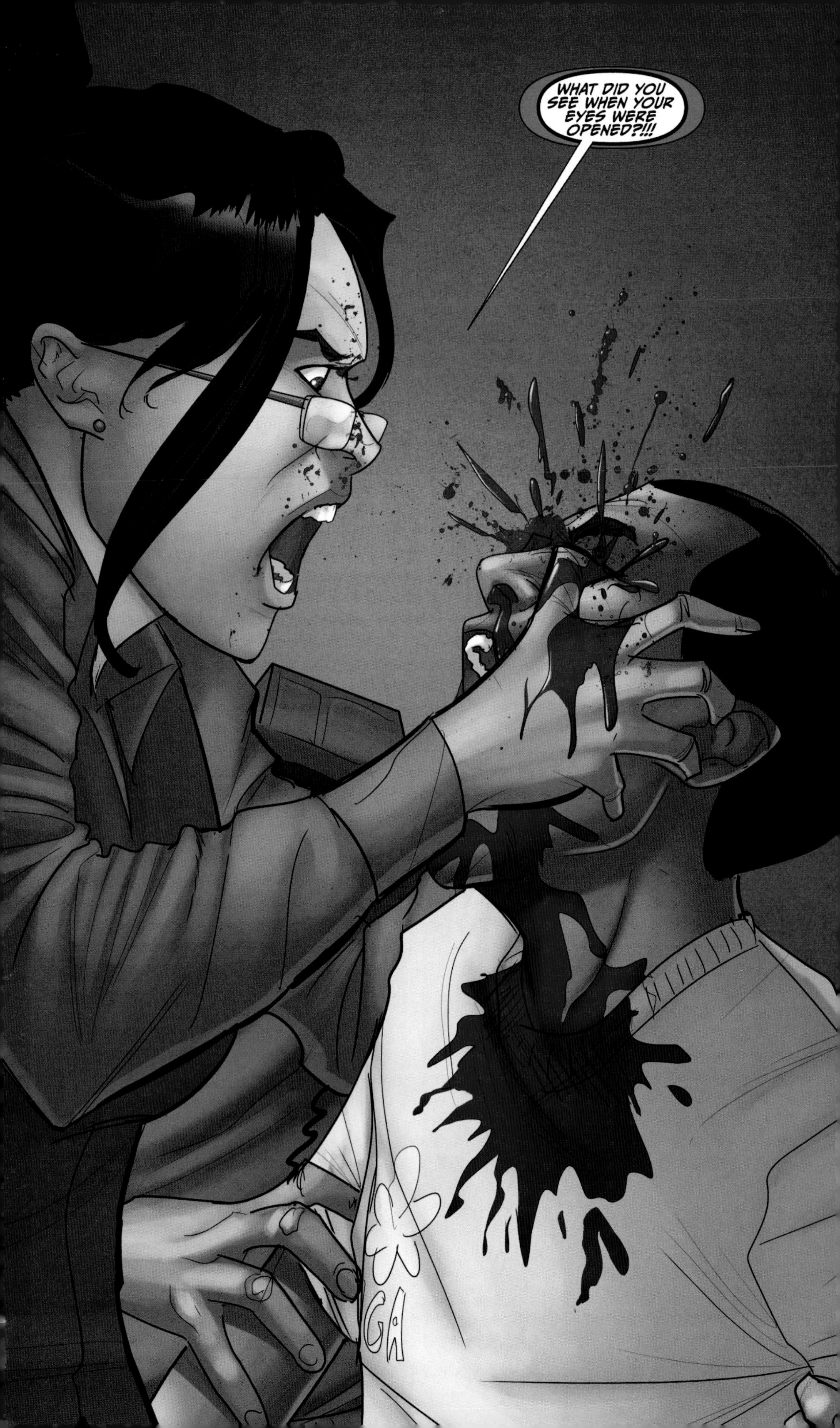
WHAT DID YOU SEE WHEN YOUR EYES WERE OPENED?!!!
GA

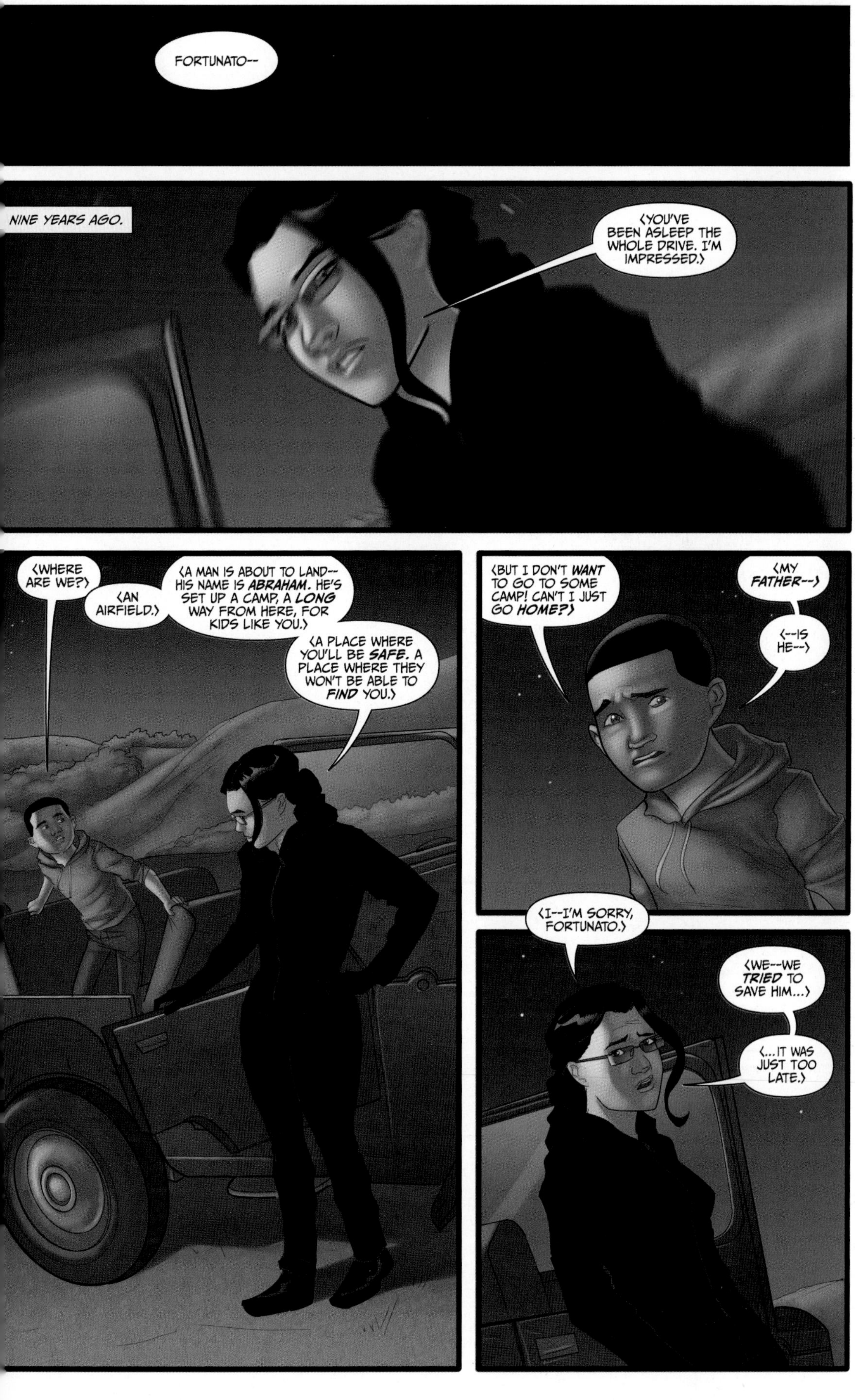
FORTUNATO--
NINE YEARS AGO.
‹YOU'VE BEEN ASLEEP THE WHOLE DRIVE. I'M IMPRESSED.›
‹WHERE ARE WE?›
‹AN AIRFIELD.›
‹A MAN IS ABOUT TO LAND-- HIS NAME IS ABRAHAM. HE'S SET UP A CAMP, A LONG WAY FROM HERE, FOR KIDS LIKE YOU.›
‹A PLACE WHERE YOU'LL BE SAFE. A PLACE WHERE THEY WON'T BE ABLE TO FIND YOU.›
‹BUT I DON'T WANT TO GO TO SOME CAMP! CAN'T I JUST GO HOME?›
‹MY FATHER--›
‹--IS HE--›
‹I--I'M SORRY, FORTUNATO.›
‹WE--WE TRIED TO SAVE HIM...›
‹...IT WAS JUST TOO LATE.›

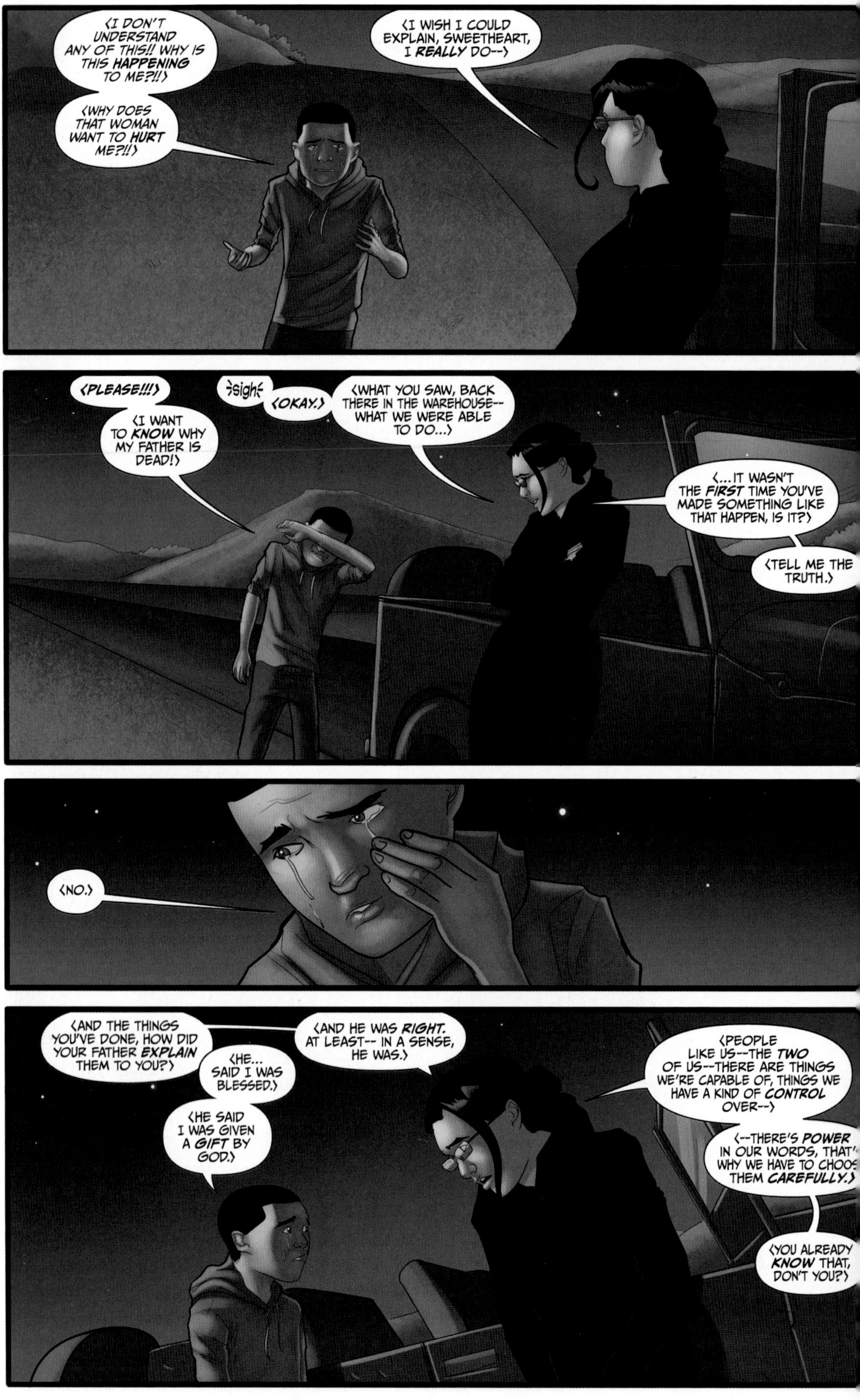

<I DON'T UNDERSTAND ANY OF THIS!! WHY IS THIS HAPPENING TO ME?!!>
<WHY DOES THAT WOMAN WANT TO HURT ME?!!>
<I WISH I COULD EXPLAIN, SWEETHEART, I REALLY DO-->
<PLEASE!!!>
<I WANT TO KNOW WHY MY FATHER IS DEAD!>
sigh
<OKAY.>
<WHAT YOU SAW, BACK THERE IN THE WAREHOUSE-- WHAT WE WERE ABLE TO DO...>
<...IT WASN'T THE FIRST TIME YOU'VE MADE SOMETHING LIKE THAT HAPPEN, IS IT?>
<TELL ME THE TRUTH.>
<NO.>
<AND THE THINGS YOU'VE DONE, HOW DID YOUR FATHER EXPLAIN THEM TO YOU?>
<HE... SAID I WAS BLESSED.>
<HE SAID I WAS GIVEN A GIFT BY GOD.>
<AND HE WAS RIGHT. AT LEAST-- IN A SENSE, HE WAS.>
<PEOPLE LIKE US--THE TWO OF US--THERE ARE THINGS WE'RE CAPABLE OF, THINGS WE HAVE A KIND OF CONTROL OVER-->
<--THERE'S POWER IN OUR WORDS, THAT' WHY WE HAVE TO CHOOS THEM CAREFULLY.>
<YOU ALREADY KNOW THAT, DON'T YOU?>

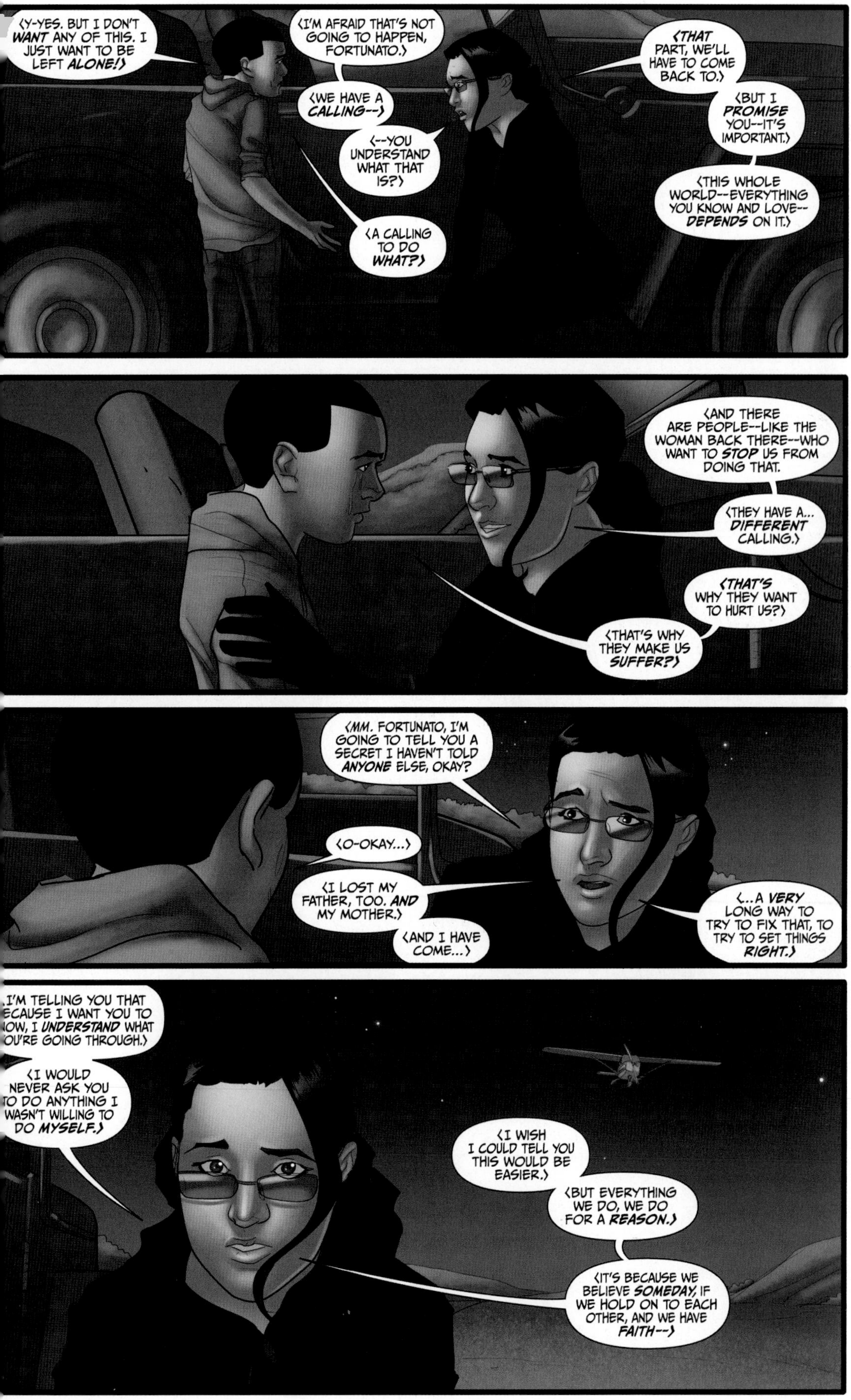

⟨Y-YES. BUT I DON'T WANT ANY OF THIS. I JUST WANT TO BE LEFT ALONE!⟩
⟨I'M AFRAID THAT'S NOT GOING TO HAPPEN, FORTUNATO.⟩
⟨WE HAVE A CALLING--⟩
⟨--YOU UNDERSTAND WHAT THAT IS?⟩
⟨A CALLING TO DO WHAT?⟩
⟨THAT PART, WE'LL HAVE TO COME BACK TO.⟩
⟨BUT I PROMISE YOU--IT'S IMPORTANT.⟩
⟨THIS WHOLE WORLD--EVERYTHING YOU KNOW AND LOVE--DEPENDS ON IT.⟩
⟨AND THERE ARE PEOPLE--LIKE THE WOMAN BACK THERE--WHO WANT TO STOP US FROM DOING THAT.
⟨THEY HAVE A... DIFFERENT CALLING.⟩
⟨THAT'S WHY THEY WANT TO HURT US?⟩
⟨THAT'S WHY THEY MAKE US SUFFER?⟩
⟨MM. FORTUNATO, I'M GOING TO TELL YOU A SECRET I HAVEN'T TOLD ANYONE ELSE, OKAY?
⟨O-OKAY...⟩
⟨I LOST MY FATHER, TOO. AND MY MOTHER.⟩
⟨AND I HAVE COME...⟩
⟨...A VERY LONG WAY TO TRY TO FIX THAT, TO TRY TO SET THINGS RIGHT.⟩
I'M TELLING YOU THAT ECAUSE I WANT YOU TO NOW, I UNDERSTAND WHAT OU'RE GOING THROUGH.⟩
⟨I WOULD NEVER ASK YOU TO DO ANYTHING I WASN'T WILLING TO DO MYSELF.⟩
⟨I WISH I COULD TELL YOU THIS WOULD BE EASIER.⟩
⟨BUT EVERYTHING WE DO, WE DO FOR A REASON.⟩
⟨IT'S BECAUSE WE BELIEVE SOMEDAY, IF WE HOLD ON TO EACH OTHER, AND WE HAVE FAITH--⟩

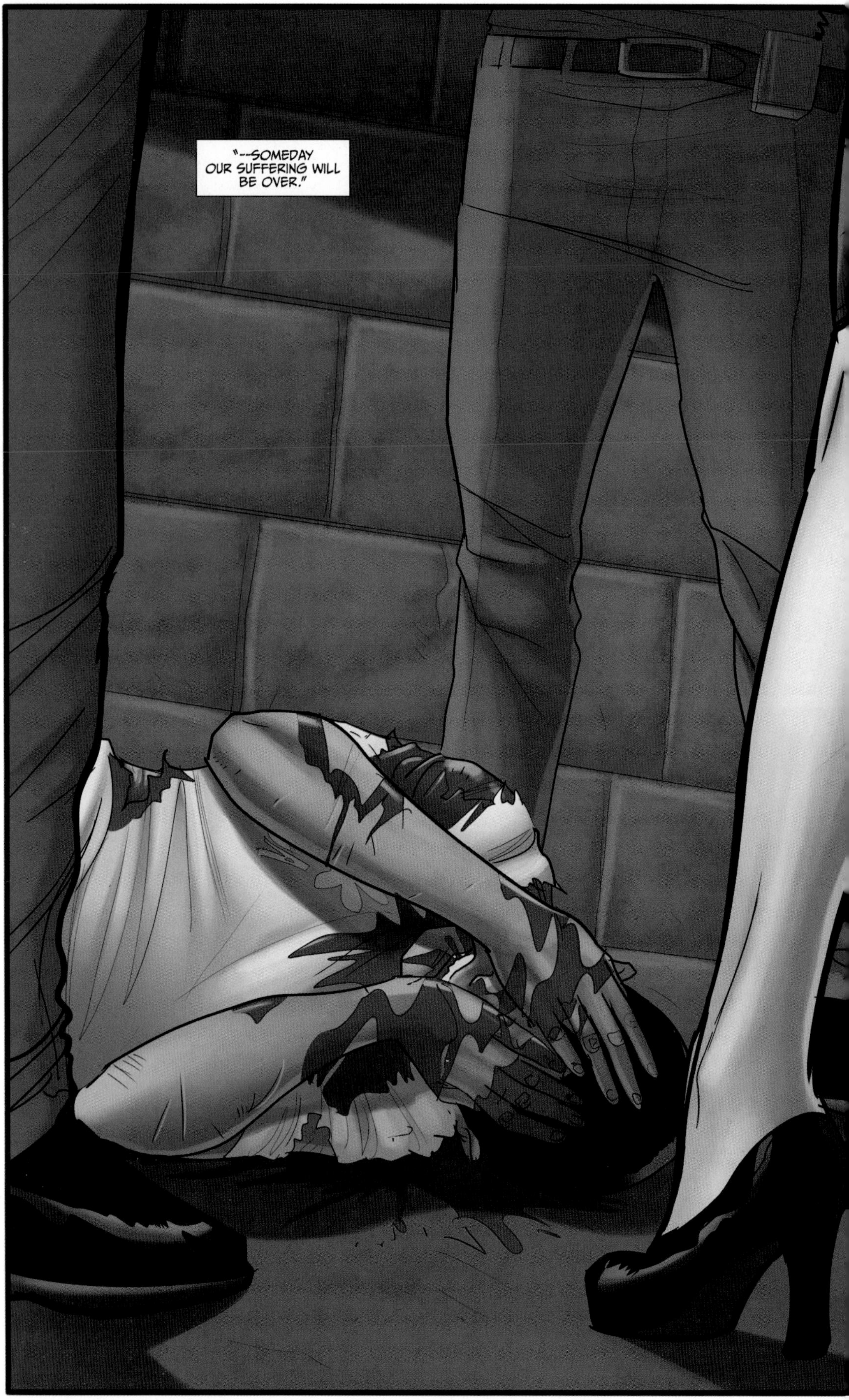
"--SOMEDAY OUR SUFFERING WILL BE OVER."

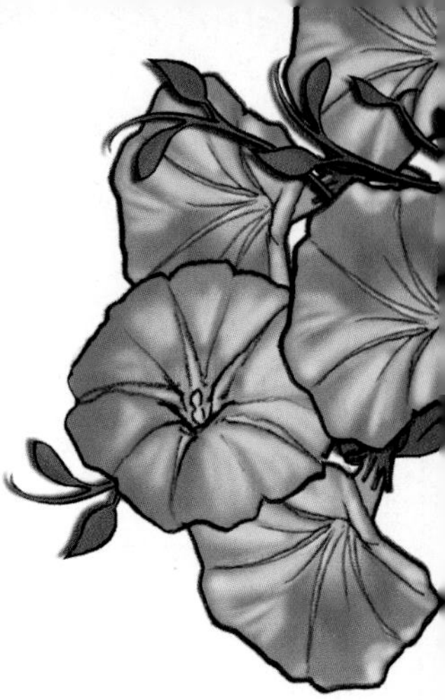

thirtysix

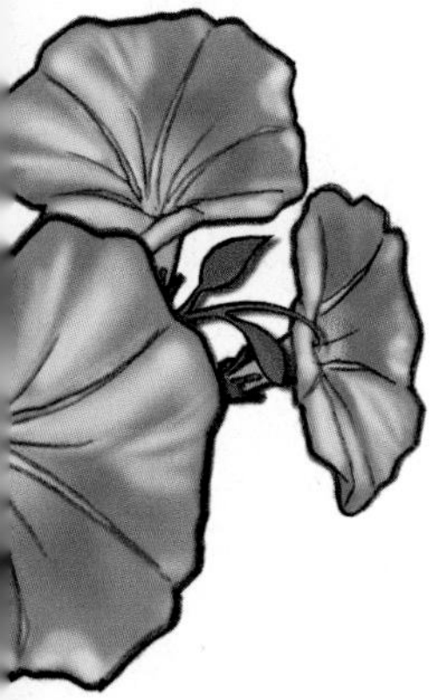

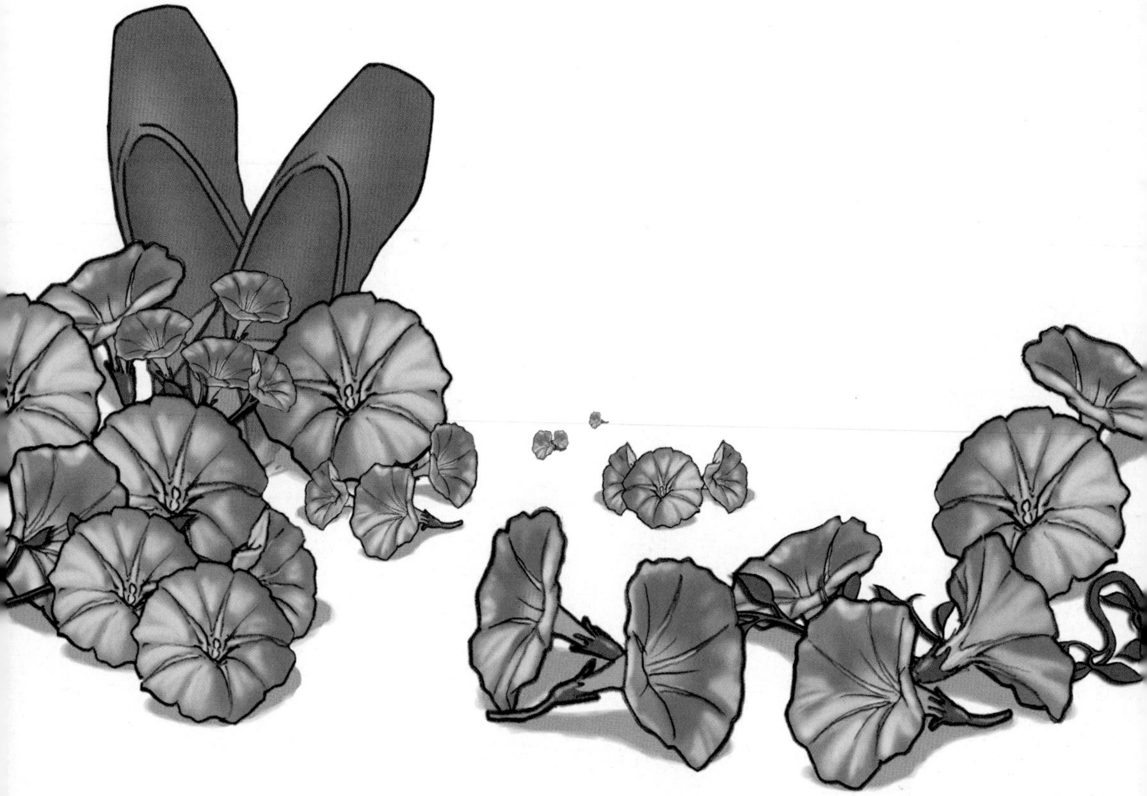

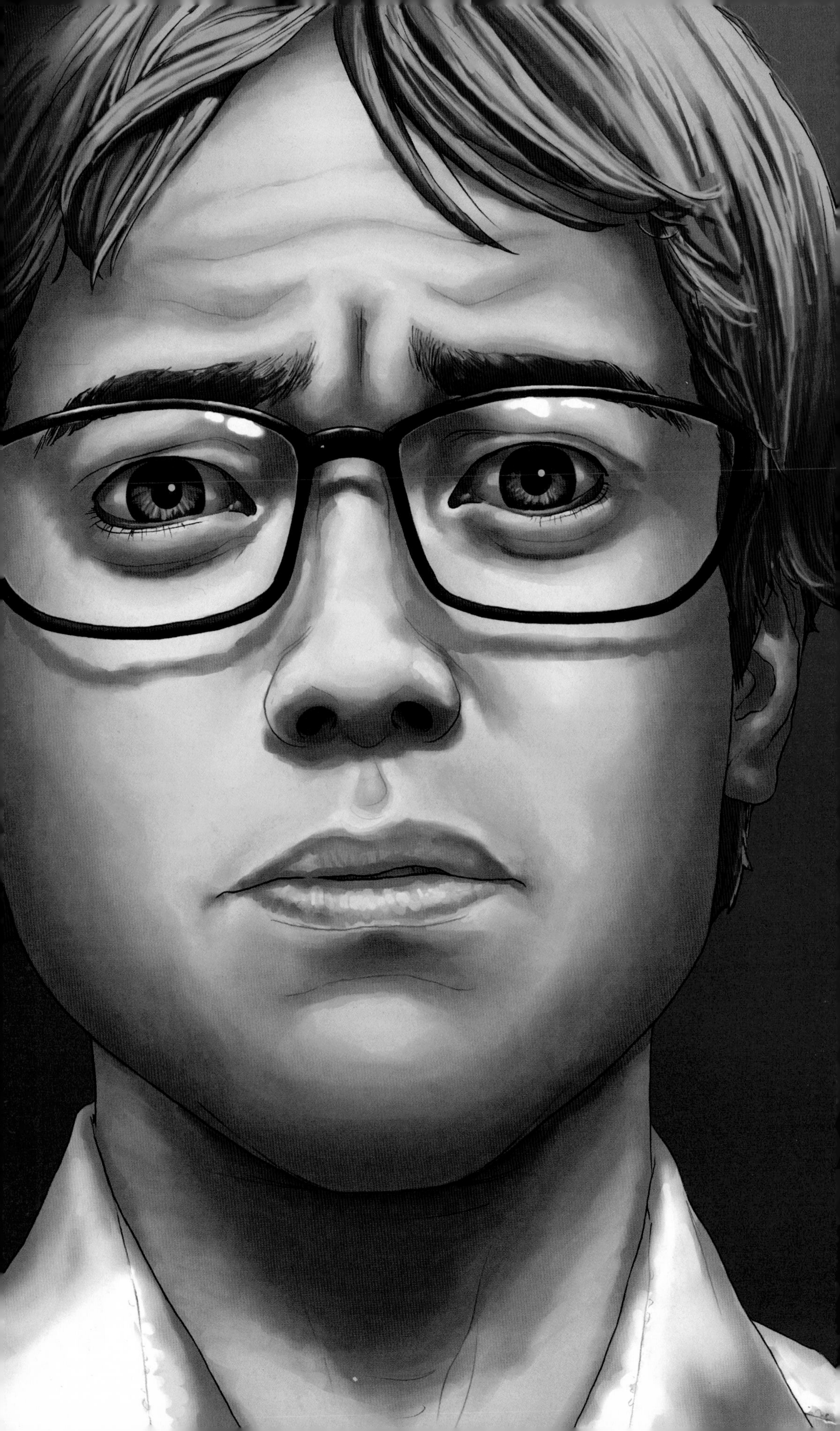

ELEVEN YEARS AGO.

YOU'VE BEEN WORKING SO *HARD* LATELY, DARLING...

...YOU *REALLY* MUST TAKE A MOMENT TO *RELAX.*

AH, WELL... YES...

...YOU SEE, I'D VERY MUCH *LIKE* TO, OF COURSE, IT'S JUST...

SHHH... ...LET ME *HELP* YOU...

AHH...

...HM--

--YES, *VERY--*

--VERY HELPFUL INDEED...

‡ahem‡

SORRY TO INTRUDE--

GAAH!

STOP, *PLEASE!*

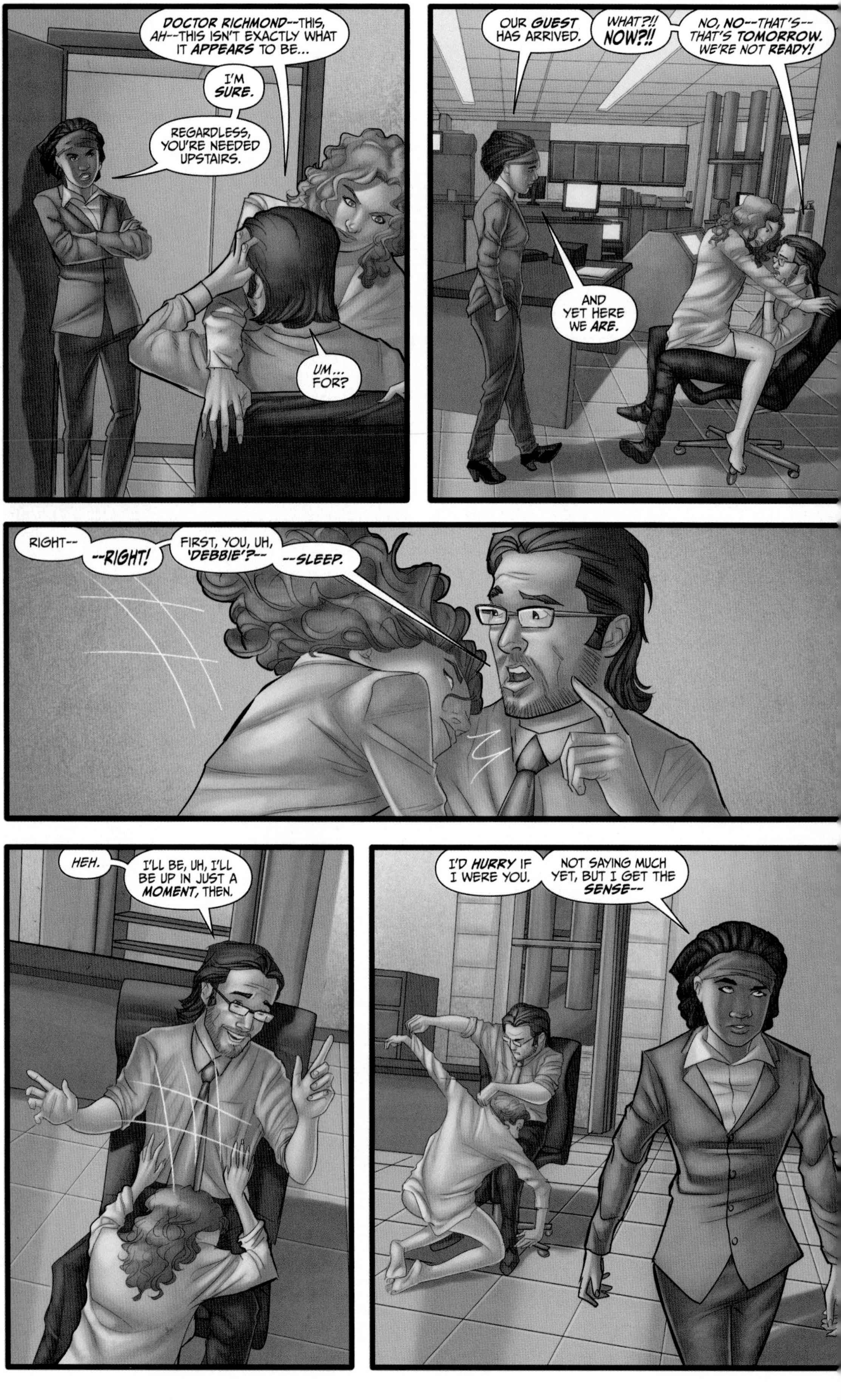
DOCTOR RICHMOND--THIS, AH--THIS ISN'T EXACTLY WHAT IT APPEARS TO BE...
I'M SURE.
REGARDLESS, YOU'RE NEEDED UPSTAIRS.
UM... FOR?
OUR GUEST HAS ARRIVED.
WHAT?!! NOW?!!
NO, NO--THAT'S--THAT'S TOMORROW. WE'RE NOT READY!
AND YET HERE WE ARE.
RIGHT--
--RIGHT!
FIRST, YOU, UH, 'DEBBIE'?--
--SLEEP.
HEH.
I'LL BE, UH, I'LL BE UP IN JUST A MOMENT, THEN.
I'D HURRY IF I WERE YOU.
NOT SAYING MUCH YET, BUT I GET THE SENSE--

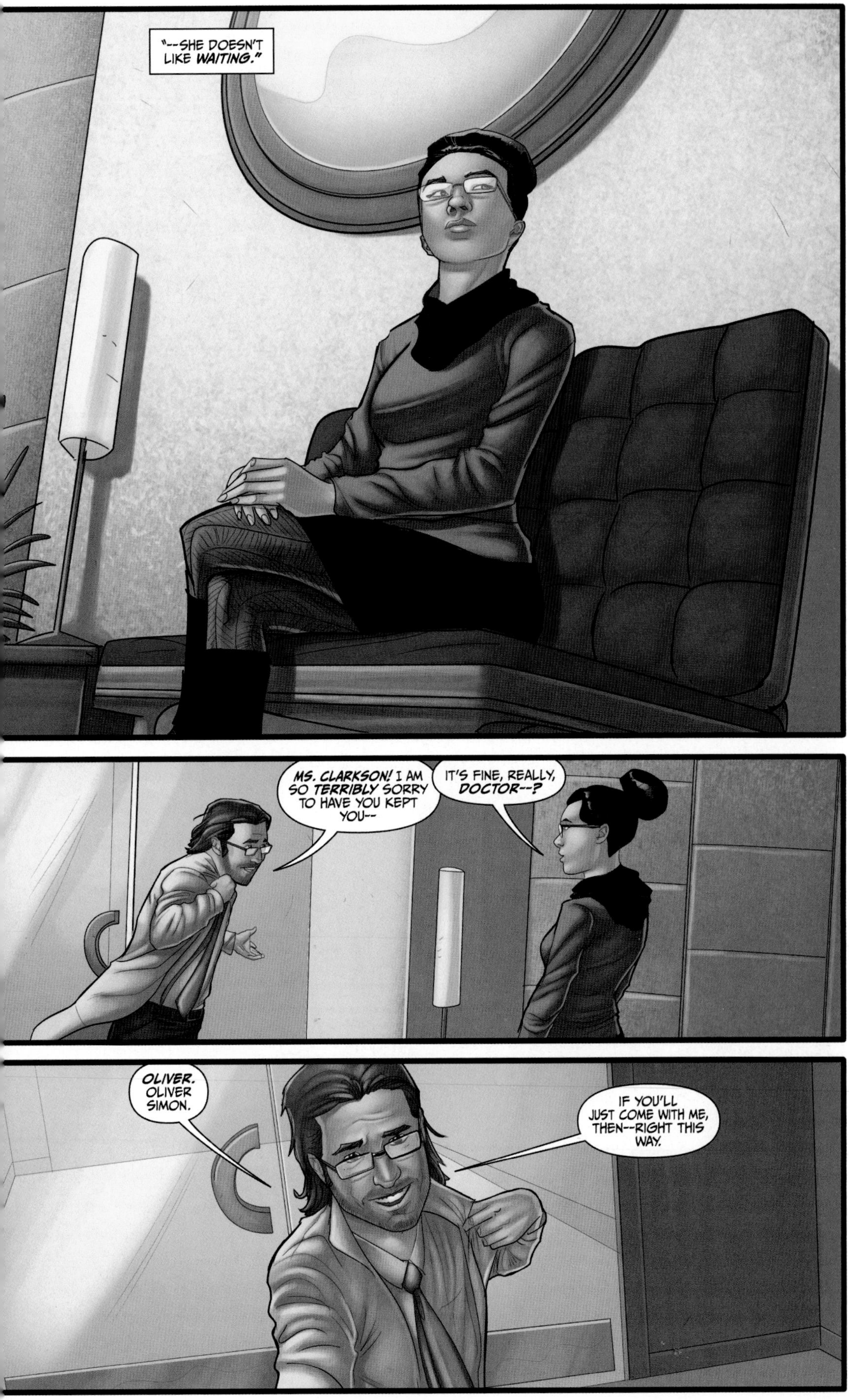
"--SHE DOESN'T LIKE *WAITING*."
MS. CLARKSON! I AM SO *TERRIBLY* SORRY TO HAVE YOU KEPT YOU--
IT'S FINE, REALLY, *DOCTOR--?*
OLIVER. OLIVER SIMON.
IF YOU'LL JUST COME WITH ME, THEN--RIGHT THIS WAY.

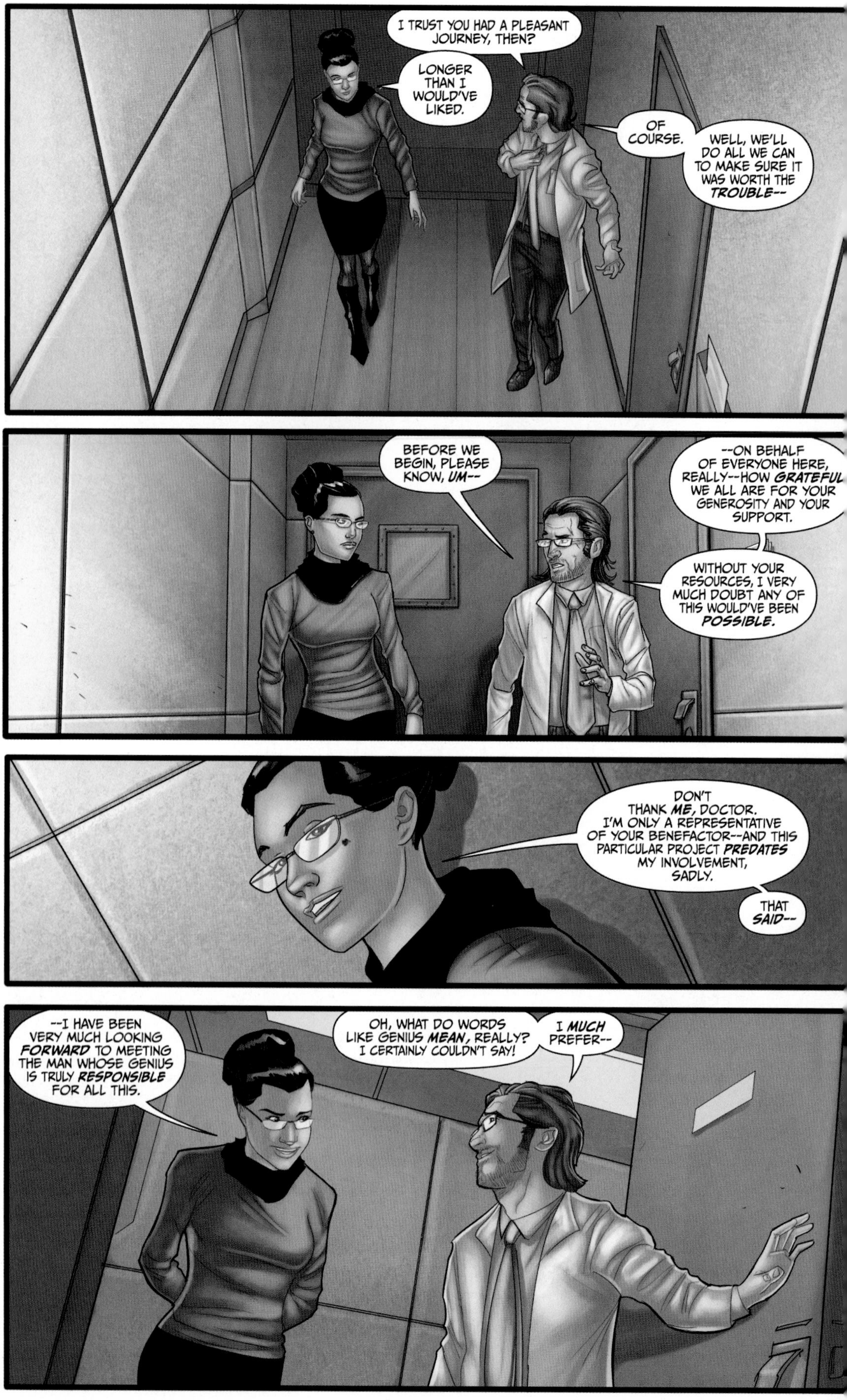
I TRUST YOU HAD A PLEASANT JOURNEY, THEN?
LONGER THAN I WOULD'VE LIKED.
OF COURSE.
WELL, WE'LL DO ALL WE CAN TO MAKE SURE IT WAS WORTH THE TROUBLE--
BEFORE WE BEGIN, PLEASE KNOW, UM--
--ON BEHALF OF EVERYONE HERE, REALLY--HOW GRATEFUL WE ALL ARE FOR YOUR GENEROSITY AND YOUR SUPPORT.
WITHOUT YOUR RESOURCES, I VERY MUCH DOUBT ANY OF THIS WOULD'VE BEEN POSSIBLE.
DON'T THANK ME, DOCTOR. I'M ONLY A REPRESENTATIVE OF YOUR BENEFACTOR--AND THIS PARTICULAR PROJECT PREDATES MY INVOLVEMENT, SADLY.
THAT SAID--
--I HAVE BEEN VERY MUCH LOOKING FORWARD TO MEETING THE MAN WHOSE GENIUS IS TRULY RESPONSIBLE FOR ALL THIS.
OH, WHAT DO WORDS LIKE GENIUS MEAN, REALLY? I CERTAINLY COULDN'T SAY!
I MUCH PREFER--

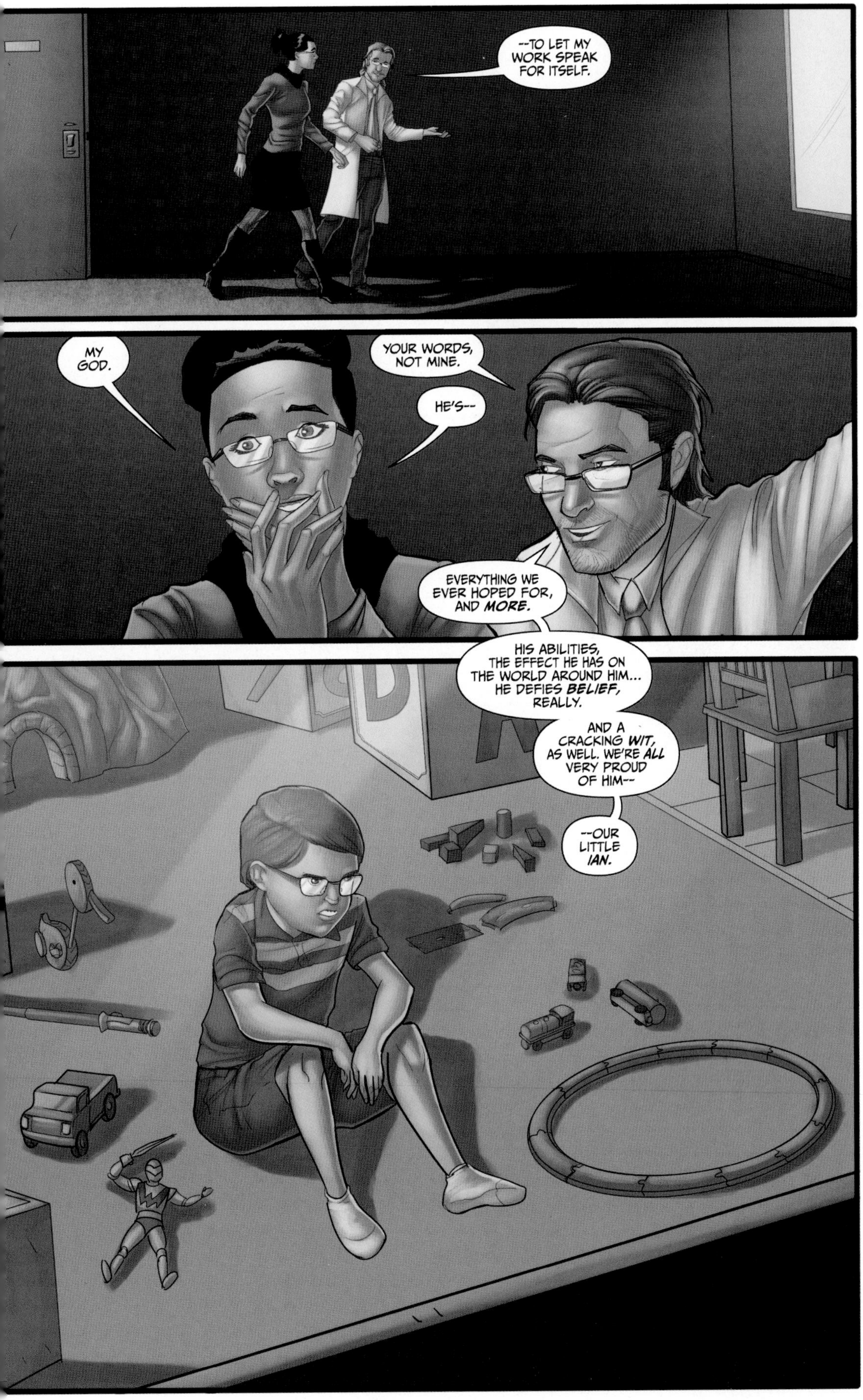
--TO LET MY WORK SPEAK FOR ITSELF.
MY GOD.
YOUR WORDS, NOT MINE.
HE'S--
EVERYTHING WE EVER HOPED FOR, AND *MORE.*
HIS ABILITIES, THE EFFECT HE HAS ON THE WORLD AROUND HIM... HE DEFIES *BELIEF,* REALLY.
AND A CRACKING *WIT,* AS WELL. WE'RE *ALL* VERY PROUD OF HIM--
--OUR LITTLE *IAN.*

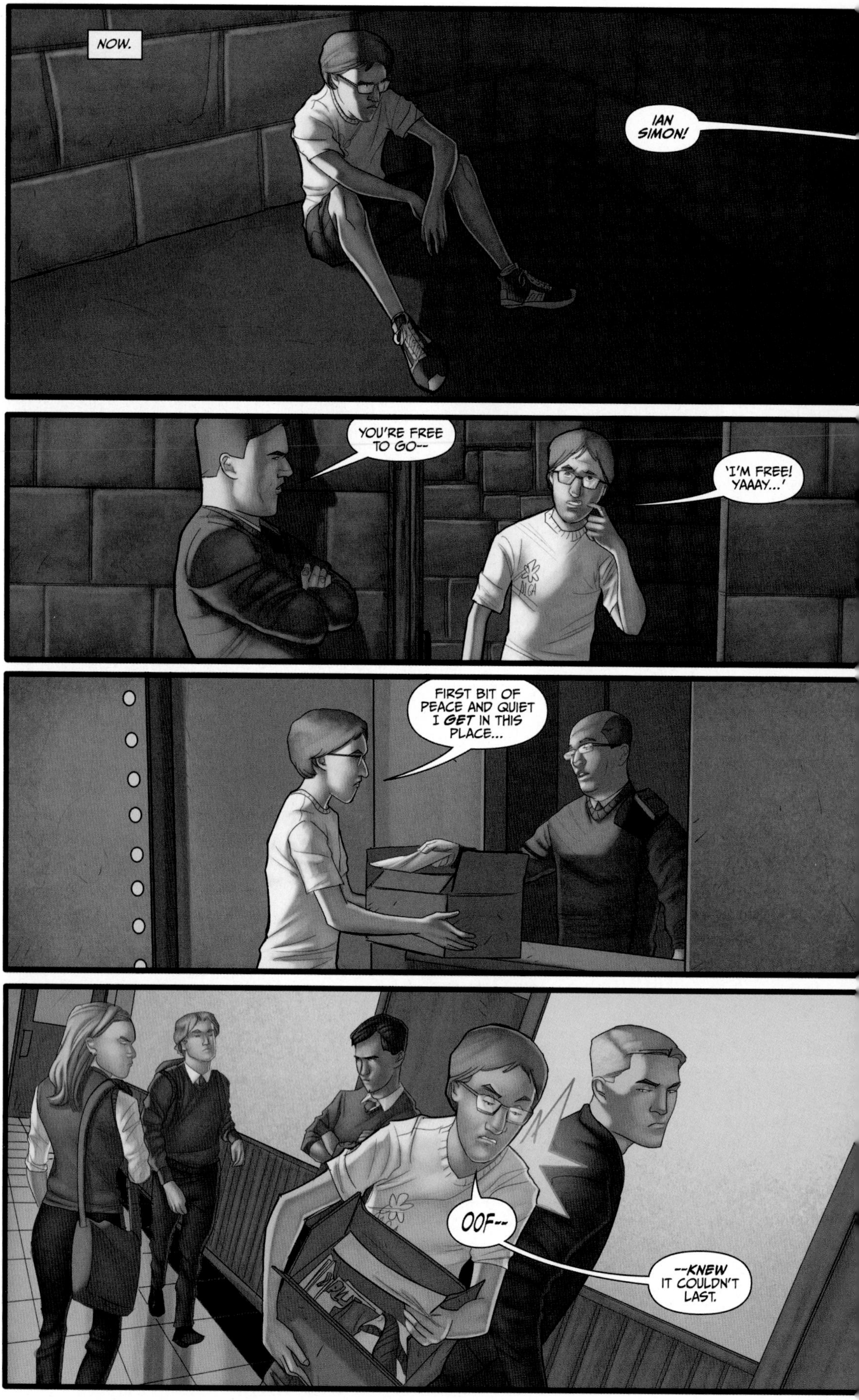
NOW.
IAN SIMON!
YOU'RE FREE TO GO--
'I'M FREE! YAAAY...'
FIRST BIT OF PEACE AND QUIET I GET IN THIS PLACE...
OOF--
--KNEW IT COULDN'T LAST.

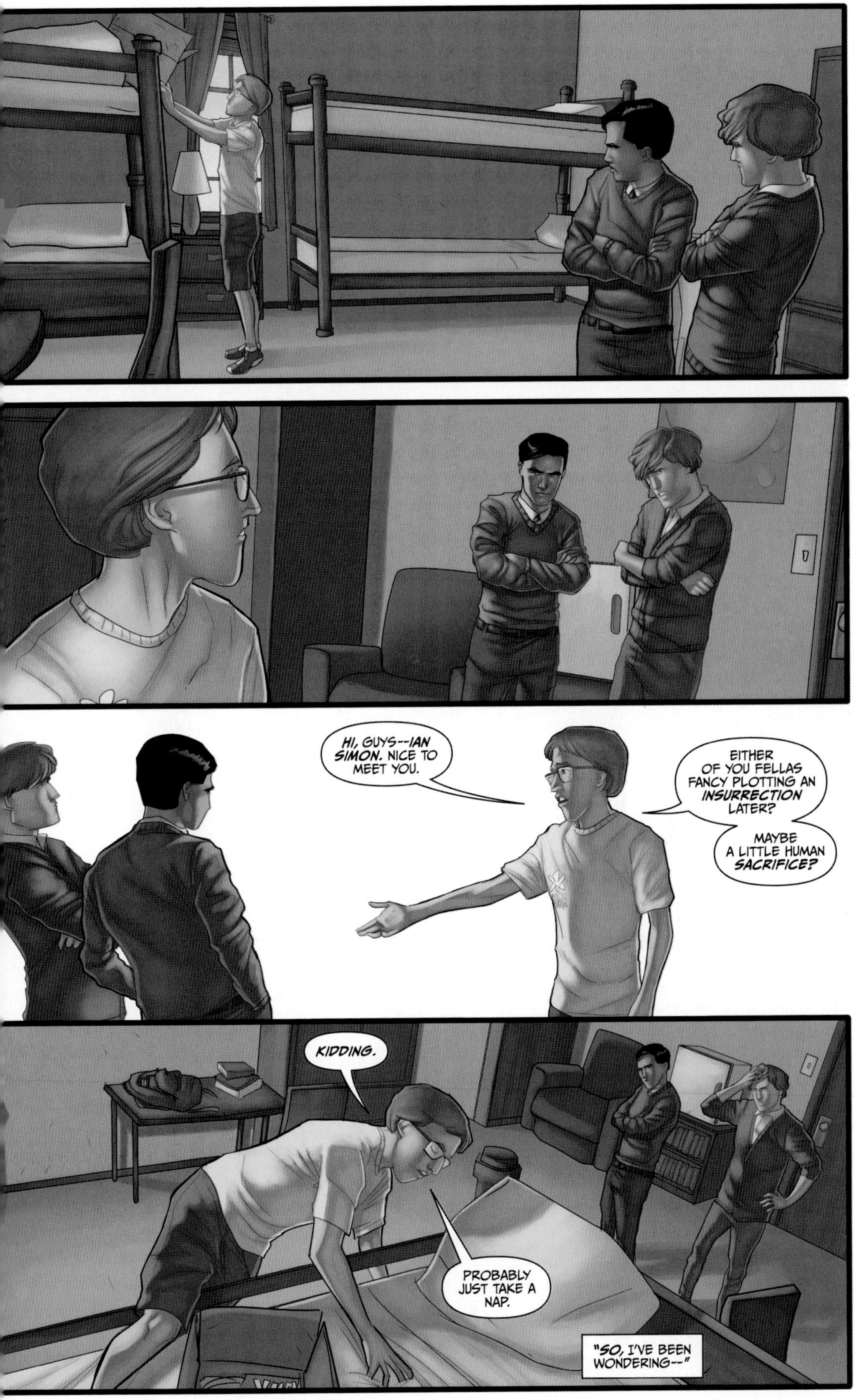
HI, GUYS--IAN SIMON. NICE TO MEET YOU.
EITHER OF YOU FELLAS FANCY PLOTTING AN INSURRECTION LATER?
MAYBE A LITTLE HUMAN SACRIFICE?
KIDDING.
PROBABLY JUST TAKE A NAP.
"SO, I'VE BEEN WONDERING--"

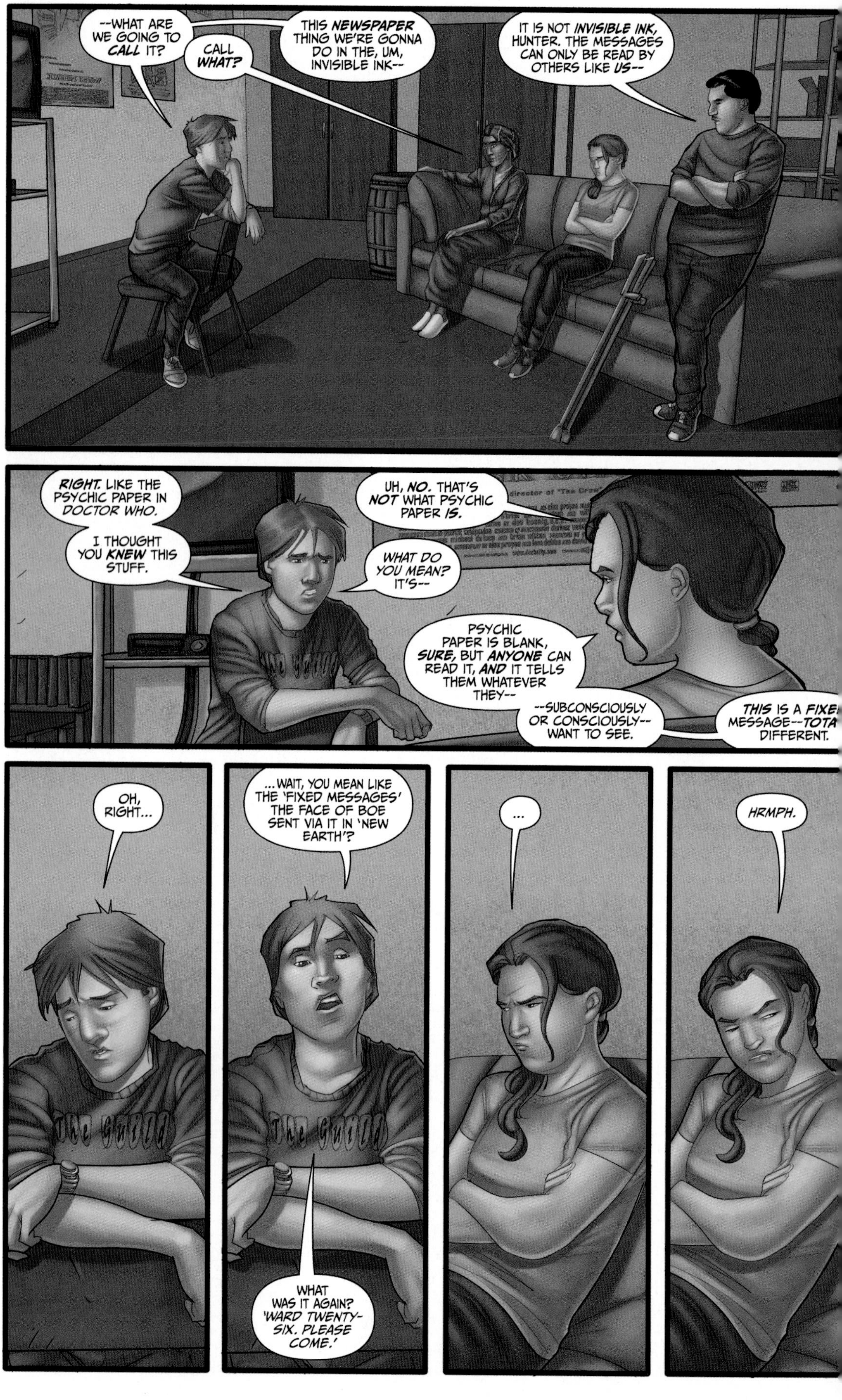
--WHAT ARE WE GOING TO CALL IT?
CALL WHAT?
THIS NEWSPAPER THING WE'RE GONNA DO IN THE, UM, INVISIBLE INK--
IT IS NOT INVISIBLE INK, HUNTER. THE MESSAGES CAN ONLY BE READ BY OTHERS LIKE US--
RIGHT. LIKE THE PSYCHIC PAPER IN DOCTOR WHO.
I THOUGHT YOU KNEW THIS STUFF.
UH, NO. THAT'S NOT WHAT PSYCHIC PAPER IS.
WHAT DO YOU MEAN? IT'S--
PSYCHIC PAPER IS BLANK, SURE, BUT ANYONE CAN READ IT, AND IT TELLS THEM WHATEVER THEY--
--SUBCONSCIOUSLY OR CONSCIOUSLY-- WANT TO SEE.
THIS IS A FIXE MESSAGE--TOTA DIFFERENT.
OH, RIGHT...
...WAIT, YOU MEAN LIKE THE 'FIXED MESSAGES' THE FACE OF BOE SENT VIA IT IN 'NEW EARTH'?
WHAT WAS IT AGAIN? 'WARD TWENTY-SIX. PLEASE COME.'
...
HRMPH.

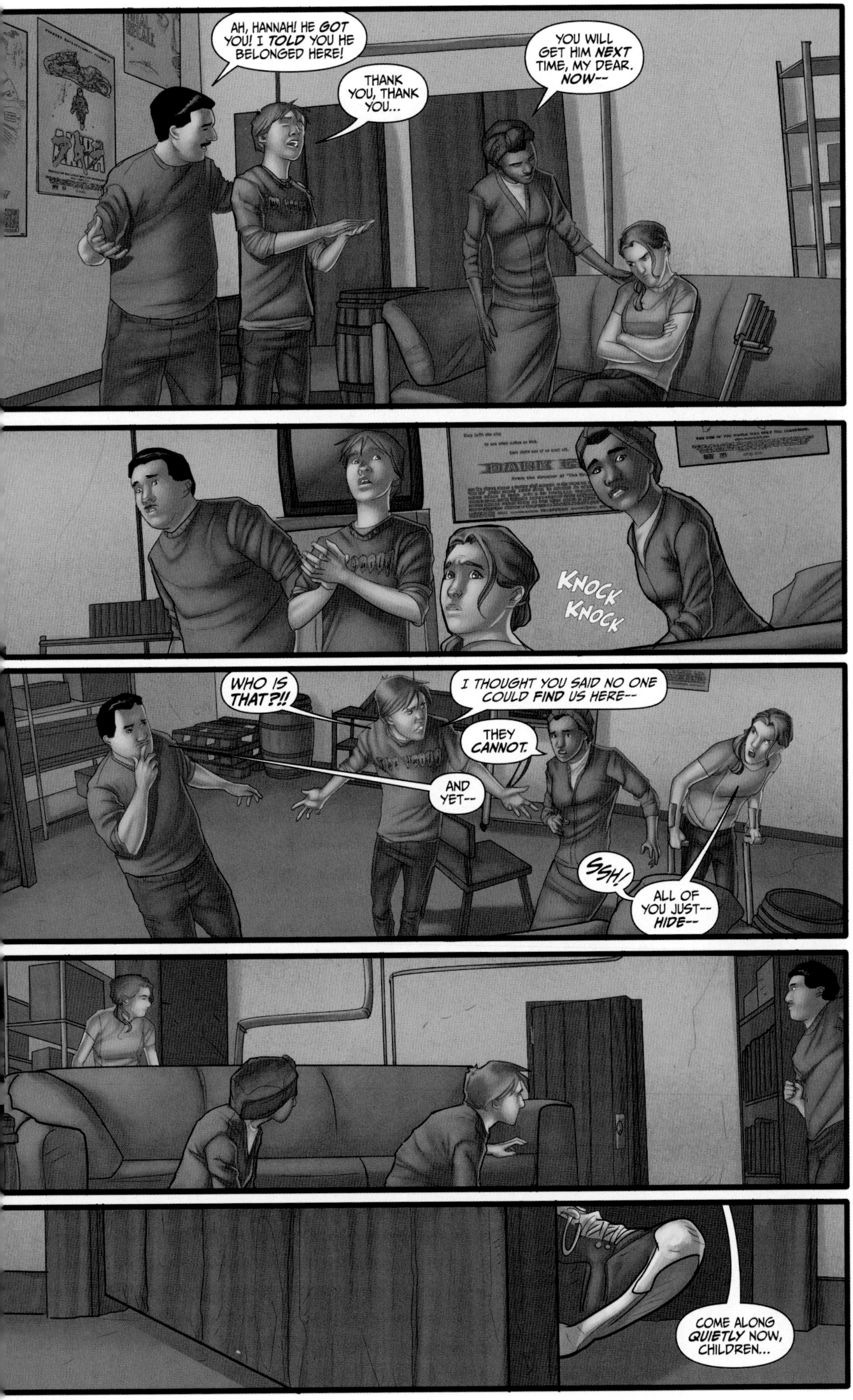
AH, HANNAH! HE GOT YOU! I TOLD YOU HE BELONGED HERE!
THANK YOU, THANK YOU...
YOU WILL GET HIM NEXT TIME, MY DEAR. NOW--
KNOCK KNOCK
WHO IS THAT?!!
I THOUGHT YOU SAID NO ONE COULD FIND US HERE--
THEY CANNOT.
AND YET--
SSH!
ALL OF YOU JUST-- HIDE--
COME ALONG QUIETLY NOW, CHILDREN...

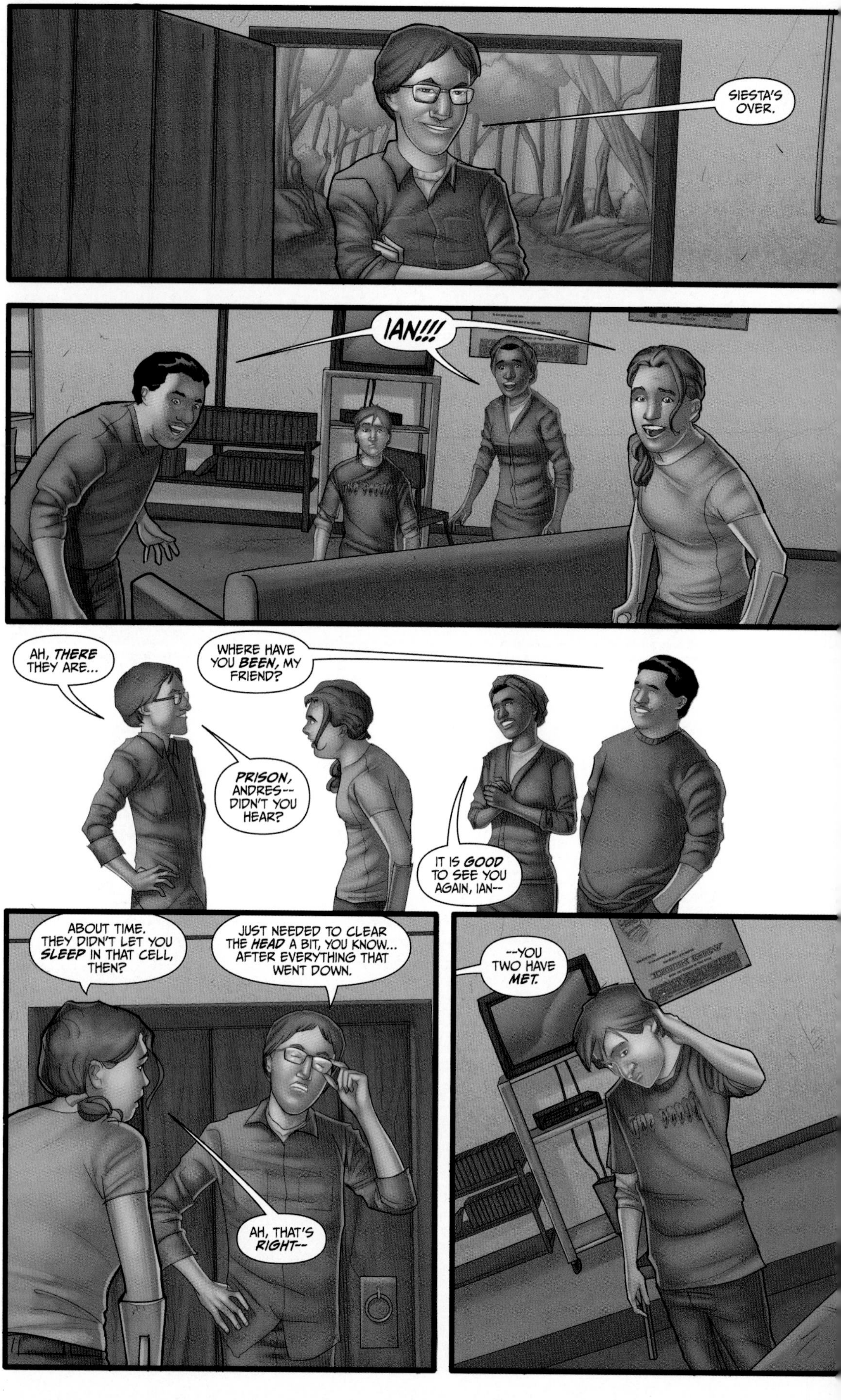
SIESTA'S OVER.
IAN!!!
AH, THERE THEY ARE...
WHERE HAVE YOU BEEN, MY FRIEND?
PRISON, ANDRES-- DIDN'T YOU HEAR?
IT IS GOOD TO SEE YOU AGAIN, IAN--
ABOUT TIME. THEY DIDN'T LET YOU SLEEP IN THAT CELL, THEN?
JUST NEEDED TO CLEAR THE HEAD A BIT, YOU KNOW... AFTER EVERYTHING THAT WENT DOWN.
AH, THAT'S RIGHT--
--YOU TWO HAVE MET.

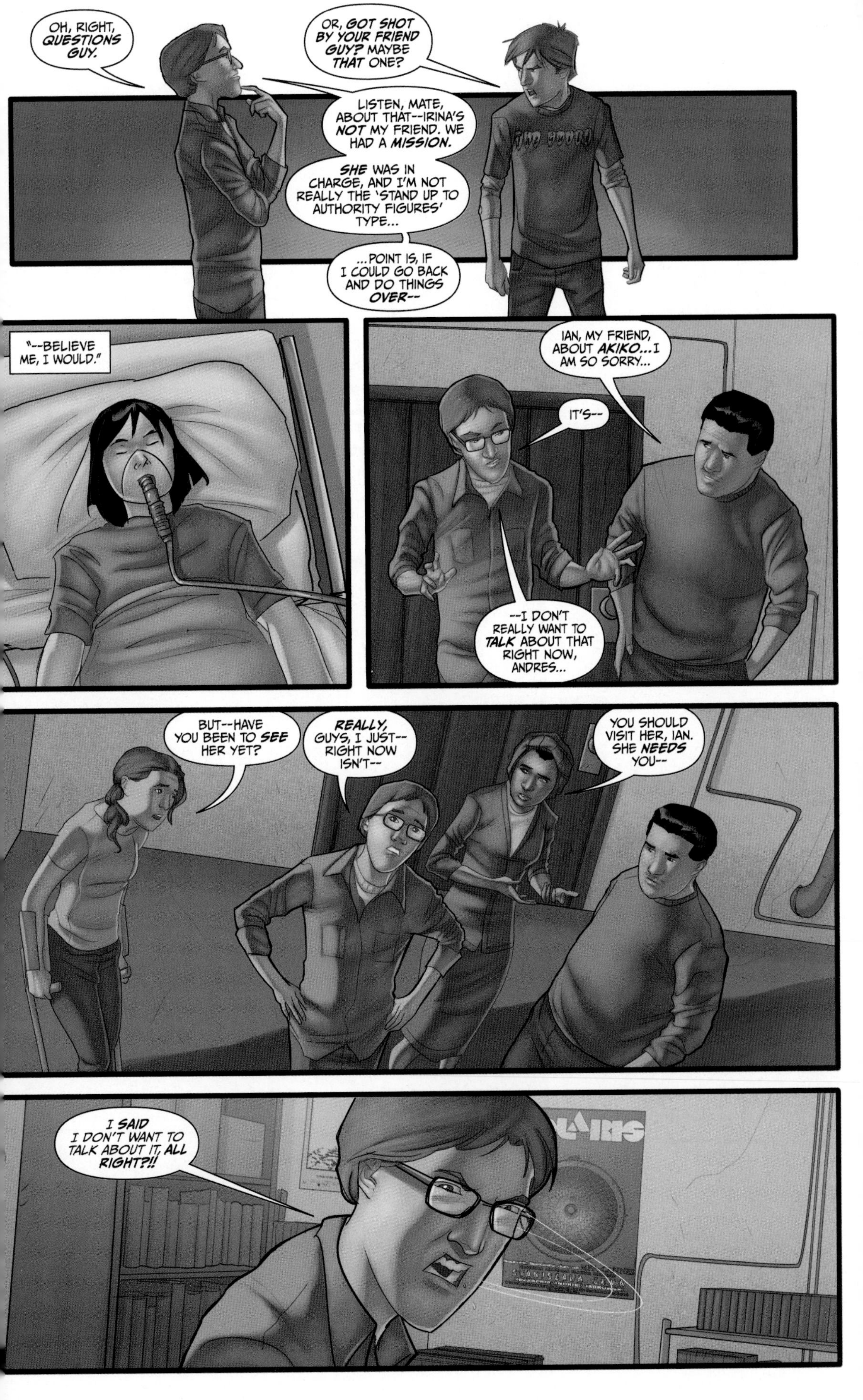
OH, RIGHT, QUESTIONS GUY.
OR, GOT SHOT BY YOUR FRIEND GUY? MAYBE THAT ONE?
LISTEN, MATE, ABOUT THAT--IRINA'S NOT MY FRIEND. WE HAD A MISSION.
SHE WAS IN CHARGE, AND I'M NOT REALLY THE 'STAND UP TO AUTHORITY FIGURES' TYPE...
...POINT IS, IF I COULD GO BACK AND DO THINGS OVER--
"--BELIEVE ME, I WOULD."
IAN, MY FRIEND, ABOUT AKIKO...I AM SO SORRY...
IT'S--
--I DON'T REALLY WANT TO TALK ABOUT THAT RIGHT NOW, ANDRES...
BUT--HAVE YOU BEEN TO SEE HER YET?
REALLY, GUYS, I JUST--RIGHT NOW ISN'T--
YOU SHOULD VISIT HER, IAN. SHE NEEDS YOU--
I SAID I DON'T WANT TO TALK ABOUT IT, ALL RIGHT?!!
SOLARIS

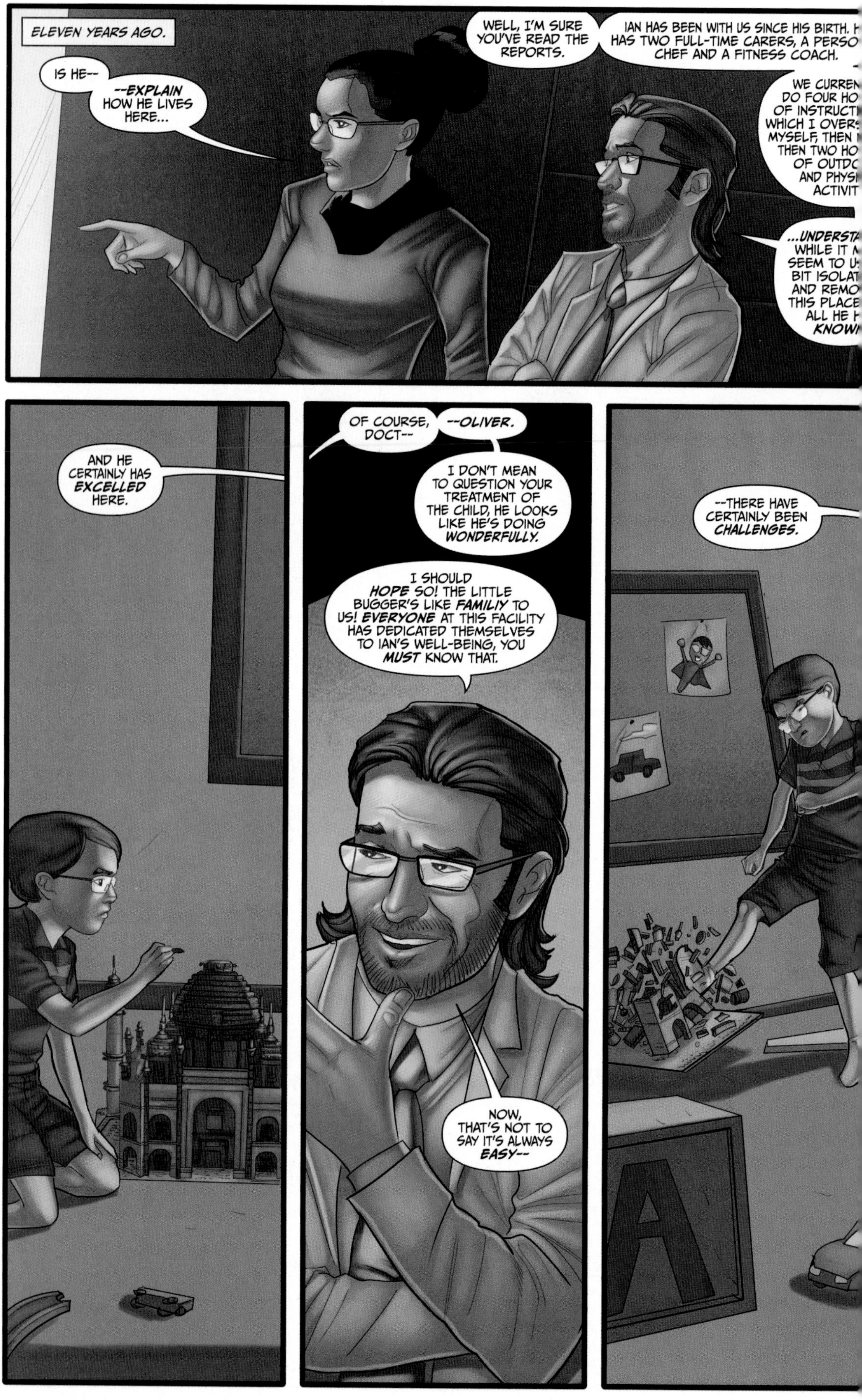

ELEVEN YEARS AGO.
IS HE--
--EXPLAIN HOW HE LIVES HERE...
WELL, I'M SURE YOU'VE READ THE REPORTS.
IAN HAS BEEN WITH US SINCE HIS BIRTH. H HAS TWO FULL-TIME CARERS, A PERSO CHEF AND A FITNESS COACH.
WE CURREN DO FOUR HO OF INSTRUCT WHICH I OVERS MYSELF, THEN THEN TWO HO OF OUTDO AND PHYS ACTIVIT
...UNDERSTA WHILE IT M SEEM TO U BIT ISOLAT AND REMO THIS PLACE ALL HE H KNOW
AND HE CERTAINLY HAS EXCELLED HERE.
OF COURSE, DOCT--
--OLIVER.
I DON'T MEAN TO QUESTION YOUR TREATMENT OF THE CHILD, HE LOOKS LIKE HE'S DOING WONDERFULLY.
I SHOULD HOPE SO! THE LITTLE BUGGER'S LIKE FAMILIY TO US! EVERYONE AT THIS FACILITY HAS DEDICATED THEMSELVES TO IAN'S WELL-BEING, YOU MUST KNOW THAT.
NOW, THAT'S NOT TO SAY IT'S ALWAYS EASY--
--THERE HAVE CERTAINLY BEEN CHALLENGES.
A

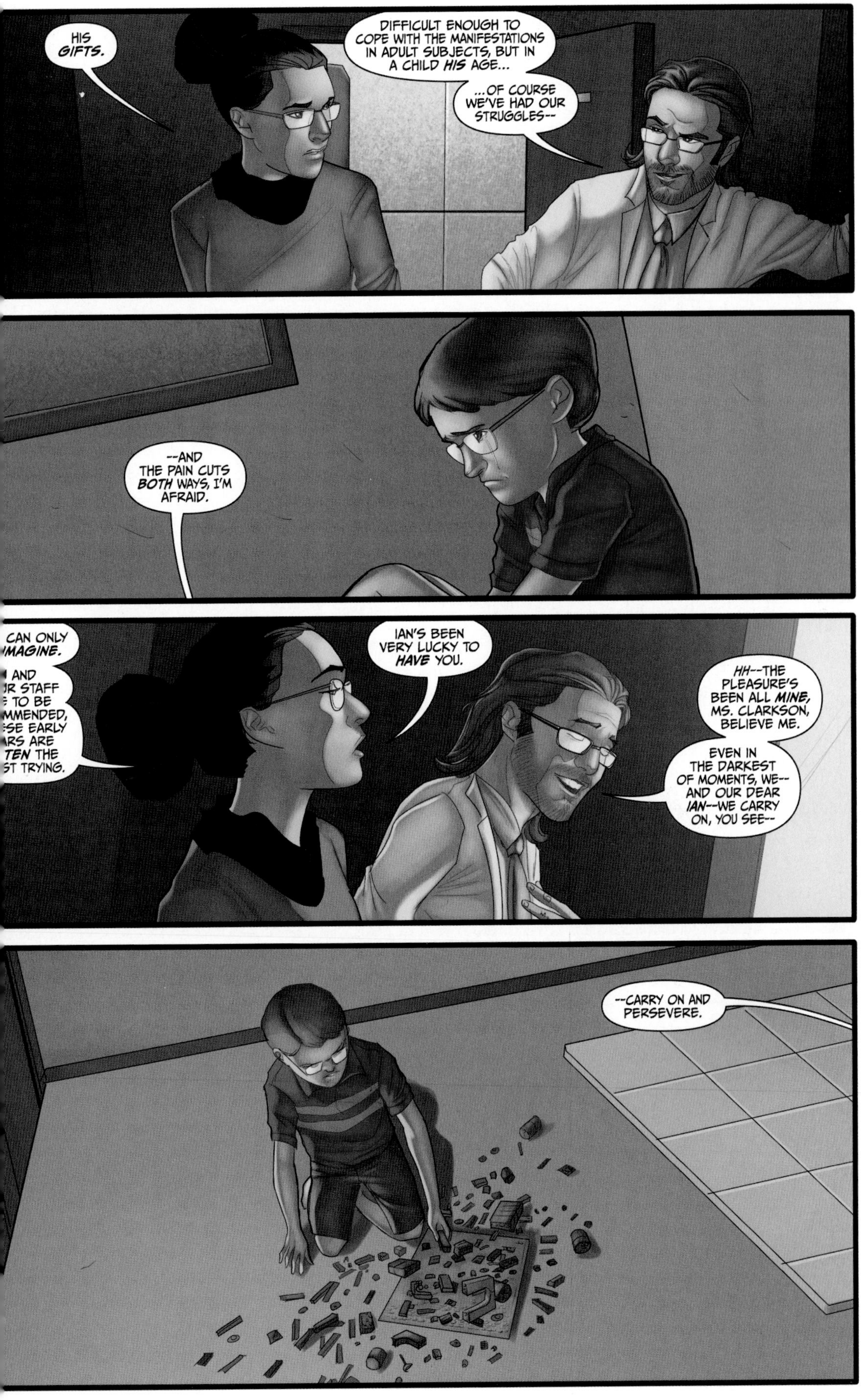
HIS *GIFTS.*
DIFFICULT ENOUGH TO COPE WITH THE MANIFESTATIONS IN ADULT SUBJECTS, BUT IN A CHILD *HIS* AGE...
...OF COURSE WE'VE HAD OUR STRUGGLES--
--AND THE PAIN CUTS *BOTH* WAYS, I'M AFRAID.
CAN ONLY *MAGINE.*
AND R STAFF E TO BE MMENDED, ESE EARLY ARS ARE *TEN* THE ST TRYING.
IAN'S BEEN VERY LUCKY TO *HAVE* YOU.
HH--THE PLEASURE'S BEEN ALL *MINE,* MS. CLARKSON, BELIEVE ME.
EVEN IN THE DARKEST OF MOMENTS, WE-- AND OUR DEAR *IAN*--WE CARRY ON, YOU SEE--
--CARRY ON AND PERSEVERE.

NOW.

I'M SORRY, GUYS--I--I DIDN'T MEAN TO BE A DICK.

I JUST-- IT'S A LOT TO *PROCESS* RIGHT NOW, BEEN THROUGH A LOT...

WE UNDERSTAND, OLD FRIEND.

WHENEVER YOU NEED US.

AND WE ARE HERE FOR YOU.

THANKS, GUYS.

SO--WHAT WERE YOU LOT DOING BEFORE *I* GOT HERE?

NOT MUCH, JUST--

THE NEWSPAPER PROJECT.

OH, RIGHT-- THE ANSWER.

YOU *NAMED* IT?

YOU'RE STUCK IN A JAIL CELL IN THAT BASEMENT, THE MIND *WANDERS.*

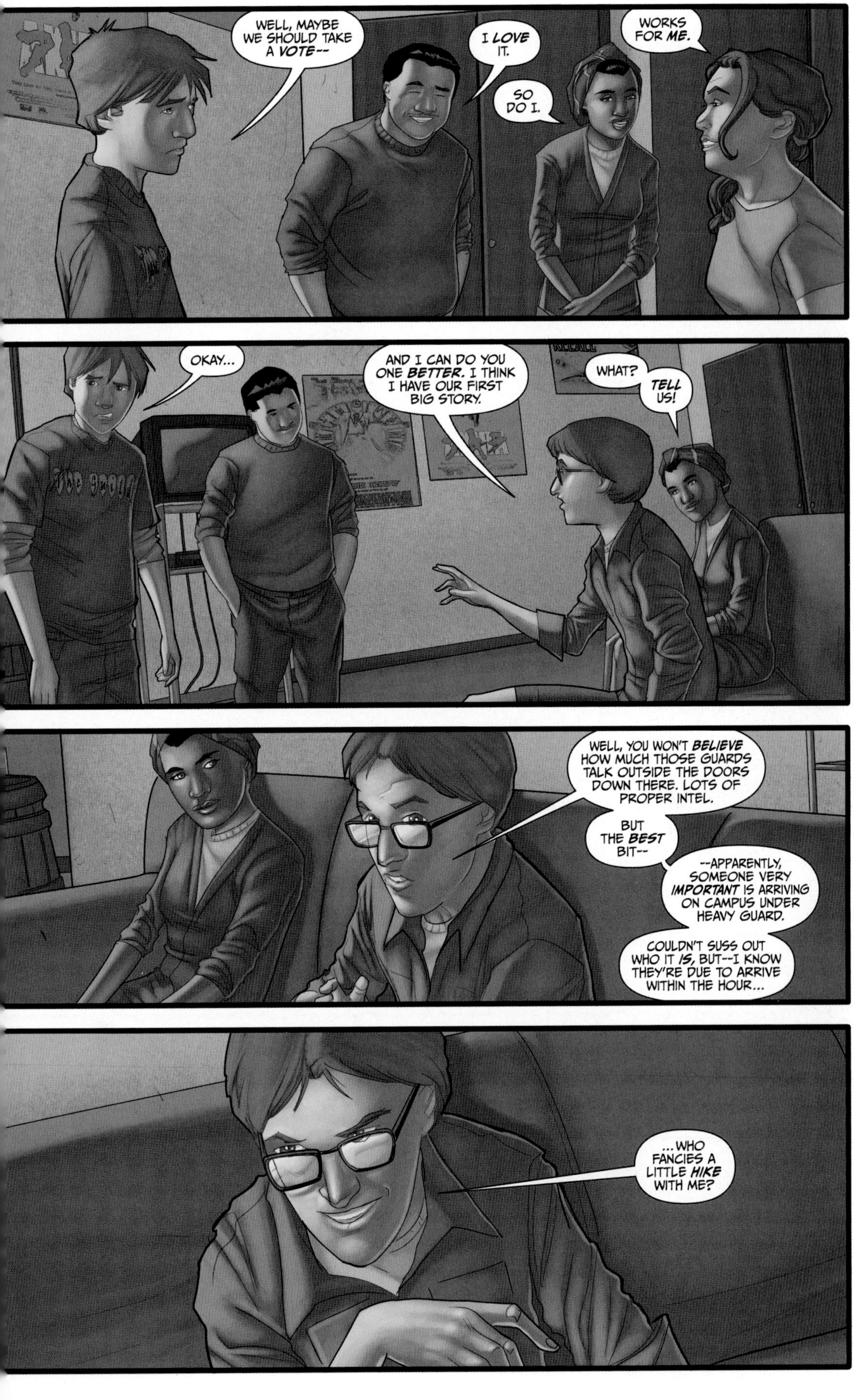
WELL, MAYBE WE SHOULD TAKE A *VOTE*--
I *LOVE* IT.
SO DO I.
WORKS FOR *ME*.
OKAY...
AND I CAN DO YOU ONE *BETTER*. I THINK I HAVE OUR FIRST BIG STORY.
WHAT?
TELL US!
WELL, YOU WON'T *BELIEVE* HOW MUCH THOSE GUARDS TALK OUTSIDE THE DOORS DOWN THERE. LOTS OF PROPER INTEL.
BUT THE *BEST* BIT--
--APPARENTLY, SOMEONE VERY *IMPORTANT* IS ARRIVING ON CAMPUS UNDER HEAVY GUARD.
COULDN'T SUSS OUT WHO IT *IS*, BUT--I KNOW THEY'RE DUE TO ARRIVE WITHIN THE HOUR...
...WHO FANCIES A LITTLE *HIKE* WITH ME?

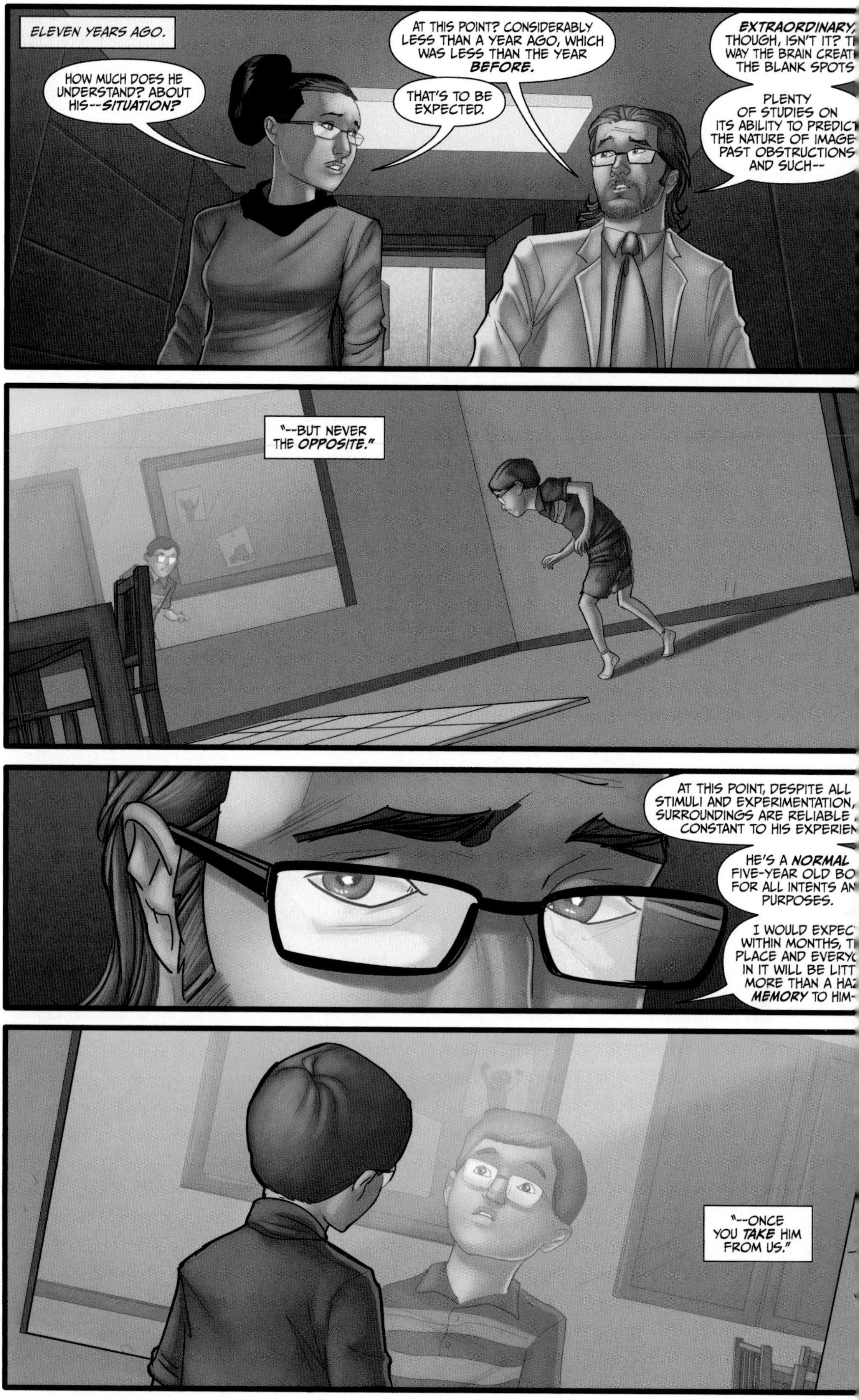
ELEVEN YEARS AGO.
HOW MUCH DOES HE UNDERSTAND? ABOUT HIS--SITUATION?
THAT'S TO BE EXPECTED.
AT THIS POINT? CONSIDERABLY LESS THAN A YEAR AGO, WHICH WAS LESS THAN THE YEAR BEFORE.
EXTRAORDINARY, THOUGH, ISN'T IT? T WAY THE BRAIN CREAT THE BLANK SPOTS
PLENTY OF STUDIES ON ITS ABILITY TO PREDIC THE NATURE OF IMAGE PAST OBSTRUCTIONS AND SUCH--
"--BUT NEVER THE OPPOSITE."
AT THIS POINT, DESPITE ALL STIMULI AND EXPERIMENTATION, SURROUNDINGS ARE RELIABLE CONSTANT TO HIS EXPERIEN
HE'S A NORMAL FIVE-YEAR OLD BO FOR ALL INTENTS AN PURPOSES.
I WOULD EXPEC WITHIN MONTHS, T PLACE AND EVERY IN IT WILL BE LITT MORE THAN A HA MEMORY TO HIM-
"--ONCE YOU TAKE HIM FROM US."

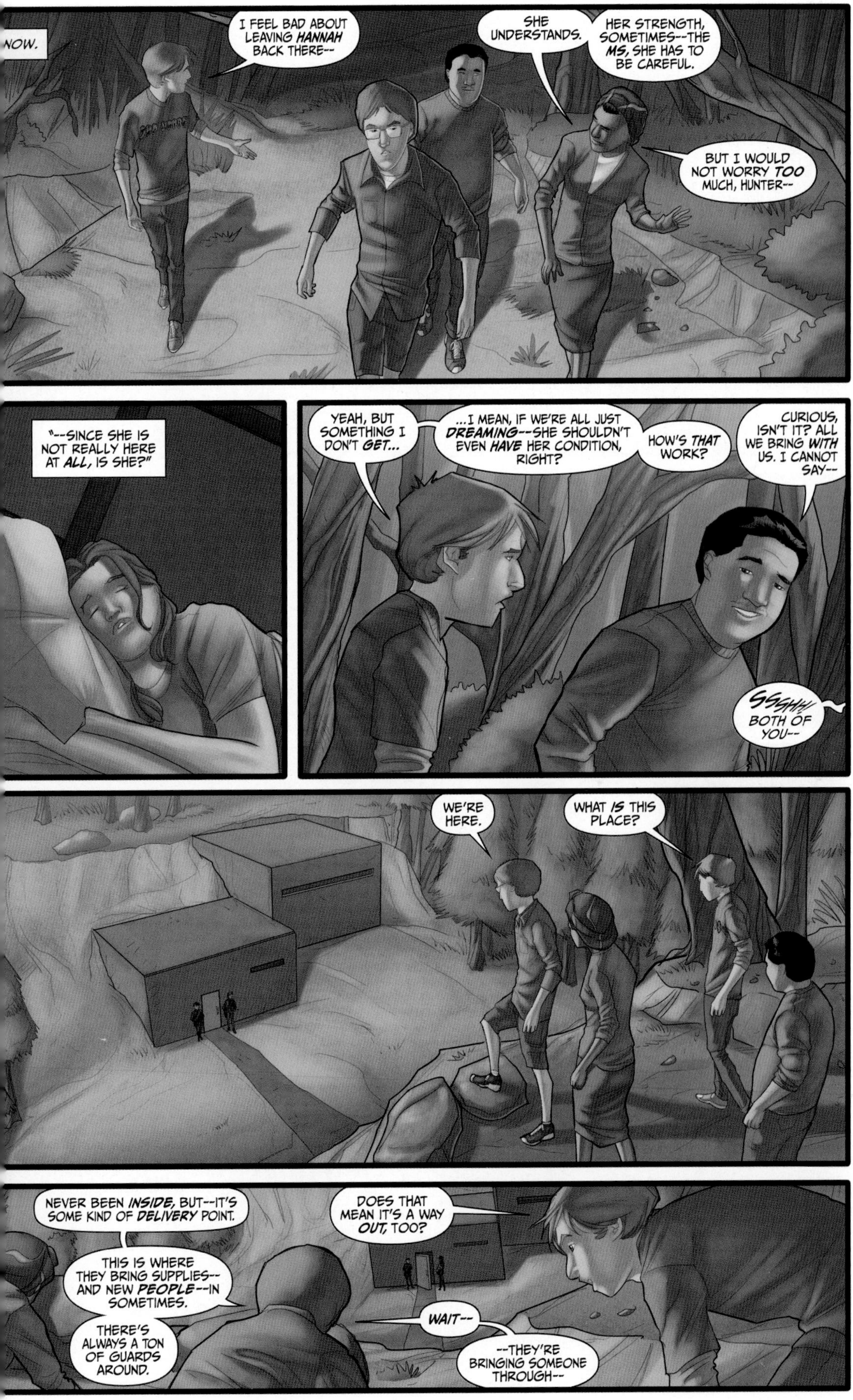
NOW.
I FEEL BAD ABOUT LEAVING HANNAH BACK THERE--
SHE UNDERSTANDS.
HER STRENGTH, SOMETIMES--THE MS, SHE HAS TO BE CAREFUL.
BUT I WOULD NOT WORRY TOO MUCH, HUNTER--
"--SINCE SHE IS NOT REALLY HERE AT ALL, IS SHE?"
YEAH, BUT SOMETHING I DON'T GET...
...I MEAN, IF WE'RE ALL JUST DREAMING--SHE SHOULDN'T EVEN HAVE HER CONDITION, RIGHT?
HOW'S THAT WORK?
CURIOUS, ISN'T IT? ALL WE BRING WITH US. I CANNOT SAY--
SSSHH! BOTH OF YOU--
WE'RE HERE.
WHAT IS THIS PLACE?
NEVER BEEN INSIDE, BUT--IT'S SOME KIND OF DELIVERY POINT.
THIS IS WHERE THEY BRING SUPPLIES--AND NEW PEOPLE--IN SOMETIMES.
THERE'S ALWAYS A TON OF GUARDS AROUND.
DOES THAT MEAN IT'S A WAY OUT, TOO?
WAIT--
--THEY'RE BRINGING SOMEONE THROUGH--

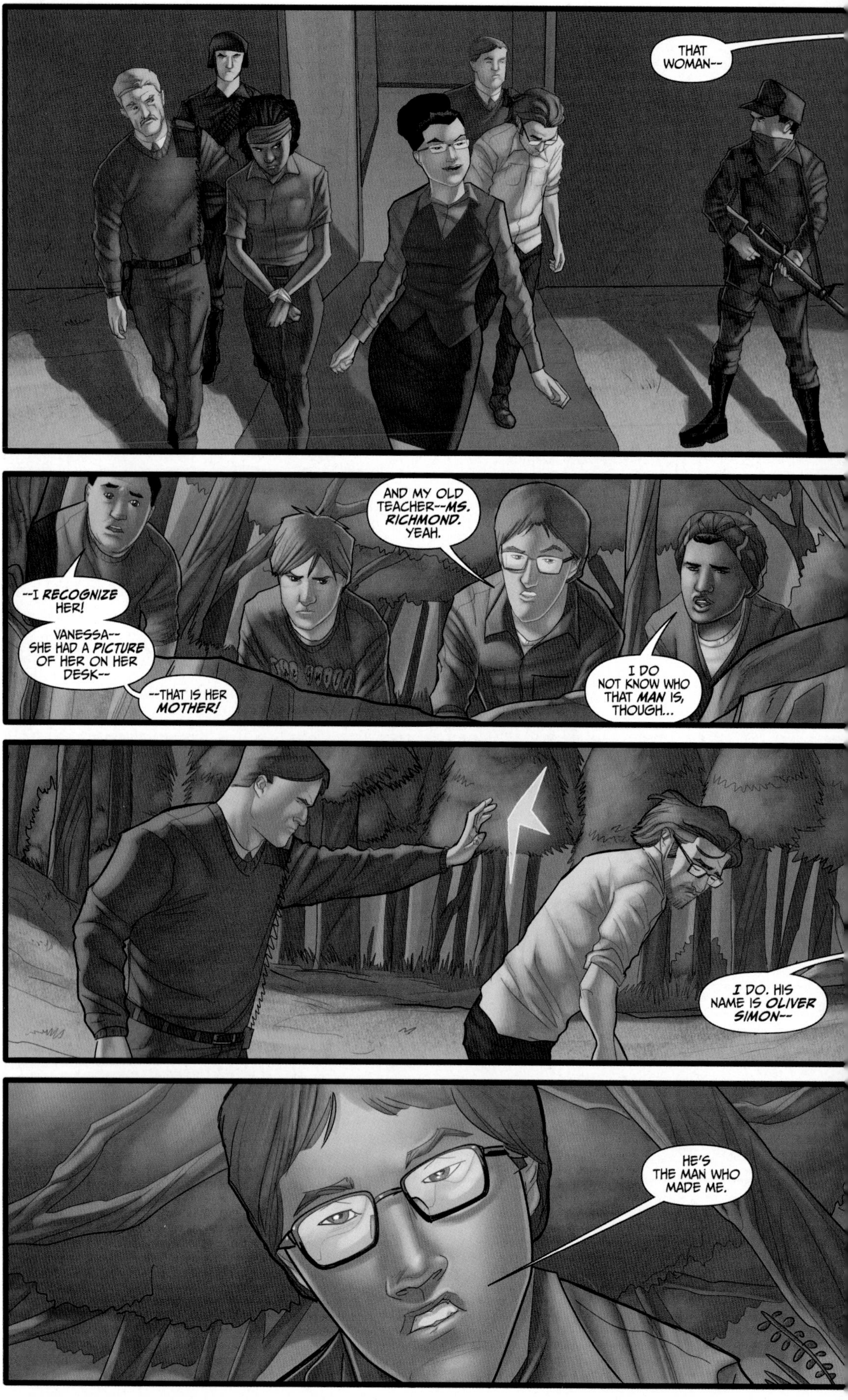
THAT WOMAN--
--I RECOGNIZE HER!
VANESSA-- SHE HAD A PICTURE OF HER ON HER DESK--
--THAT IS HER MOTHER!
AND MY OLD TEACHER--MS. RICHMOND. YEAH.
I DO NOT KNOW WHO THAT MAN IS, THOUGH...
I DO. HIS NAME IS OLIVER SIMON--
HE'S THE MAN WHO MADE ME.

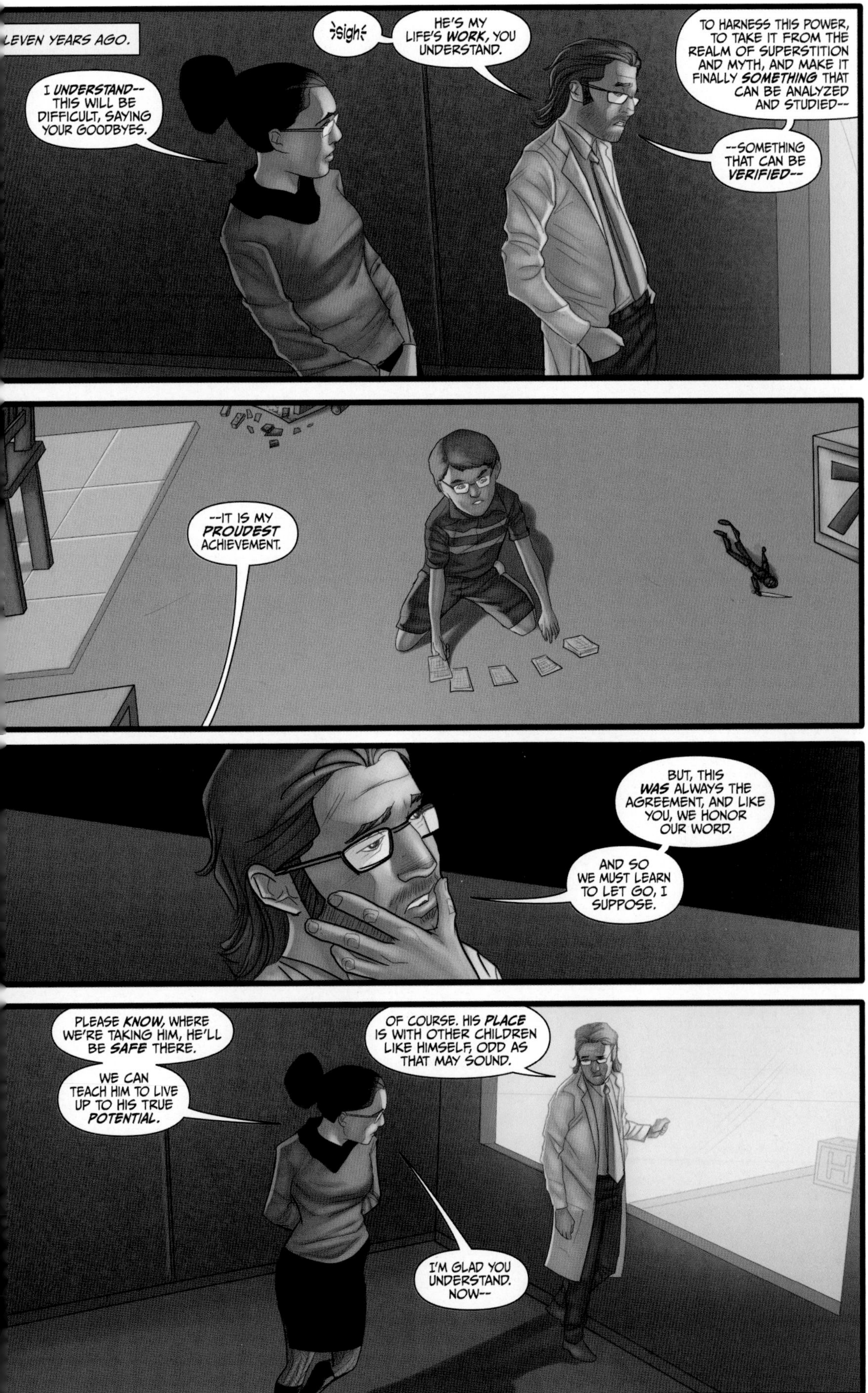
LEVEN YEARS AGO.
I UNDERSTAND-- THIS WILL BE DIFFICULT, SAYING YOUR GOODBYES.
sigh
HE'S MY LIFE'S WORK, YOU UNDERSTAND.
TO HARNESS THIS POWER, TO TAKE IT FROM THE REALM OF SUPERSTITION AND MYTH, AND MAKE IT FINALLY SOMETHING THAT CAN BE ANALYZED AND STUDIED--
--SOMETHING THAT CAN BE VERIFIED--
--IT IS MY PROUDEST ACHIEVEMENT.
BUT, THIS WAS ALWAYS THE AGREEMENT, AND LIKE YOU, WE HONOR OUR WORD.
AND SO WE MUST LEARN TO LET GO, I SUPPOSE.
PLEASE KNOW, WHERE WE'RE TAKING HIM, HE'LL BE SAFE THERE.
WE CAN TEACH HIM TO LIVE UP TO HIS TRUE POTENTIAL.
OF COURSE. HIS PLACE IS WITH OTHER CHILDREN LIKE HIMSELF, ODD AS THAT MAY SOUND.
I'M GLAD YOU UNDERSTAND. NOW--

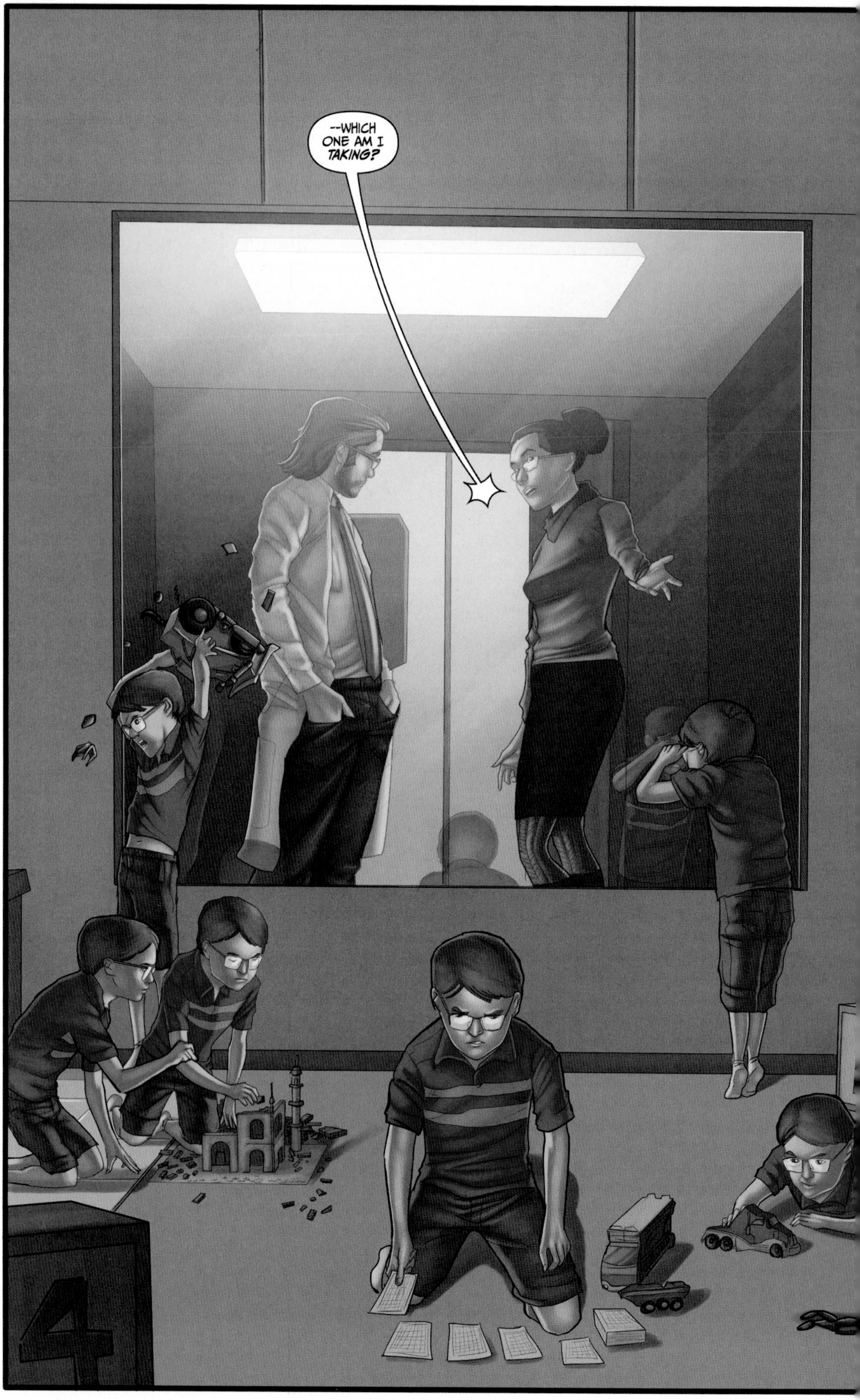
--WHICH ONE AM I TAKING?

thirtyseven

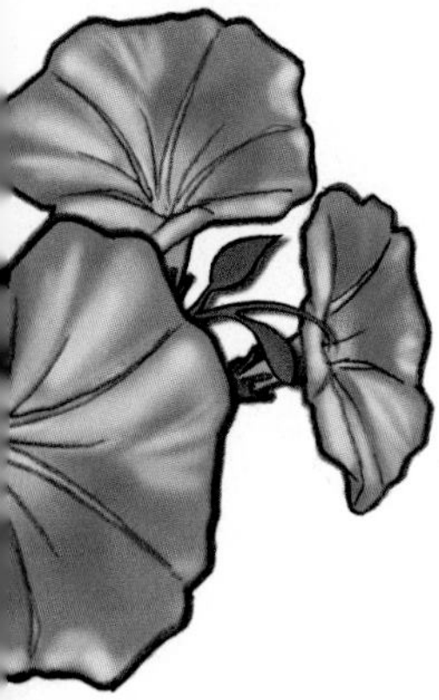

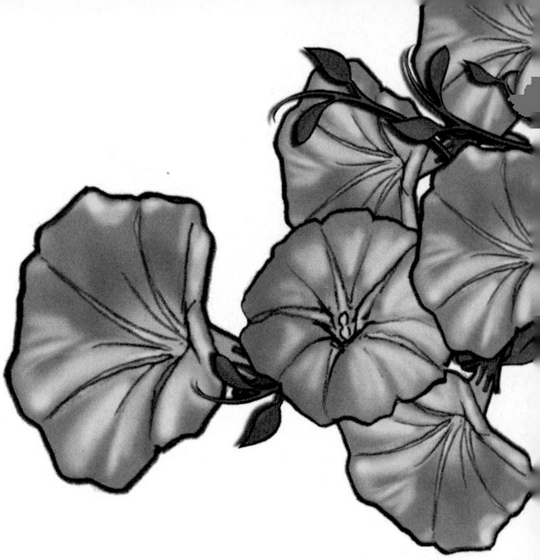

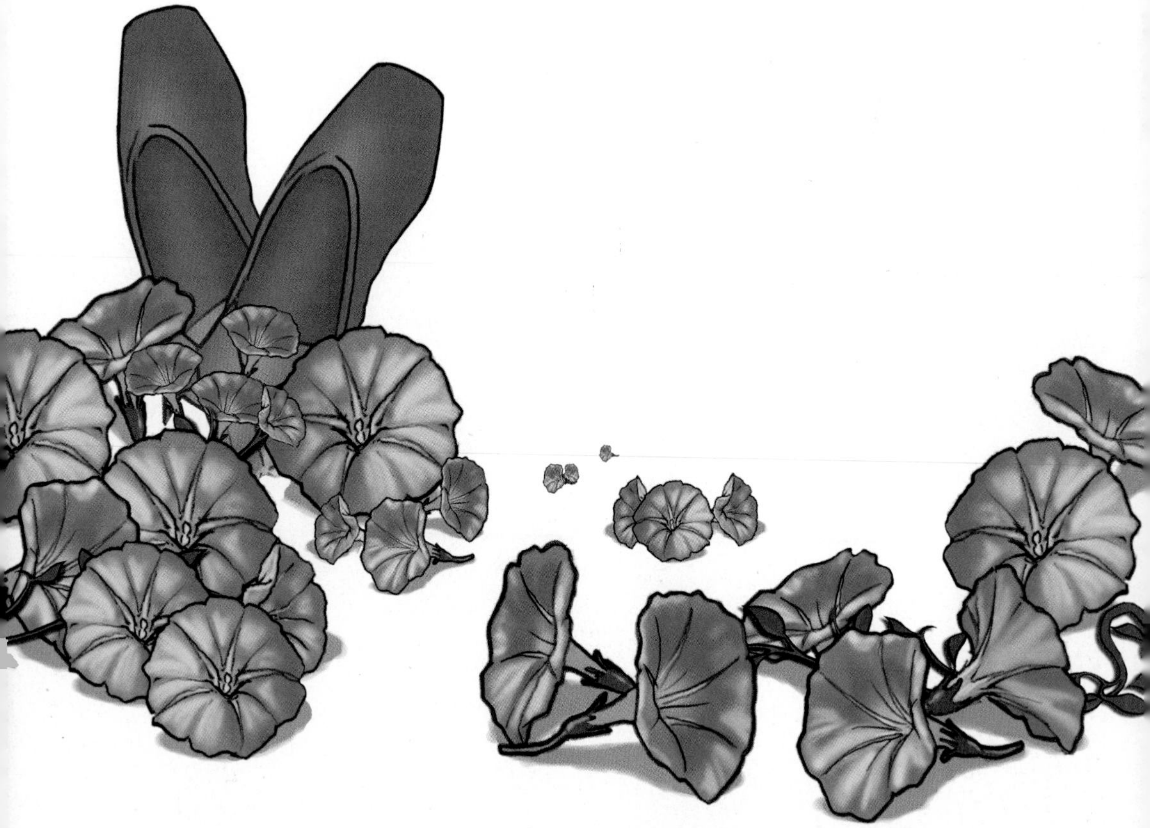

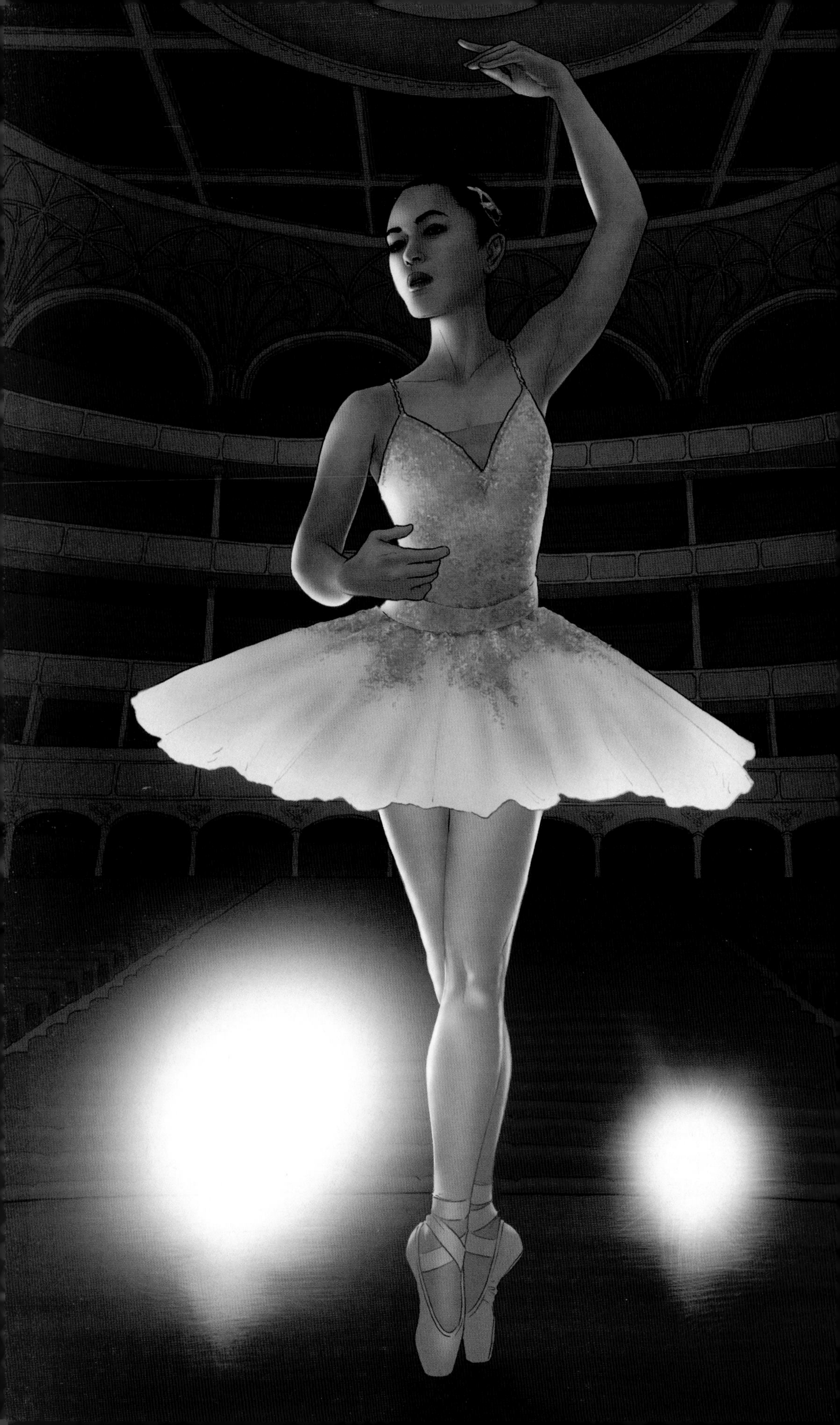

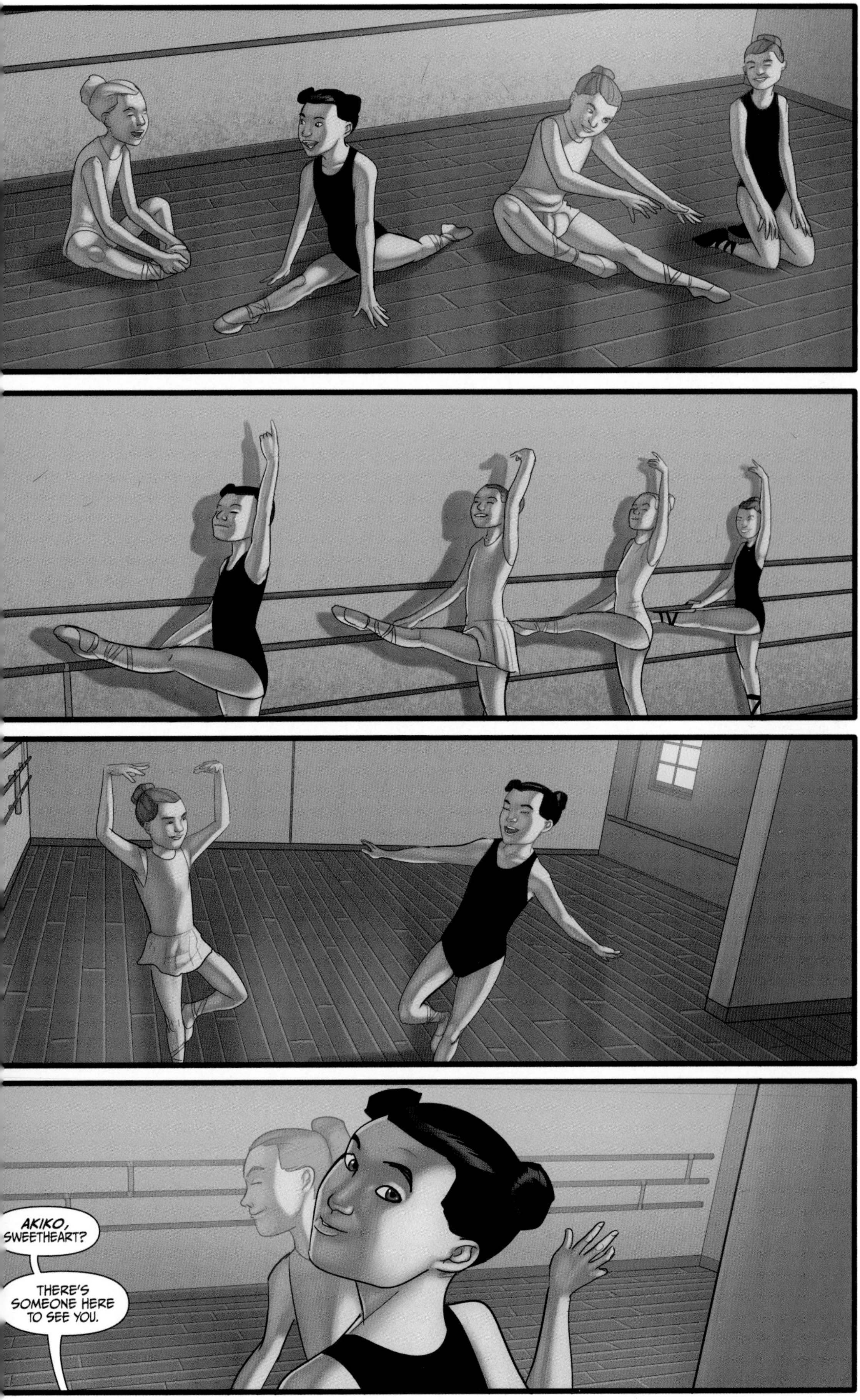
AKIKO, SWEETHEART?
THERE'S SOMEONE HERE TO SEE YOU.

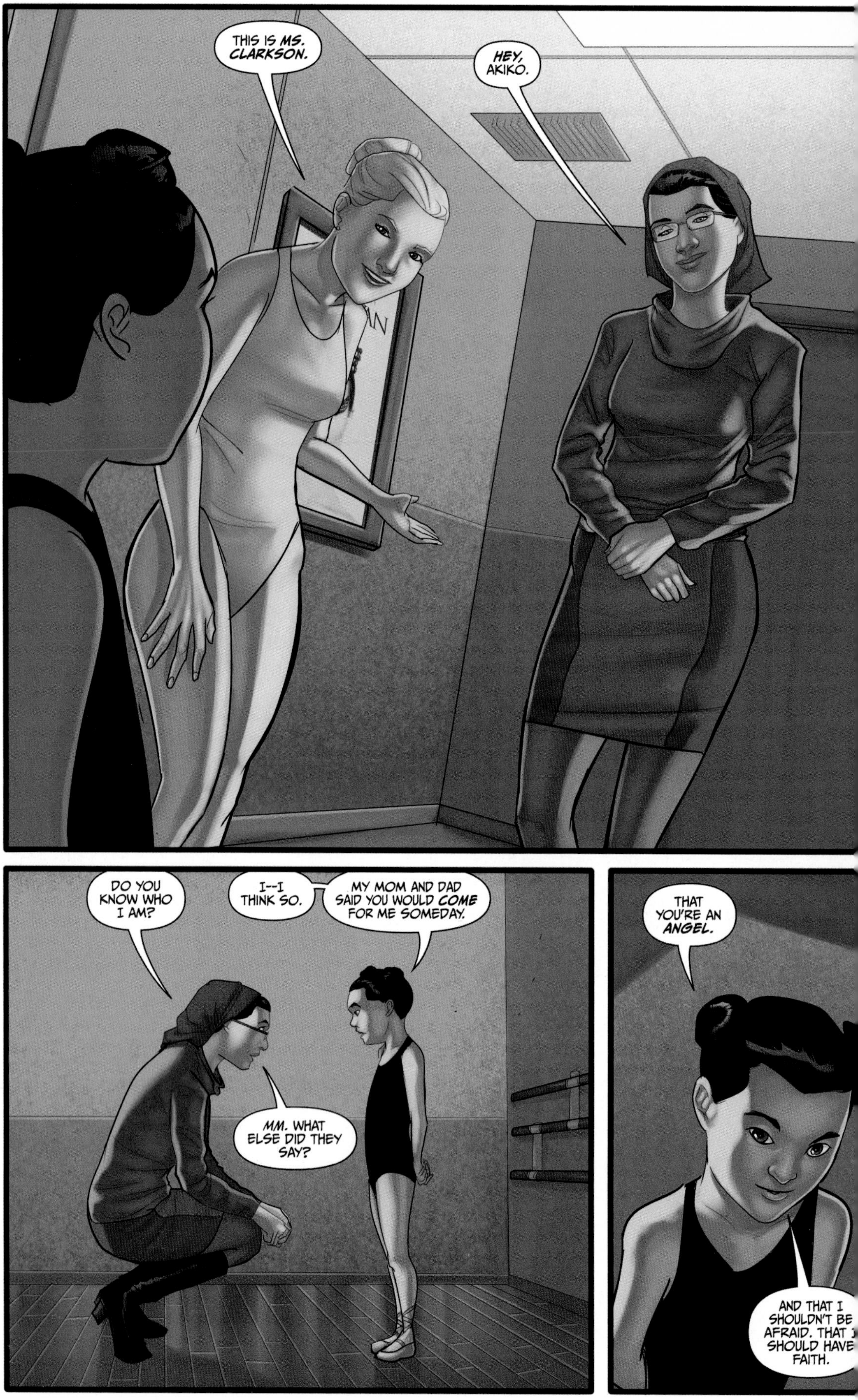
THIS IS MS. CLARKSON.
HEY, AKIKO.
DO YOU KNOW WHO I AM?
I--I THINK SO.
MY MOM AND DAD SAID YOU WOULD COME FOR ME SOMEDAY.
MM. WHAT ELSE DID THEY SAY?
THAT YOU'RE AN ANGEL.
AND THAT I SHOULDN'T BE AFRAID. THAT I SHOULD HAVE FAITH.

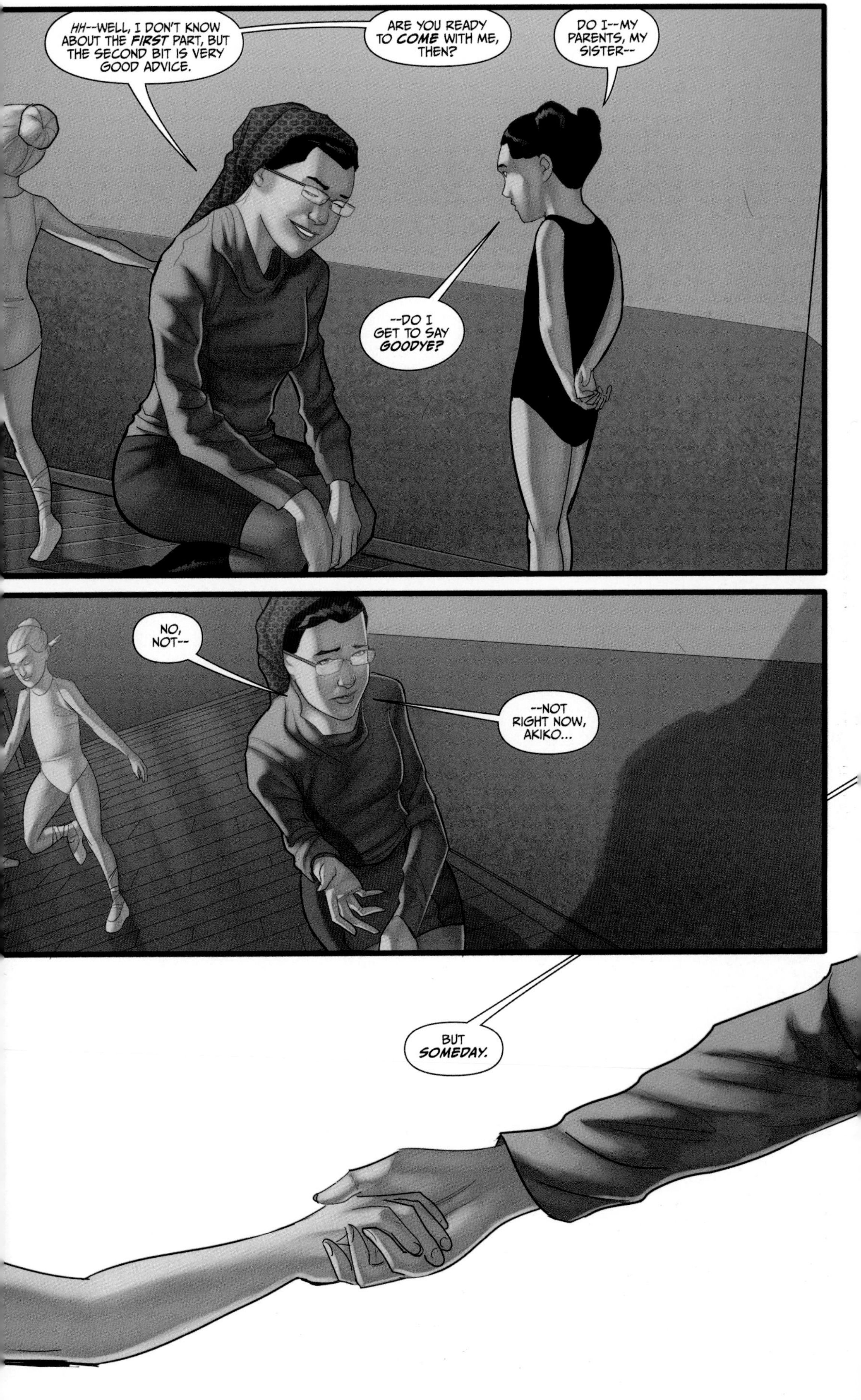
HH--WELL, I DON'T KNOW ABOUT THE FIRST PART, BUT THE SECOND BIT IS VERY GOOD ADVICE.
ARE YOU READY TO COME WITH ME, THEN?
DO I--MY PARENTS, MY SISTER--
--DO I GET TO SAY GOODYE?
NO, NOT--
--NOT RIGHT NOW, AKIKO...
BUT SOMEDAY.

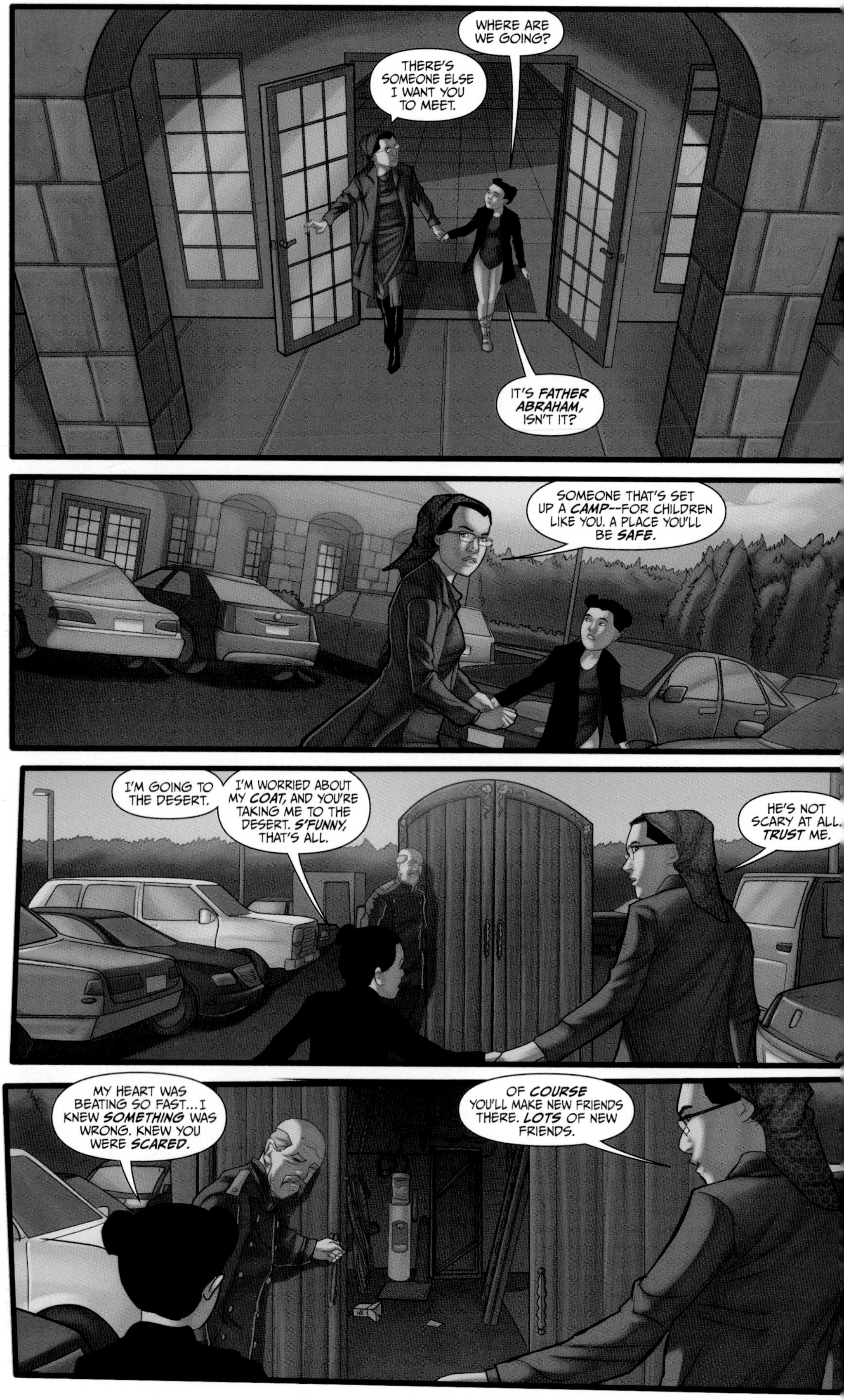
WHERE ARE WE GOING?
THERE'S SOMEONE ELSE I WANT YOU TO MEET.
IT'S FATHER ABRAHAM, ISN'T IT?
SOMEONE THAT'S SET UP A CAMP--FOR CHILDREN LIKE YOU. A PLACE YOU'LL BE SAFE.
I'M GOING TO THE DESERT.
I'M WORRIED ABOUT MY COAT, AND YOU'RE TAKING ME TO THE DESERT. S'FUNNY, THAT'S ALL.
HE'S NOT SCARY AT ALL. TRUST ME.
MY HEART WAS BEATING SO FAST... I KNEW SOMETHING WAS WRONG. KNEW YOU WERE SCARED.
OF COURSE YOU'LL MAKE NEW FRIENDS THERE. LOTS OF NEW FRIENDS.

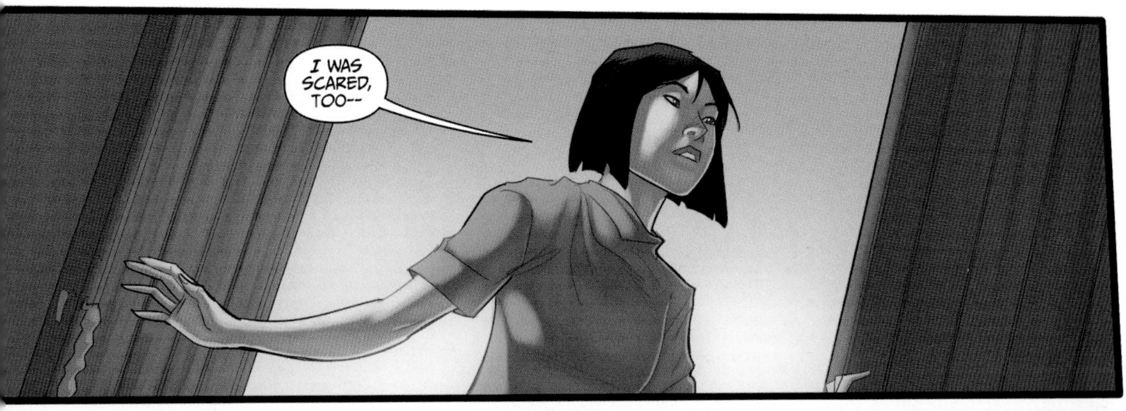
I WAS SCARED, TOO--

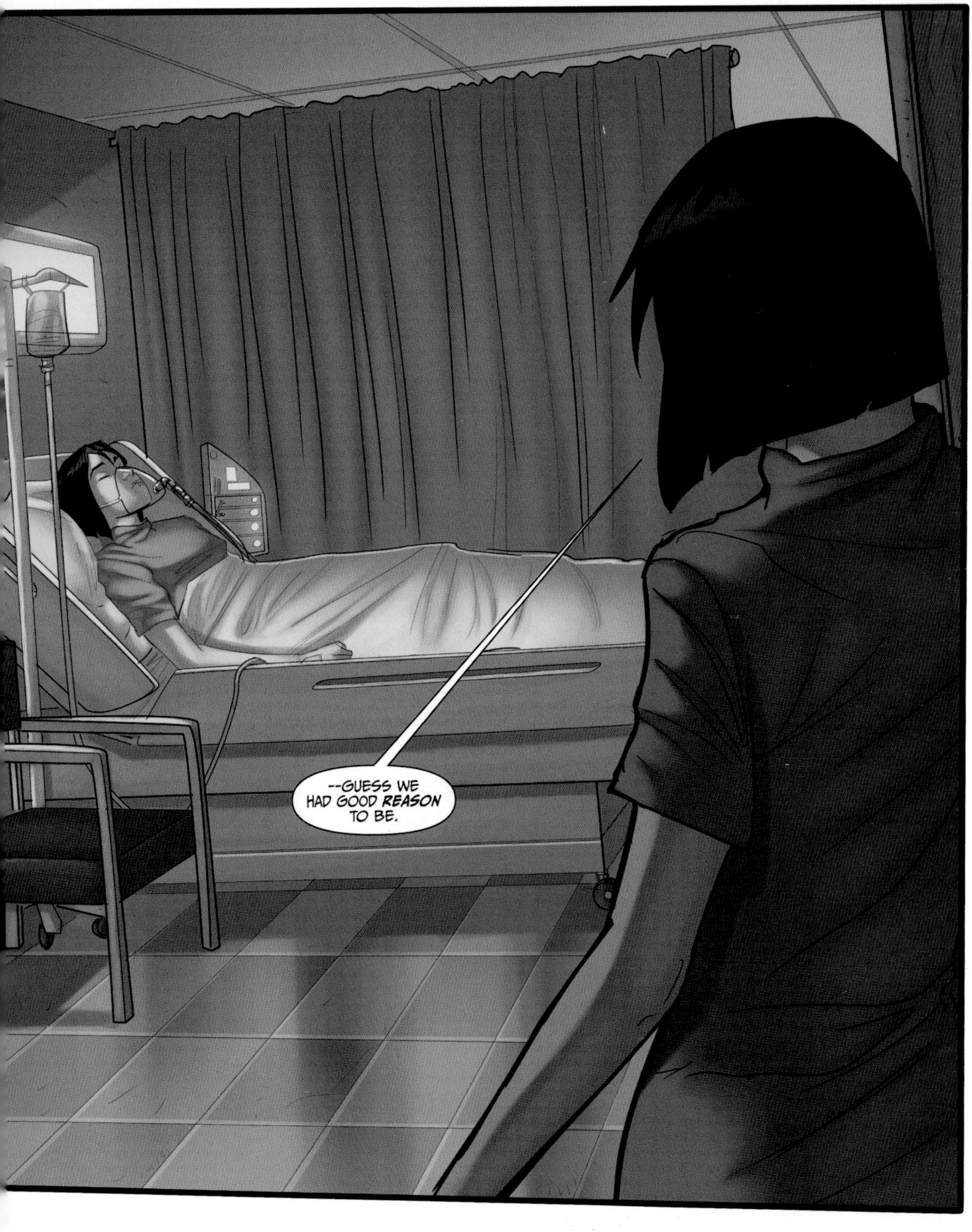
--GUESS WE HAD GOOD REASON TO BE.

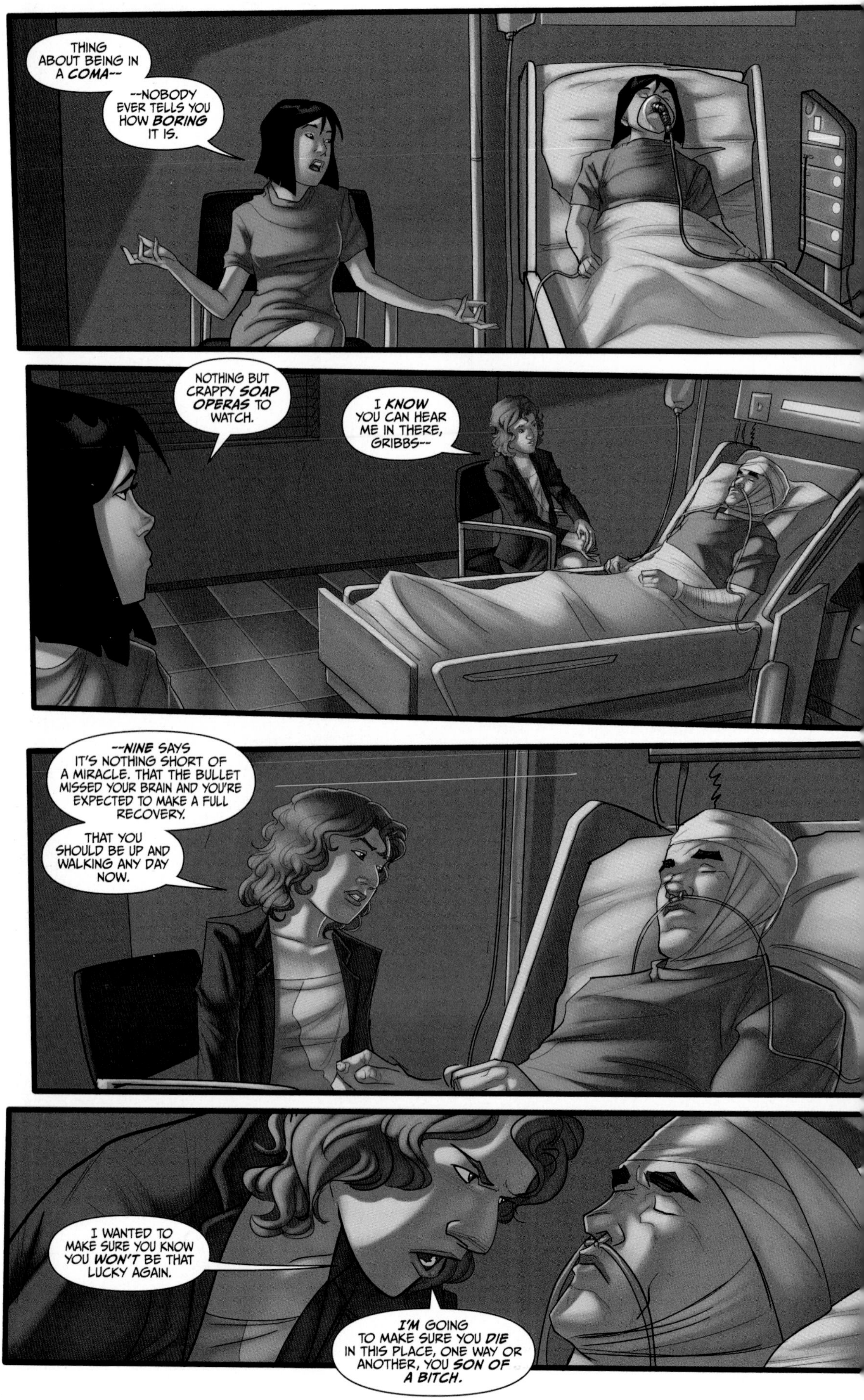
THING ABOUT BEING IN A COMA--
--NOBODY EVER TELLS YOU HOW BORING IT IS.
NOTHING BUT CRAPPY SOAP OPERAS TO WATCH.
I KNOW YOU CAN HEAR ME IN THERE, GRIBBS--
--NINE SAYS IT'S NOTHING SHORT OF A MIRACLE. THAT THE BULLET MISSED YOUR BRAIN AND YOU'RE EXPECTED TO MAKE A FULL RECOVERY.
THAT YOU SHOULD BE UP AND WALKING ANY DAY NOW.
I WANTED TO MAKE SURE YOU KNOW YOU WON'T BE THAT LUCKY AGAIN.
I'M GOING TO MAKE SURE YOU DIE IN THIS PLACE, ONE WAY OR ANOTHER, YOU SON OF A BITCH.

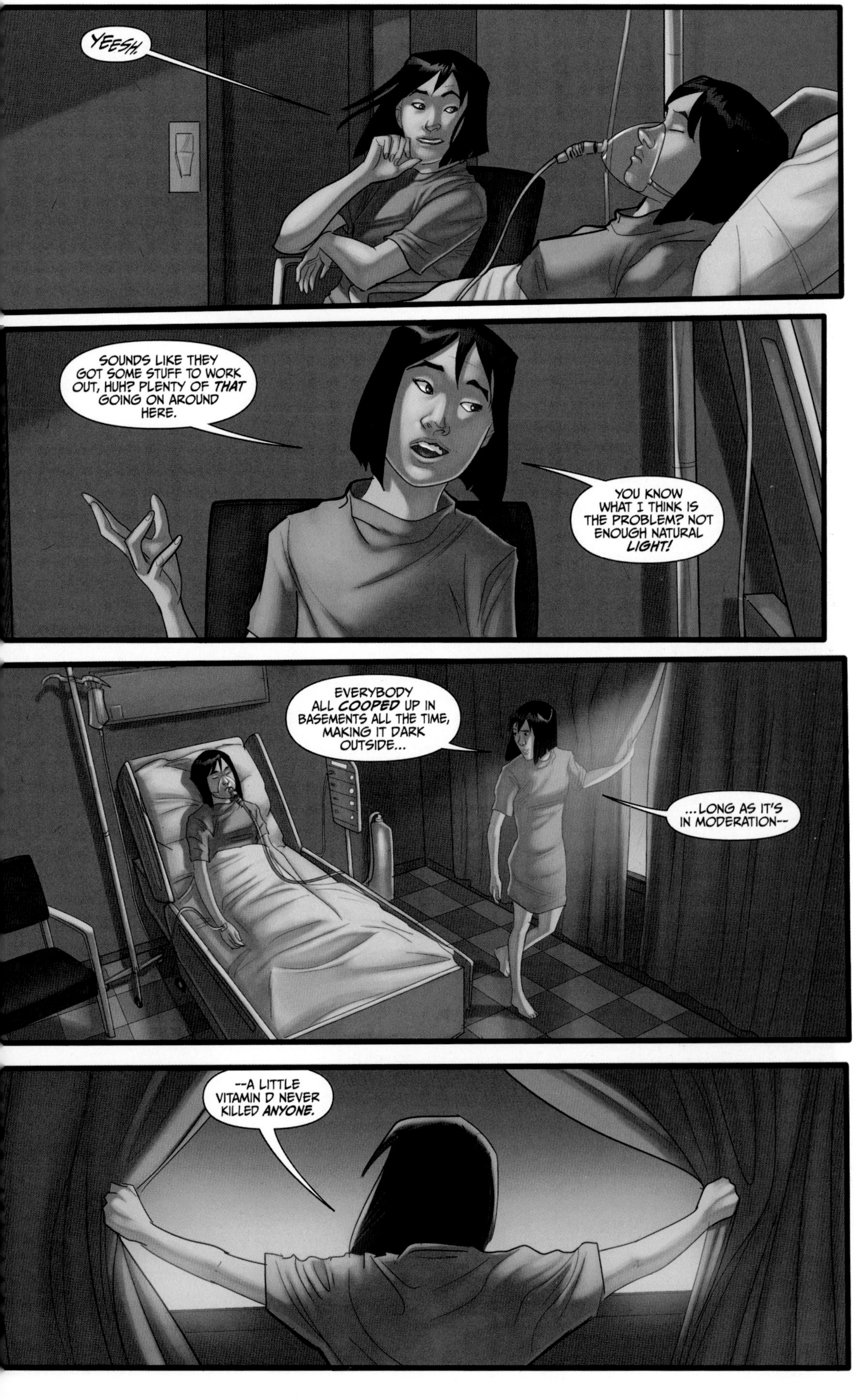
YEESH.
SOUNDS LIKE THEY GOT SOME STUFF TO WORK OUT, HUH? PLENTY OF *THAT* GOING ON AROUND HERE.
YOU KNOW WHAT I THINK IS THE PROBLEM? NOT ENOUGH NATURAL *LIGHT!*
EVERYBODY ALL *COOPED* UP IN BASEMENTS ALL THE TIME, MAKING IT DARK OUTSIDE...
...LONG AS IT'S IN MODERATION--
--A LITTLE VITAMIN D NEVER KILLED *ANYONE.*

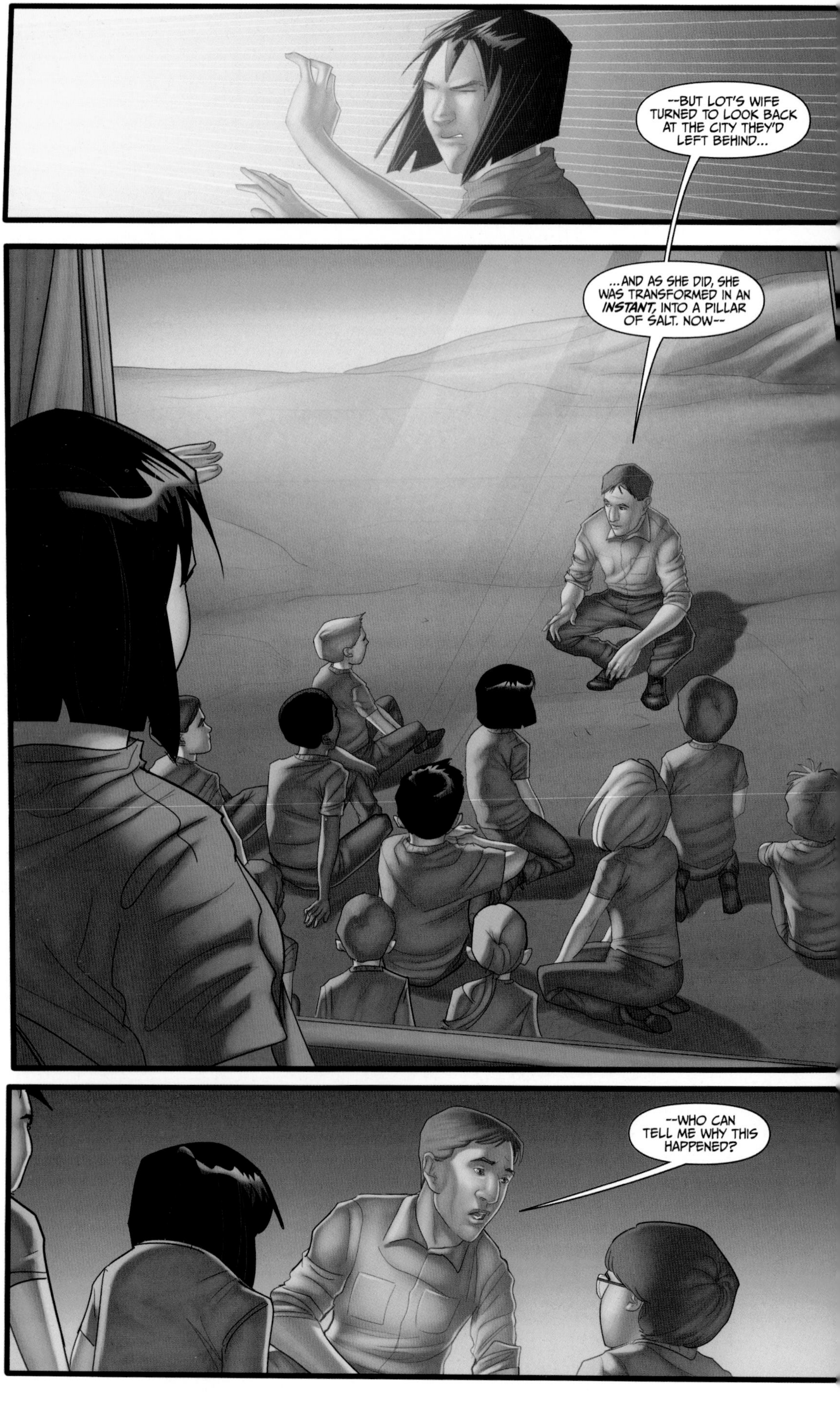
--BUT LOT'S WIFE TURNED TO LOOK BACK AT THE CITY THEY'D LEFT BEHIND...
...AND AS SHE DID, SHE WAS TRANSFORMED IN AN *INSTANT,* INTO A PILLAR OF SALT. NOW--
--WHO CAN TELL ME WHY THIS HAPPENED?

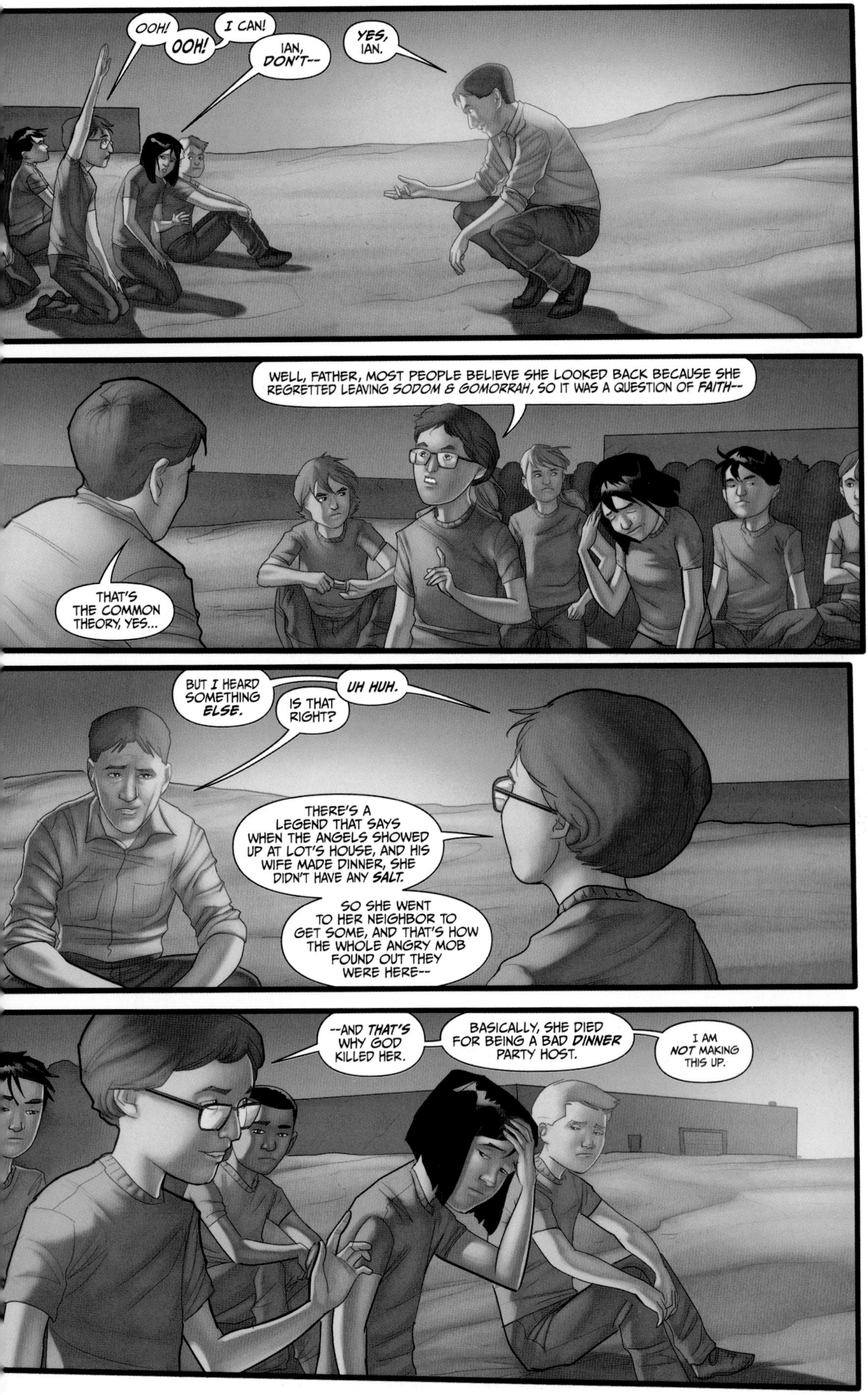
OOH!
OOH!
I CAN!
IAN, DON'T--
YES, IAN.
WELL, FATHER, MOST PEOPLE BELIEVE SHE LOOKED BACK BECAUSE SHE REGRETTED LEAVING SODOM & GOMORRAH, SO IT WAS A QUESTION OF FAITH--
THAT'S THE COMMON THEORY, YES...
BUT I HEARD SOMETHING ELSE.
IS THAT RIGHT?
UH HUH.
THERE'S A LEGEND THAT SAYS WHEN THE ANGELS SHOWED UP AT LOT'S HOUSE, AND HIS WIFE MADE DINNER, SHE DIDN'T HAVE ANY SALT.
SO SHE WENT TO HER NEIGHBOR TO GET SOME, AND THAT'S HOW THE WHOLE ANGRY MOB FOUND OUT THEY WERE HERE--
--AND THAT'S WHY GOD KILLED HER.
BASICALLY, SHE DIED FOR BEING A BAD DINNER PARTY HOST.
I AM NOT MAKING THIS UP.

HH. AND THAT SOUNDS *TRUE* TO YOU?

I DON'T KNOW--

--GOD DOES ALL *KINDS* OF CRAZY THINGS AT THE BEGINNING OF THE BOOK--WRESTLING MATCHES, DEADLY PLAGUES...

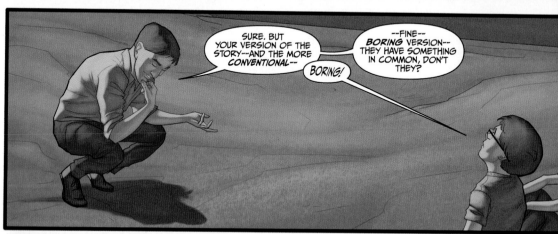

SURE. BUT YOUR VERSION OF THE STORY--AND THE MORE *CONVENTIONAL*--

BORING!

--FINE-- *BORING* VERSION-- THEY HAVE SOMETHING IN COMMON, DON'T THEY?

THEY BOTH ASSUME GOD WAS *PUNISHING* LOT'S WIFE.

EVER SINCE MAN'S FIRST MISTAKE, IN THE GARDEN OF EDEN--HE'S BEEN *AFRAID* OF GOD, *HIDING* FROM HIM.

HE'S SO *ASHAMED*, AND SO OVERCOME BY *GUILT*, THAT HE CAN'T IMAGINE GOD WOULD WANT ANYTHING ELSE FROM HIM OTHER *THAN* TO PUNISH HIM.

AND SO THEY TELL THESE STORIES OF AN *ANGRY* GOD, HIS *JUDGEMENT* AND HIS *WRATH.* THEY FILL THEIR RELIGIONS WITH RULES AND RITUALS *IMPOSSIBLE* TO FULFILL. THAT PUT *DISTANCE* BETWEEN US AND HIM.

BUT GOD MADE US SO THAT HE WOULD NOT *BE* ALONE. *ALL* GOD REALLY WANTS MAN TO DO--

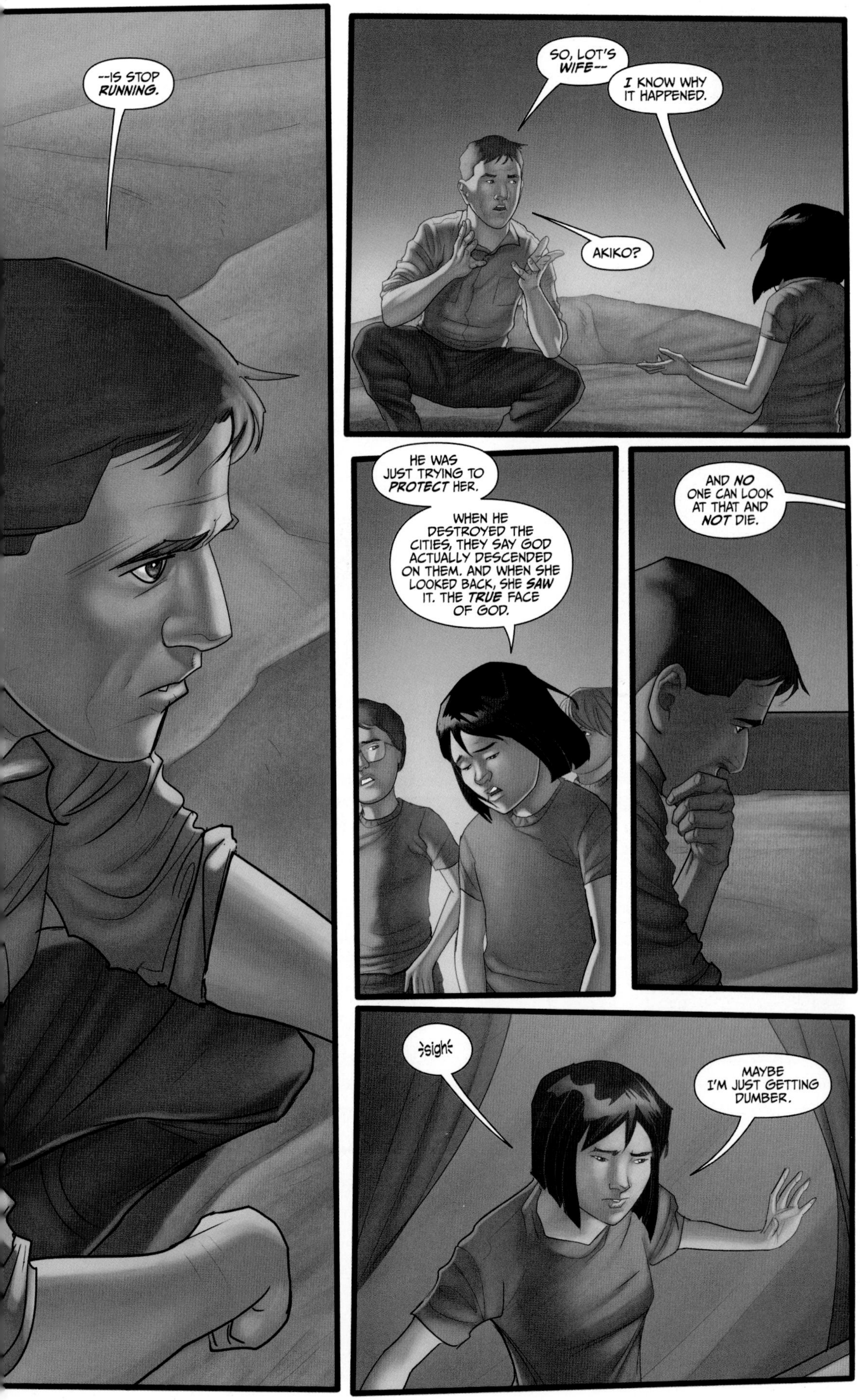
--IS STOP RUNNING.
SO, LOT'S WIFE--
I KNOW WHY IT HAPPENED.
AKIKO?
HE WAS JUST TRYING TO PROTECT HER.
WHEN HE DESTROYED THE CITIES, THEY SAY GOD ACTUALLY DESCENDED ON THEM. AND WHEN SHE LOOKED BACK, SHE SAW IT. THE TRUE FACE OF GOD.
AND NO ONE CAN LOOK AT THAT AND NOT DIE.
sigh
MAYBE I'M JUST GETTING DUMBER.

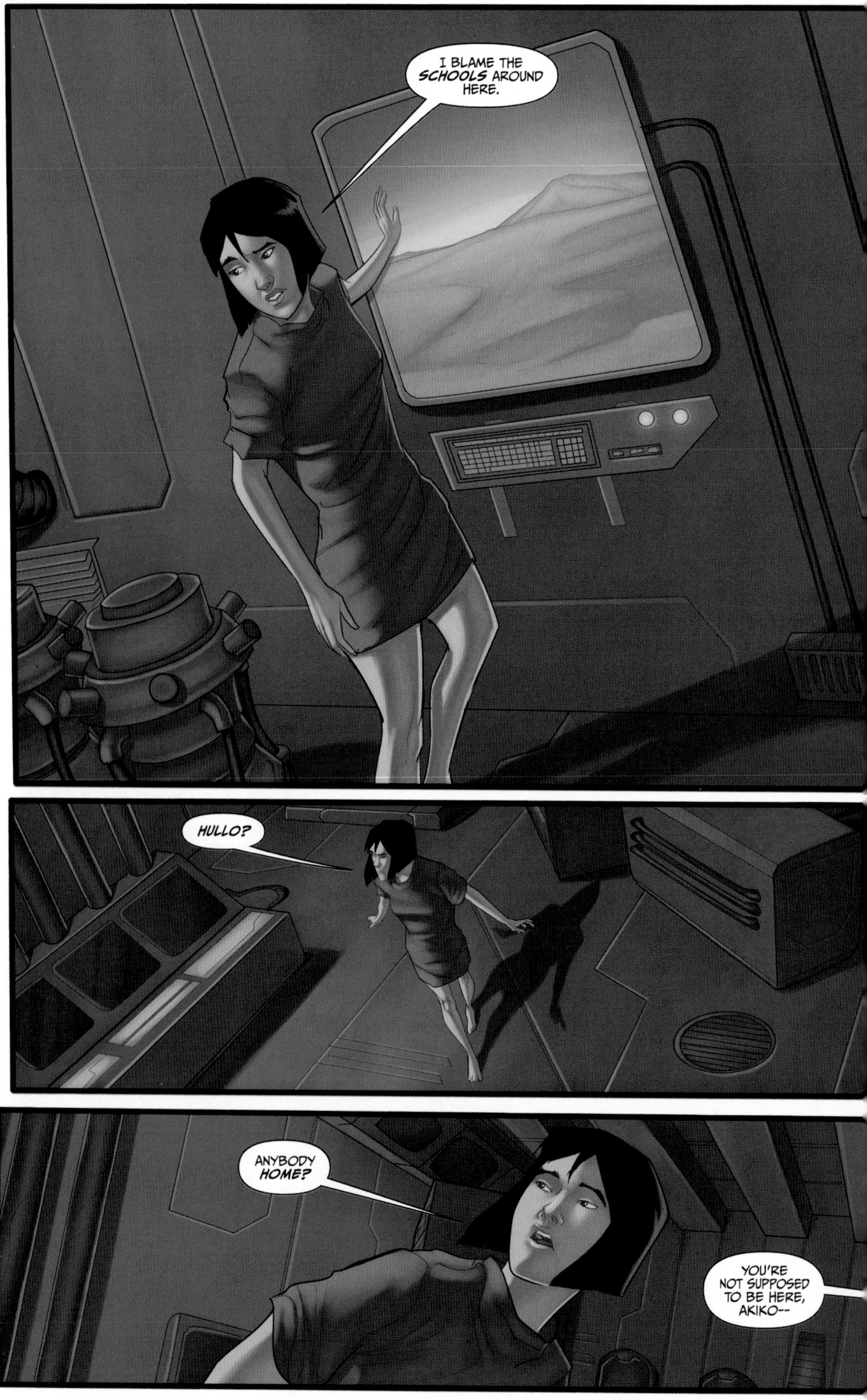
I BLAME THE SCHOOLS AROUND HERE.
HULLO?
ANYBODY HOME?
YOU'RE NOT SUPPOSED TO BE HERE, AKIKO--

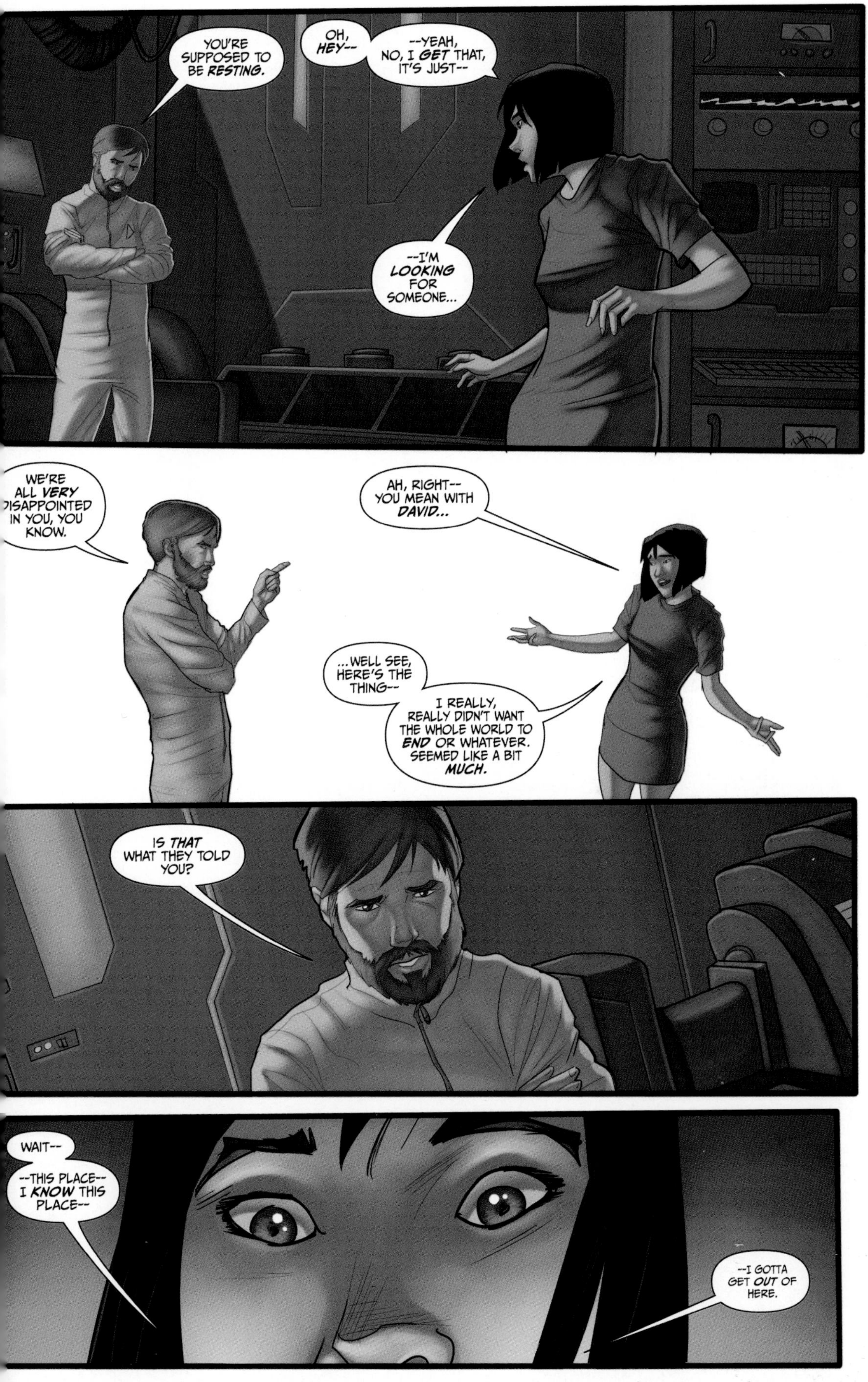
YOU'RE SUPPOSED TO BE RESTING.
OH, HEY--
--YEAH, NO, I GET THAT, IT'S JUST--
--I'M LOOKING FOR SOMEONE...
WE'RE ALL VERY DISAPPOINTED IN YOU, YOU KNOW.
AH, RIGHT-- YOU MEAN WITH DAVID...
...WELL SEE, HERE'S THE THING--
I REALLY, REALLY DIDN'T WANT THE WHOLE WORLD TO END OR WHATEVER. SEEMED LIKE A BIT MUCH.
IS THAT WHAT THEY TOLD YOU?
WAIT--
--THIS PLACE-- I KNOW THIS PLACE--
--I GOTTA GET OUT OF HERE.

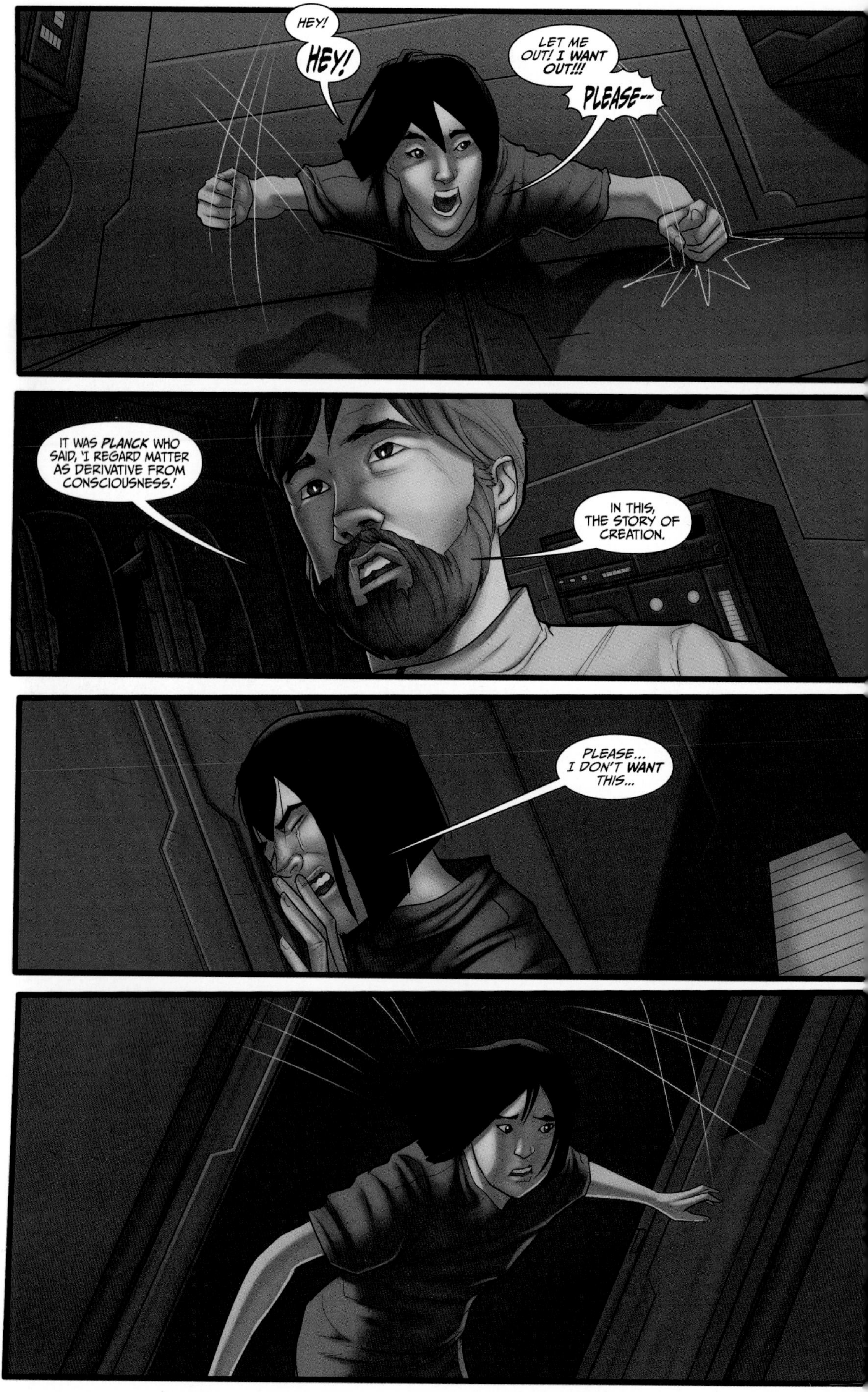
HEY!
HEY!
LET ME OUT! I WANT OUT!!!
PLEASE--
IT WAS PLANCK WHO SAID, 'I REGARD MATTER AS DERIVATIVE FROM CONSCIOUSNESS.'
IN THIS, THE STORY OF CREATION.
PLEASE... I DON'T WANT THIS...

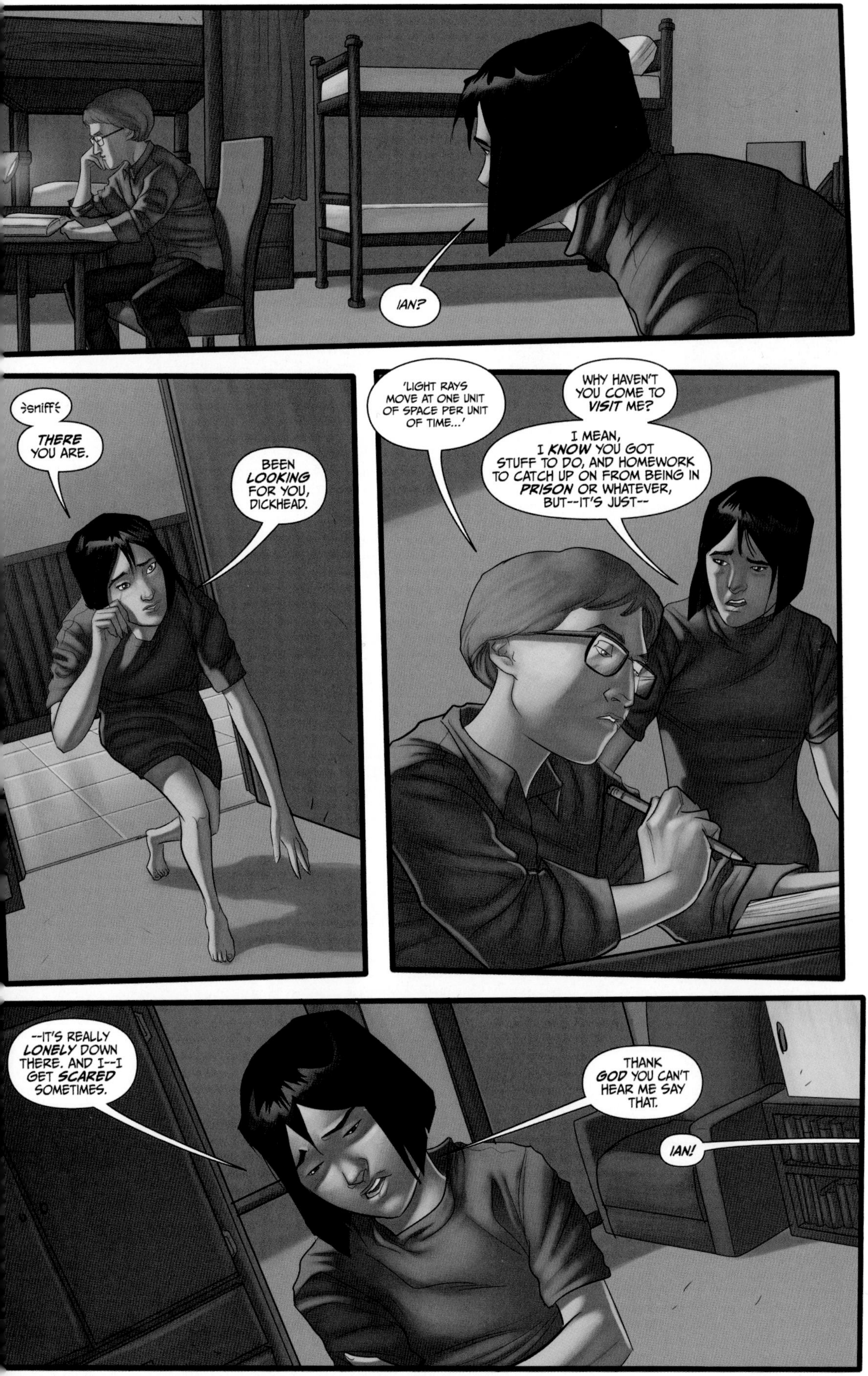
IAN?
ƐsniffƐ
THERE YOU ARE.
BEEN LOOKING FOR YOU, DICKHEAD.
'LIGHT RAYS MOVE AT ONE UNIT OF SPACE PER UNIT OF TIME...'
WHY HAVEN'T YOU COME TO VISIT ME?
I MEAN, I KNOW YOU GOT STUFF TO DO, AND HOMEWORK TO CATCH UP ON FROM BEING IN PRISON OR WHATEVER, BUT--IT'S JUST--
--IT'S REALLY LONELY DOWN THERE. AND I--I GET SCARED SOMETIMES.
THANK GOD YOU CAN'T HEAR ME SAY THAT.
IAN!

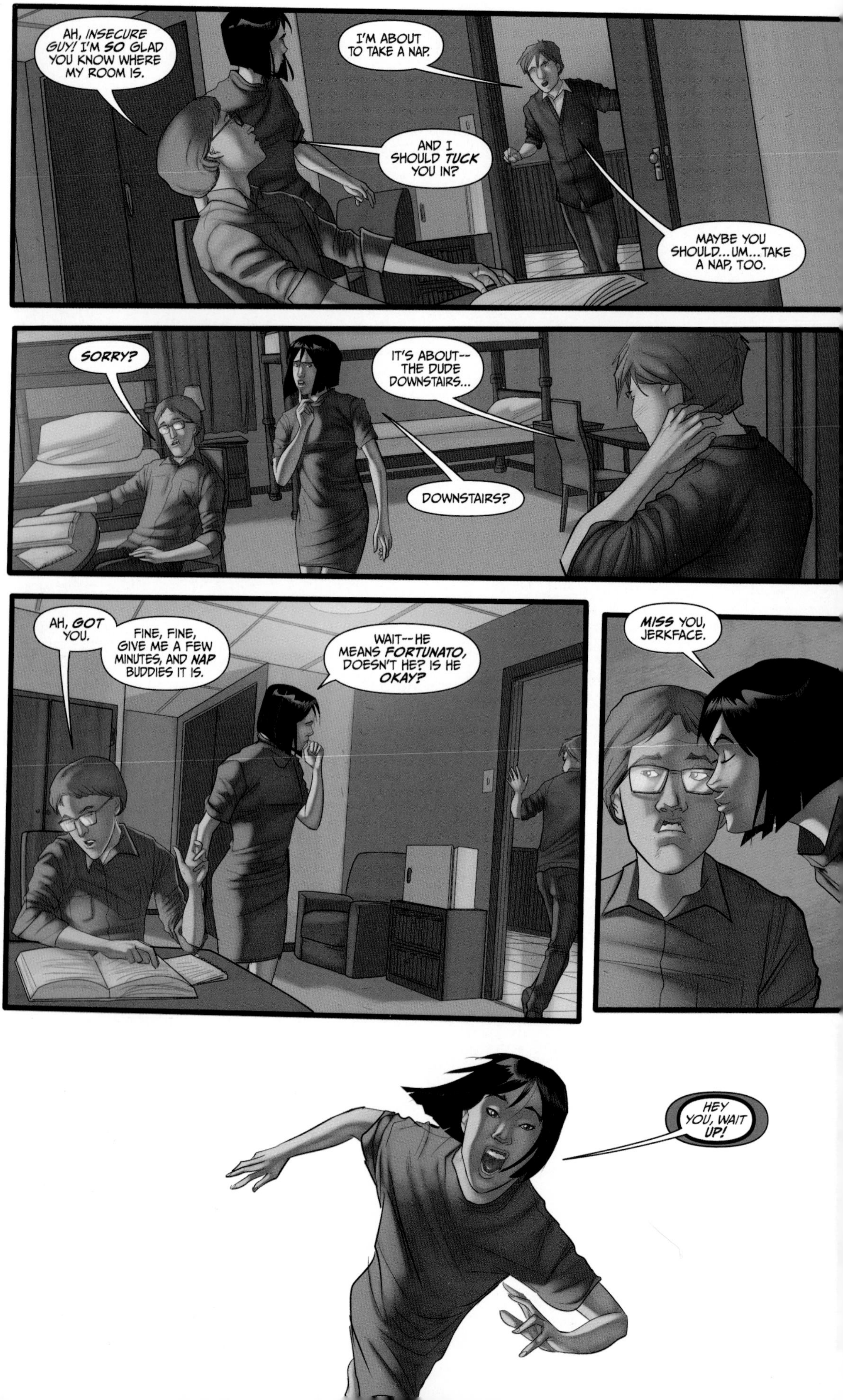
AH, INSECURE GUY! I'M SO GLAD YOU KNOW WHERE MY ROOM IS.
I'M ABOUT TO TAKE A NAP.
AND I SHOULD TUCK YOU IN?
MAYBE YOU SHOULD...UM...TAKE A NAP, TOO.
SORRY?
IT'S ABOUT-- THE DUDE DOWNSTAIRS...
DOWNSTAIRS?
AH, GOT YOU.
FINE, FINE, GIVE ME A FEW MINUTES, AND NAP BUDDIES IT IS.
WAIT--HE MEANS FORTUNATO, DOESN'T HE? IS HE OKAY?
MISS YOU, JERKFACE.
HEY YOU, WAIT UP!

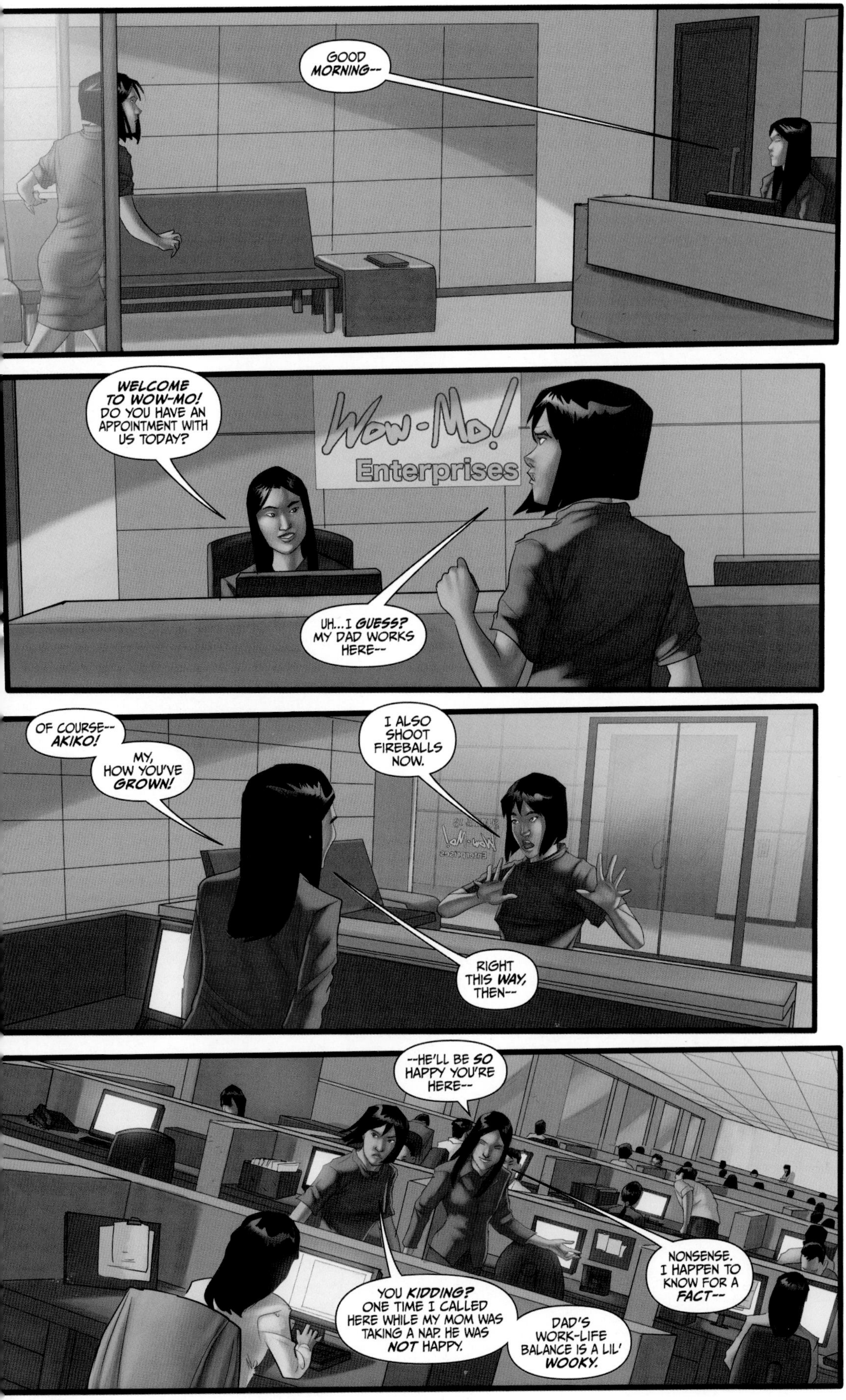
GOOD MORNING--
WELCOME TO WOW-MO! DO YOU HAVE AN APPOINTMENT WITH US TODAY?
Wow-Mo! Enterprises
UH...I GUESS? MY DAD WORKS HERE--
OF COURSE-- AKIKO!
MY, HOW YOU'VE GROWN!
I ALSO SHOOT FIREBALLS NOW.
RIGHT THIS WAY, THEN--
--HE'LL BE SO HAPPY YOU'RE HERE--
YOU KIDDING? ONE TIME I CALLED HERE WHILE MY MOM WAS TAKING A NAP. HE WAS NOT HAPPY.
NONSENSE. I HAPPEN TO KNOW FOR A FACT--
DAD'S WORK-LIFE BALANCE IS A LIL' WOOKY.

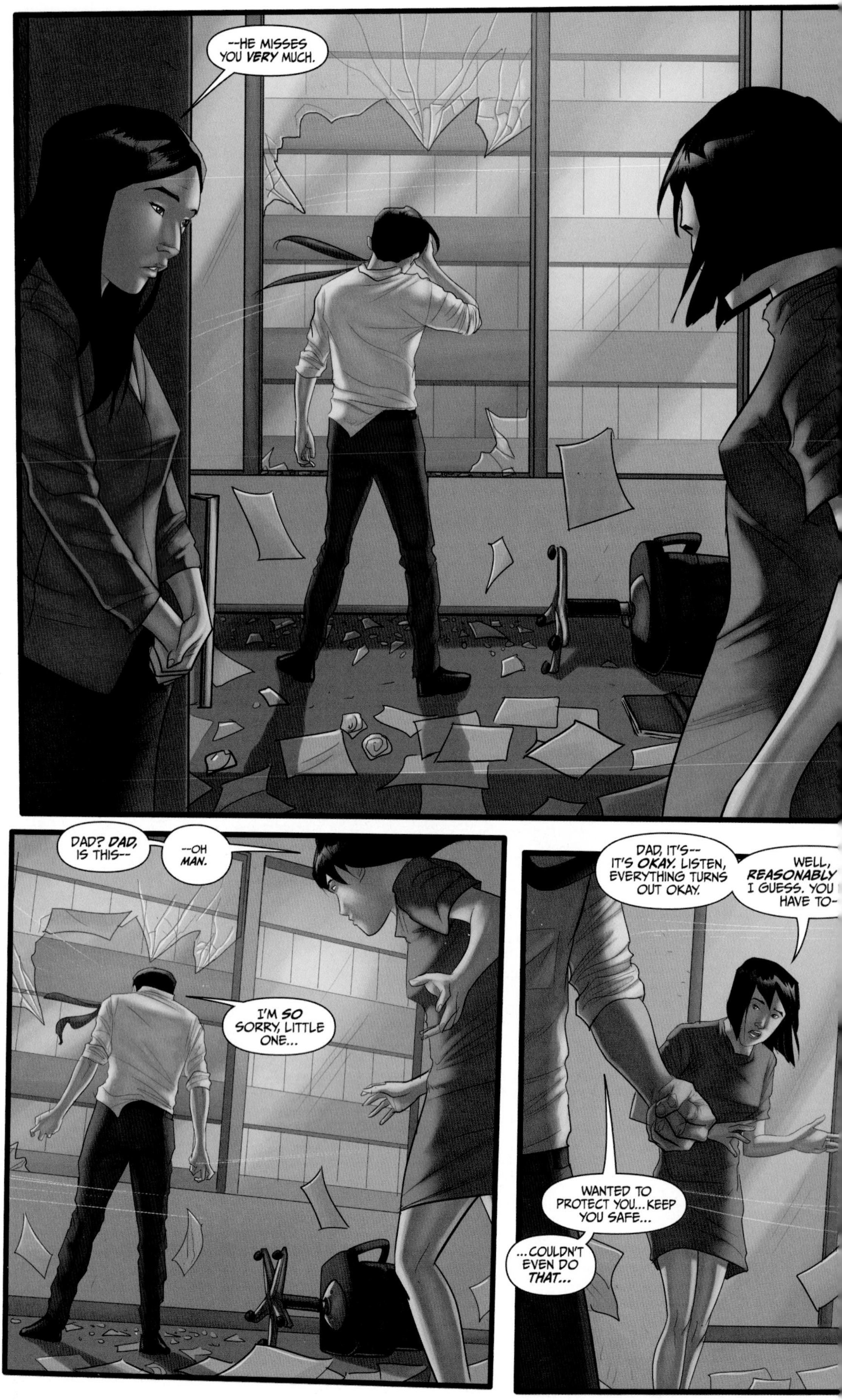
--HE MISSES YOU VERY MUCH.
DAD? DAD, IS THIS--
--OH MAN.
I'M SO SORRY, LITTLE ONE...
DAD, IT'S-- IT'S OKAY. LISTEN, EVERYTHING TURNS OUT OKAY.
WELL, REASONABLY I GUESS. YOU HAVE TO-
WANTED TO PROTECT YOU...KEEP YOU SAFE...
...COULDN'T EVEN DO THAT...

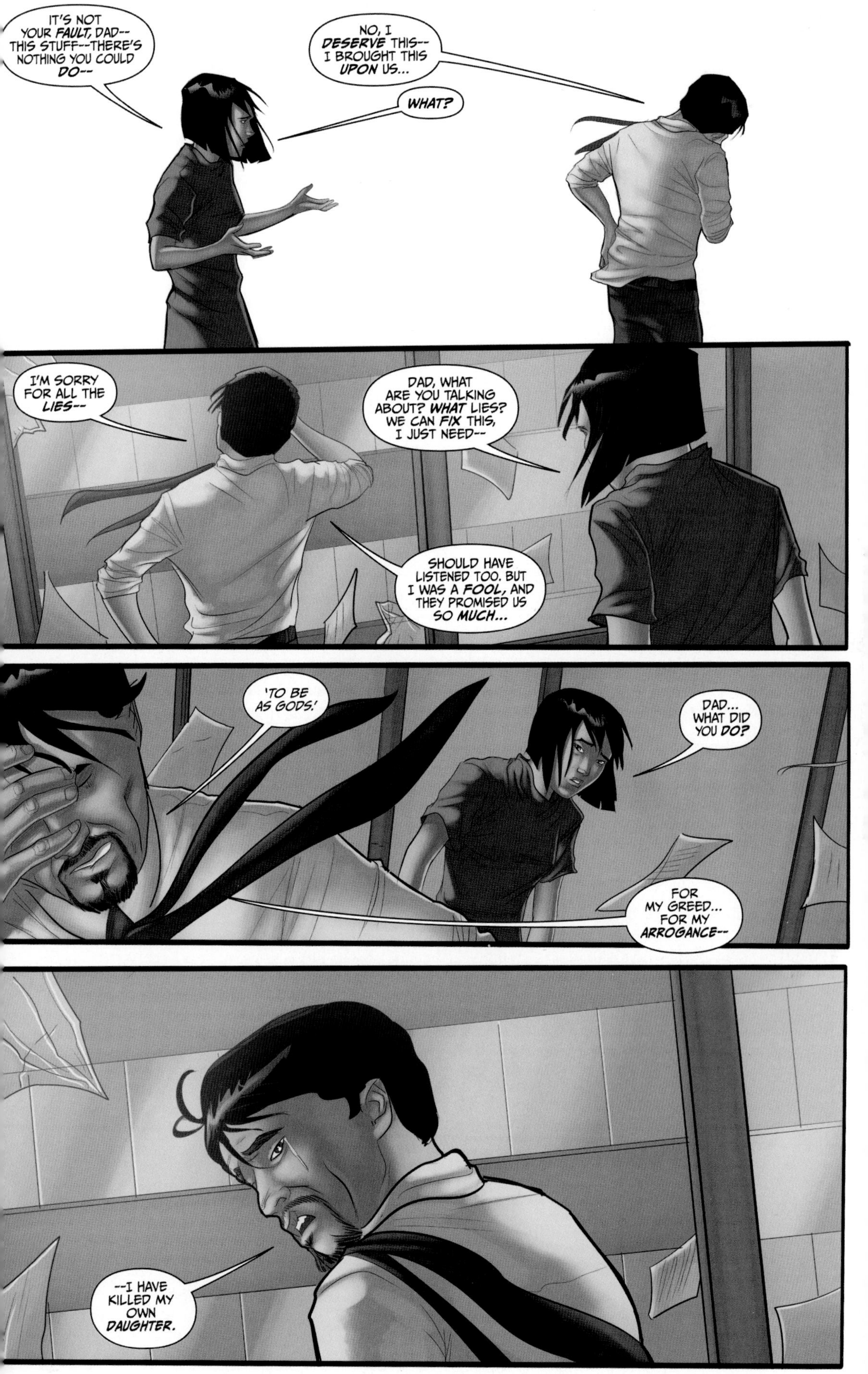
IT'S NOT YOUR FAULT, DAD-- THIS STUFF--THERE'S NOTHING YOU COULD DO--
NO, I DESERVE THIS-- I BROUGHT THIS UPON US...
WHAT?
I'M SORRY FOR ALL THE LIES--
DAD, WHAT ARE YOU TALKING ABOUT? WHAT LIES? WE CAN FIX THIS, I JUST NEED--
SHOULD HAVE LISTENED TOO. BUT I WAS A FOOL, AND THEY PROMISED US SO MUCH...
'TO BE AS GODS.'
DAD... WHAT DID YOU DO?
FOR MY GREED... FOR MY ARROGANCE--
--I HAVE KILLED MY OWN DAUGHTER.

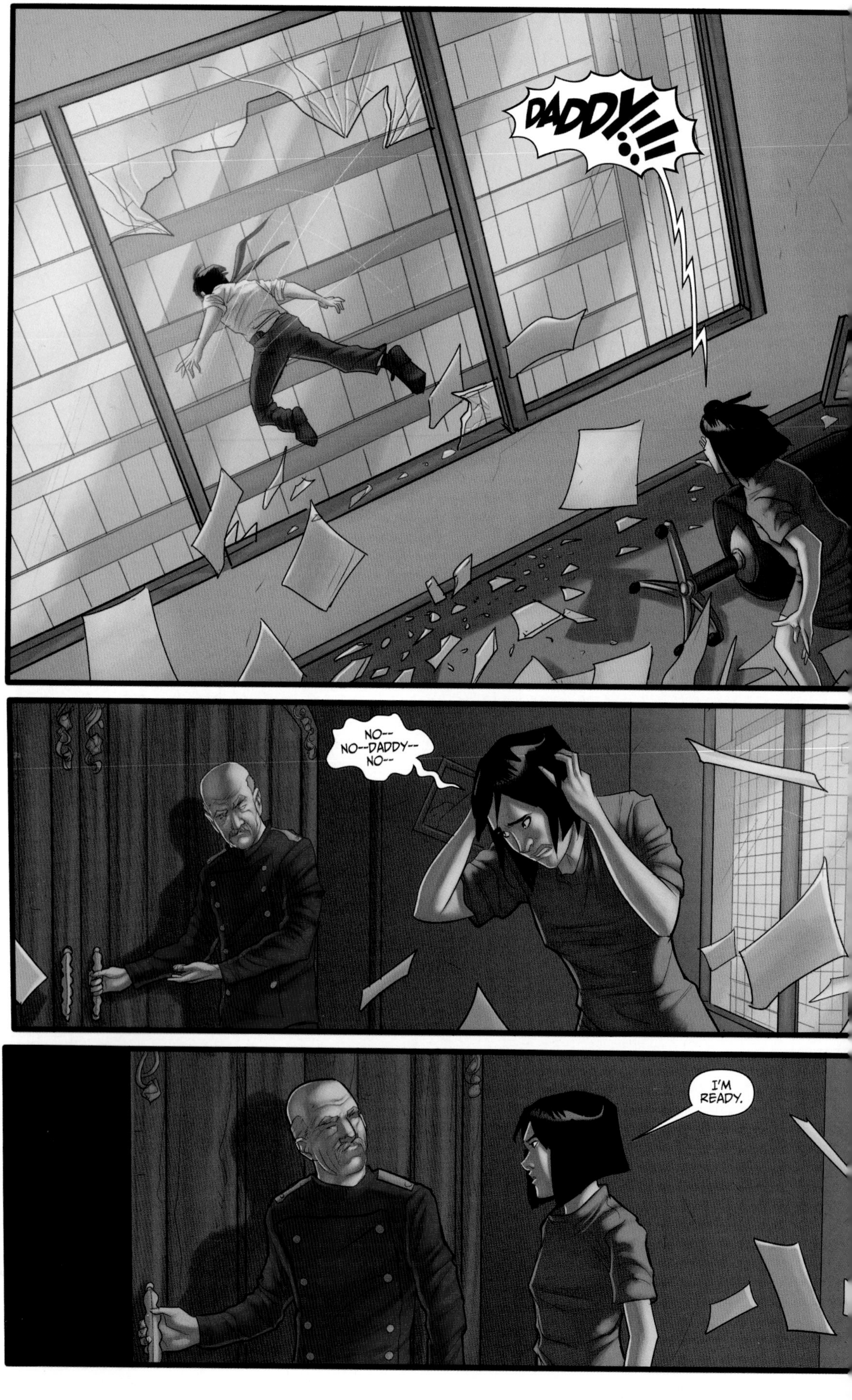
DADDY!!!
NO-- NO--DADDY-- NO--
I'M READY.

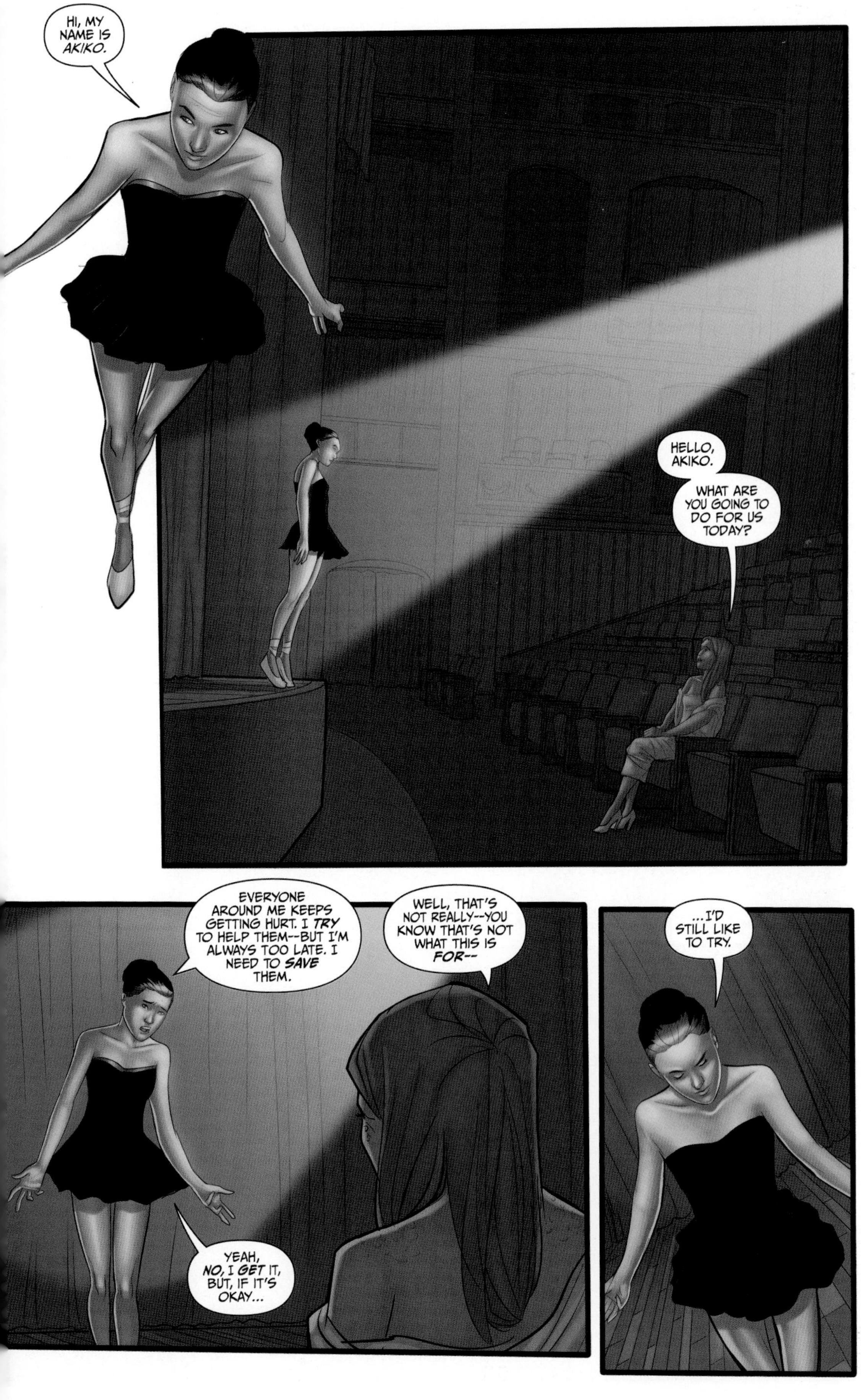
HI, MY NAME IS AKIKO.
HELLO, AKIKO.
WHAT ARE YOU GOING TO DO FOR US TODAY?
EVERYONE AROUND ME KEEPS GETTING HURT. I TRY TO HELP THEM--BUT I'M ALWAYS TOO LATE. I NEED TO SAVE THEM.
WELL, THAT'S NOT REALLY--YOU KNOW THAT'S NOT WHAT THIS IS FOR--
YEAH, NO, I GET IT, BUT, IF IT'S OKAY...
...I'D STILL LIKE TO TRY.

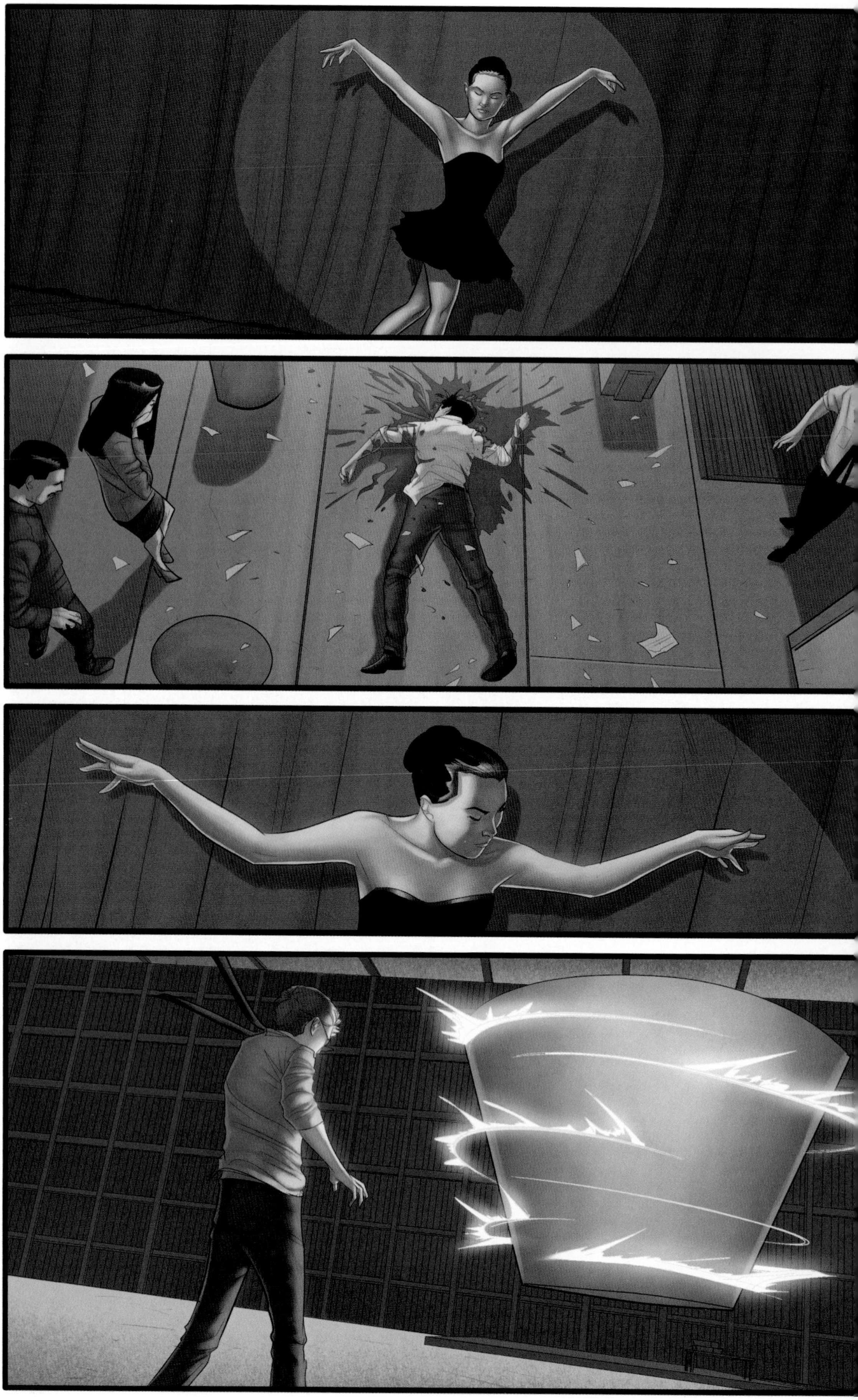

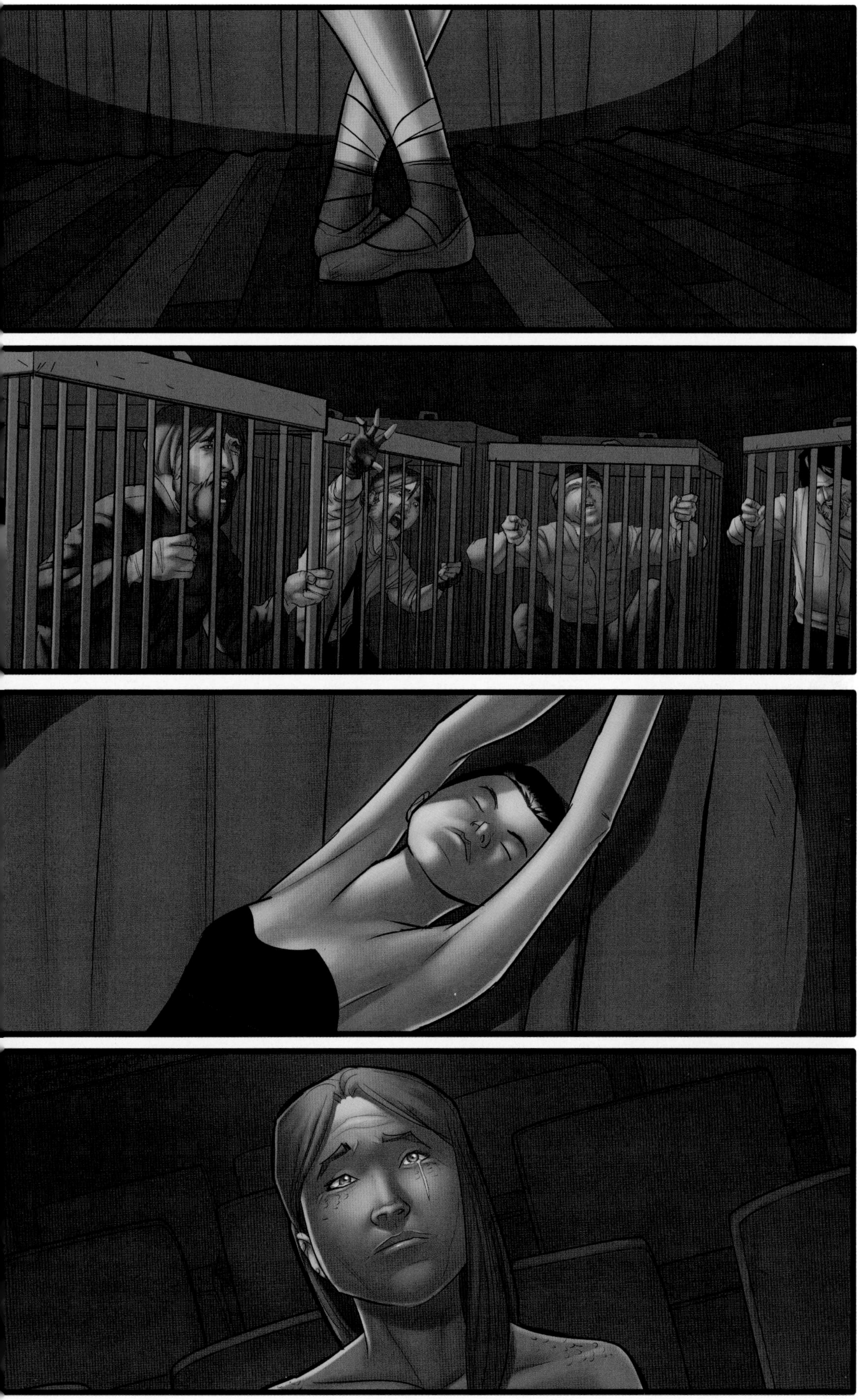

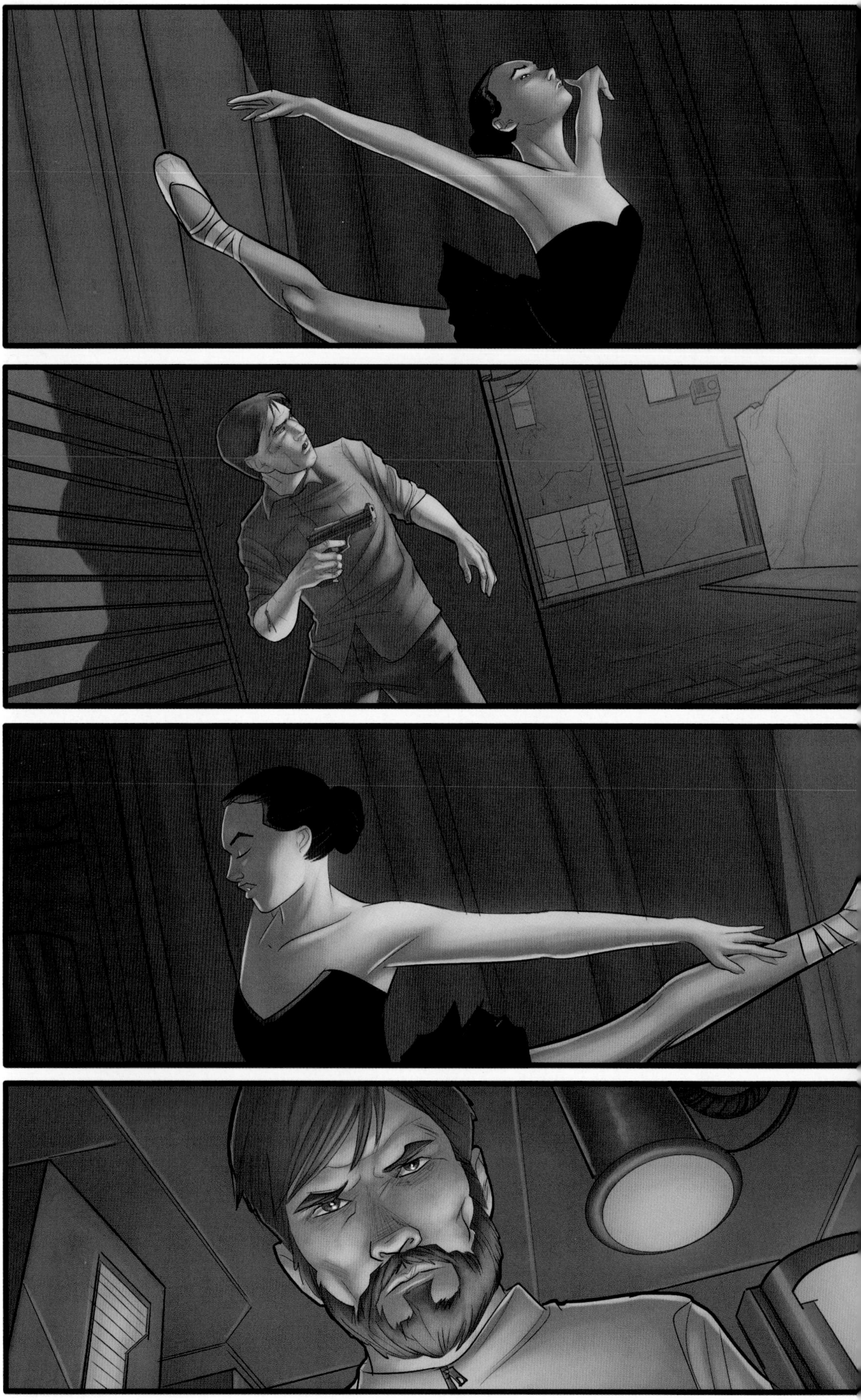

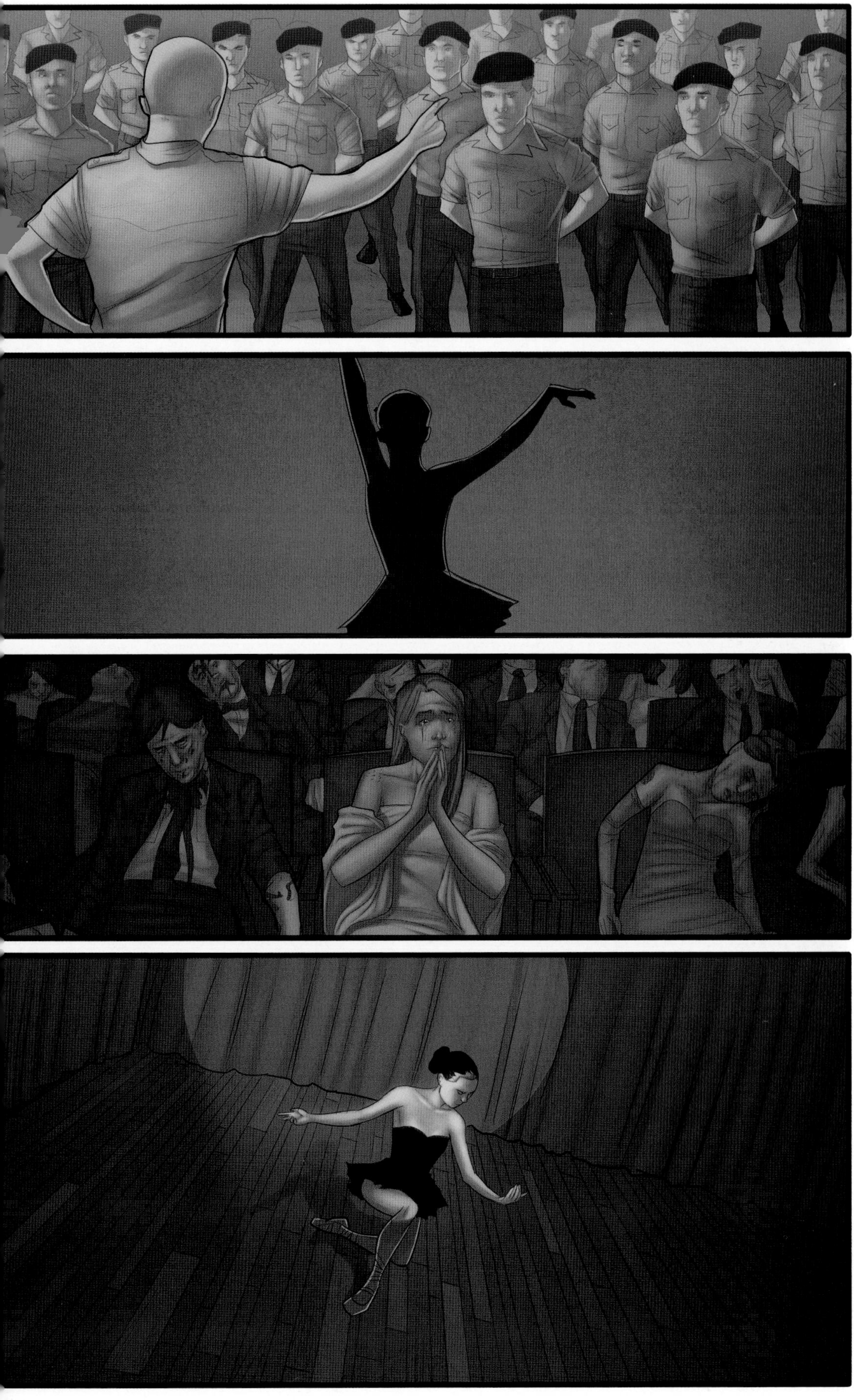

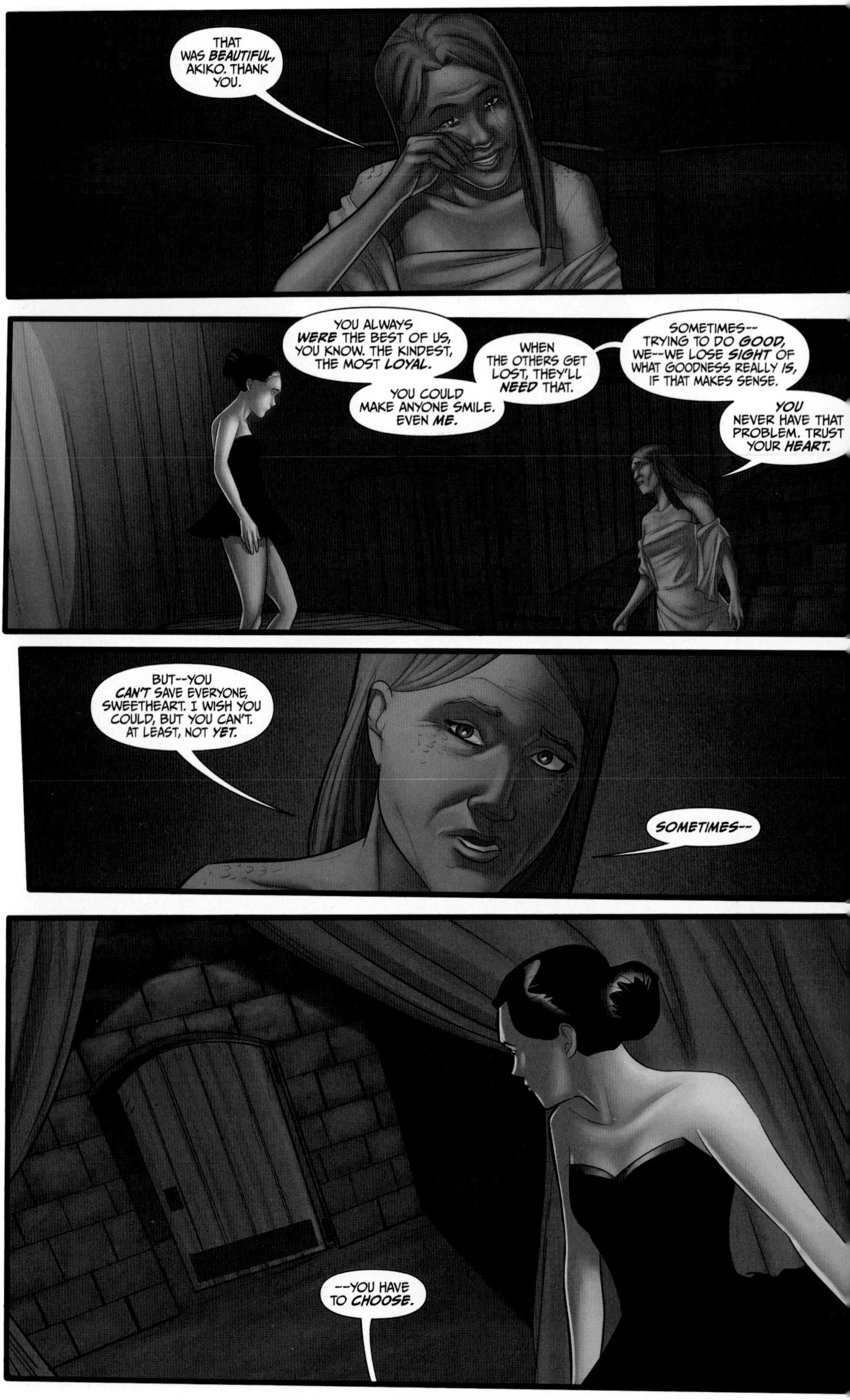
THAT WAS BEAUTIFUL, AKIKO. THANK YOU.
YOU ALWAYS WERE THE BEST OF US, YOU KNOW. THE KINDEST, THE MOST LOYAL.
YOU COULD MAKE ANYONE SMILE. EVEN ME.
WHEN THE OTHERS GET LOST, THEY'LL NEED THAT.
SOMETIMES-- TRYING TO DO GOOD, WE--WE LOSE SIGHT OF WHAT GOODNESS REALLY IS, IF THAT MAKES SENSE.
YOU NEVER HAVE THAT PROBLEM. TRUST YOUR HEART.
BUT--YOU CAN'T SAVE EVERYONE, SWEETHEART. I WISH YOU COULD, BUT YOU CAN'T. AT LEAST, NOT YET.
SOMETIMES--
--YOU HAVE TO CHOOSE.

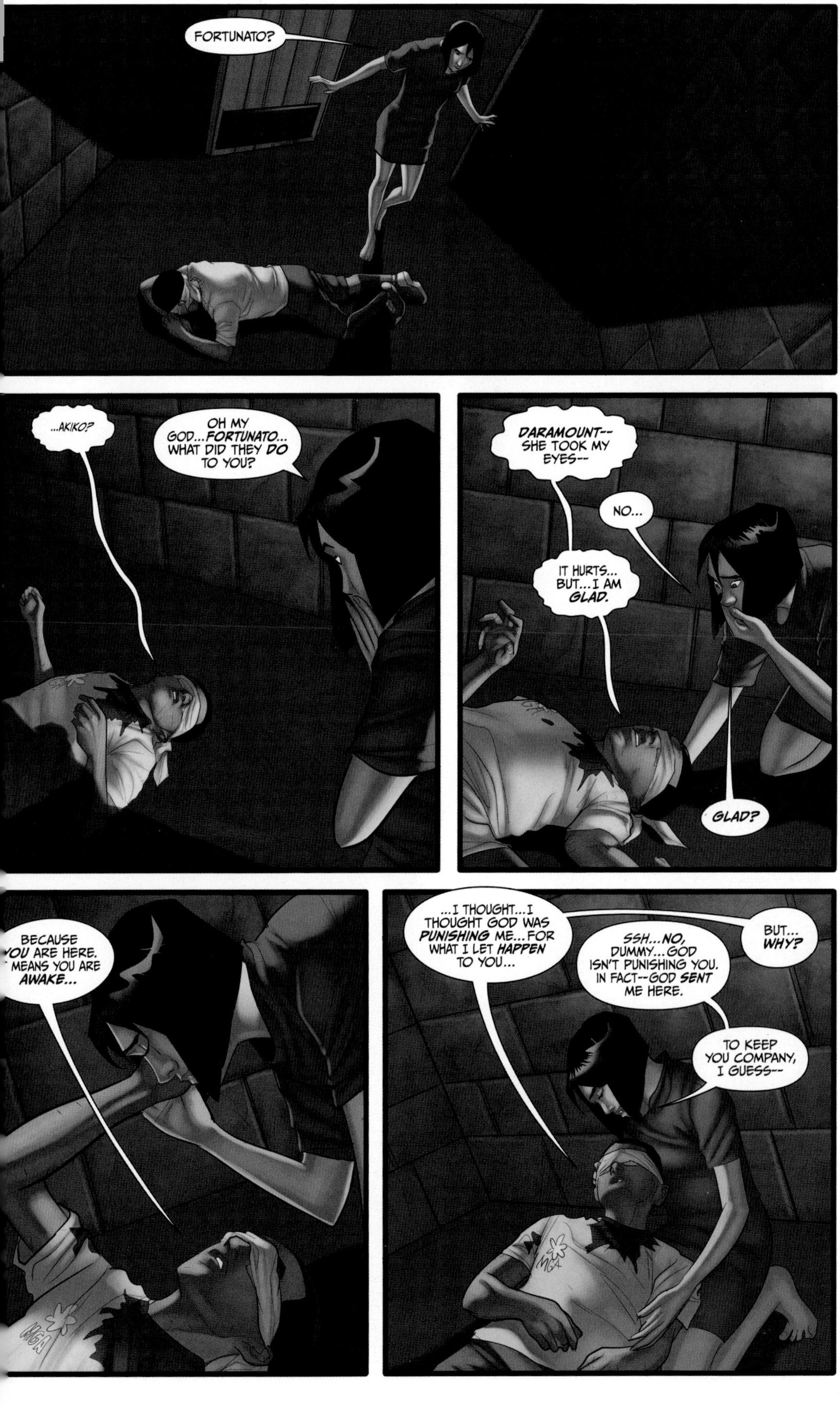

FORTUNATO?
...AKIKO?
OH MY GOD...FORTUNATO... WHAT DID THEY DO TO YOU?
DARAMOUNT-- SHE TOOK MY EYES--
NO...
IT HURTS... BUT...I AM GLAD.
GLAD?
BECAUSE YOU ARE HERE. IT MEANS YOU ARE AWAKE...
...I THOUGHT...I THOUGHT GOD WAS PUNISHING ME...FOR WHAT I LET HAPPEN TO YOU...
BUT... WHY?
SSH...NO, DUMMY...GOD ISN'T PUNISHING YOU. IN FACT--GOD SENT ME HERE.
TO KEEP YOU COMPANY, I GUESS--

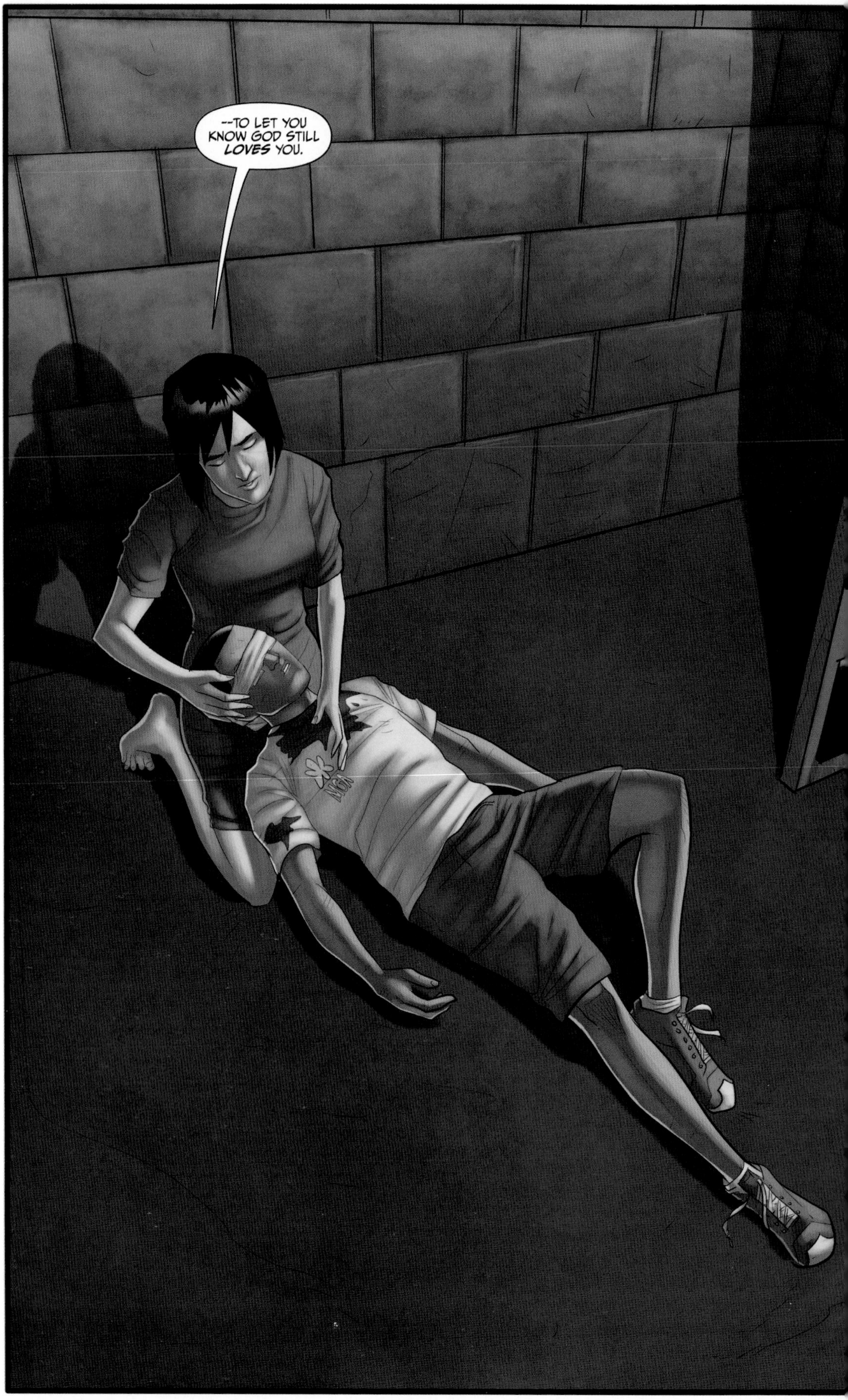
--TO LET YOU KNOW GOD STILL *LOVES* YOU.

thirtyeight

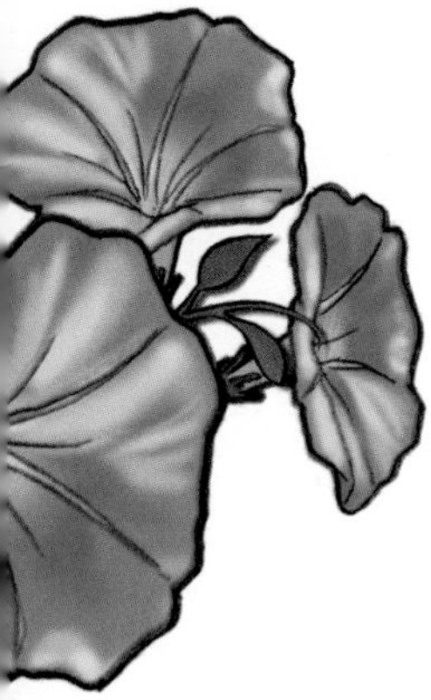

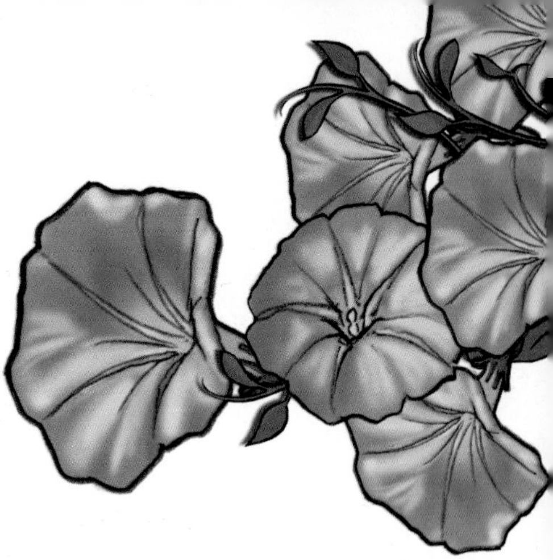

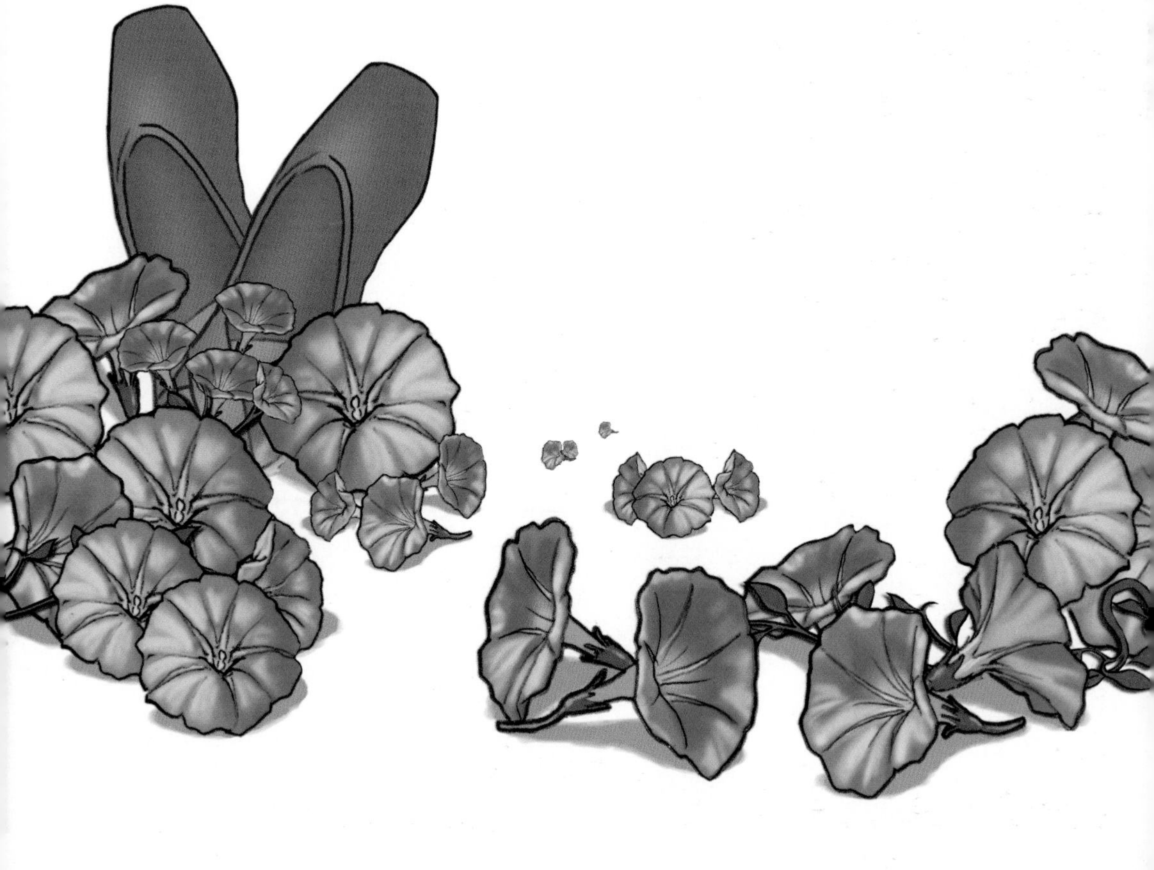

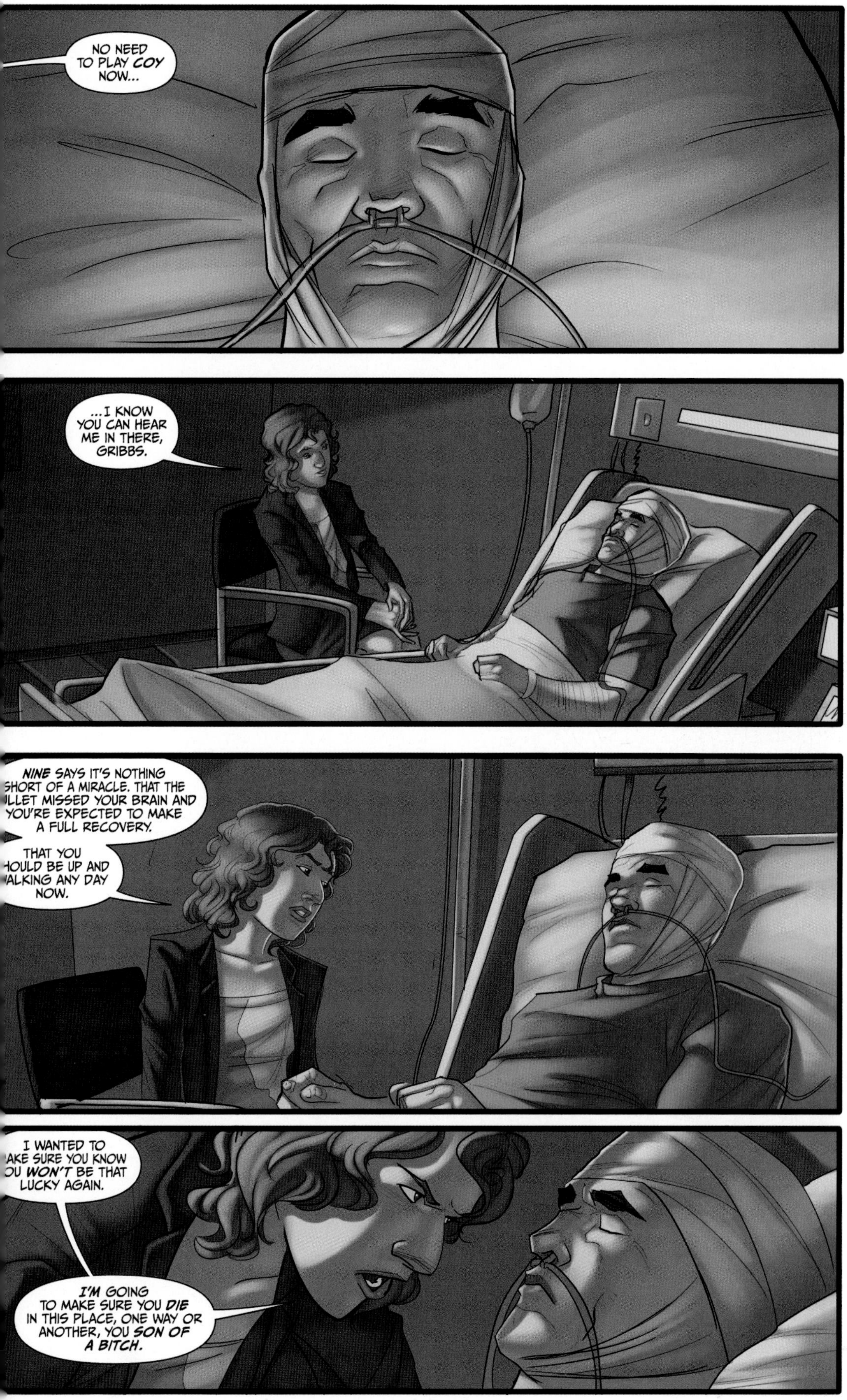
NO NEED TO PLAY *COY* NOW...
...I KNOW YOU CAN HEAR ME IN THERE, GRIBBS.
NINE SAYS IT'S NOTHING SHORT OF A MIRACLE. THAT THE ULLET MISSED YOUR BRAIN AND YOU'RE EXPECTED TO MAKE A FULL RECOVERY.
THAT YOU HOULD BE UP AND ALKING ANY DAY NOW.
I WANTED TO AKE SURE YOU KNOW OU *WON'T* BE THAT LUCKY AGAIN.
I'M GOING TO MAKE SURE YOU *DIE* IN THIS PLACE, ONE WAY OR ANOTHER, YOU *SON OF A BITCH.*

WELL--IT CERTAINLY DID FEEL GOOD TO GET *THAT* OFF MY CHEST.

IT'S *GOOD* THAT WE CAN STILL BE HONEST WITH ONE ANOTHER, AFTER ALL WE'VE BEEN THROUGH, YEAH?

AND HEY, IF YOU EVER NEED SOMEONE TO TALK TO--

--YOU KNOW WHERE TO *FIND* ME.

I IMAGINE YOU'LL NEED ALL THE SUPPORT YOU CAN *GET*, AFTER ALL--

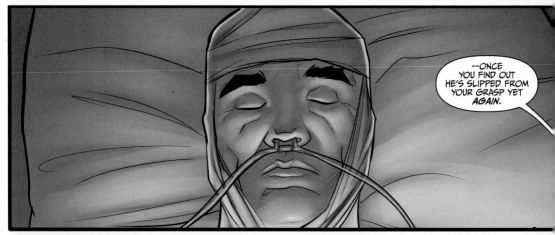

--ONCE YOU FIND OUT HE'S SLIPPED FROM YOUR GRASP YET *AGAIN*.

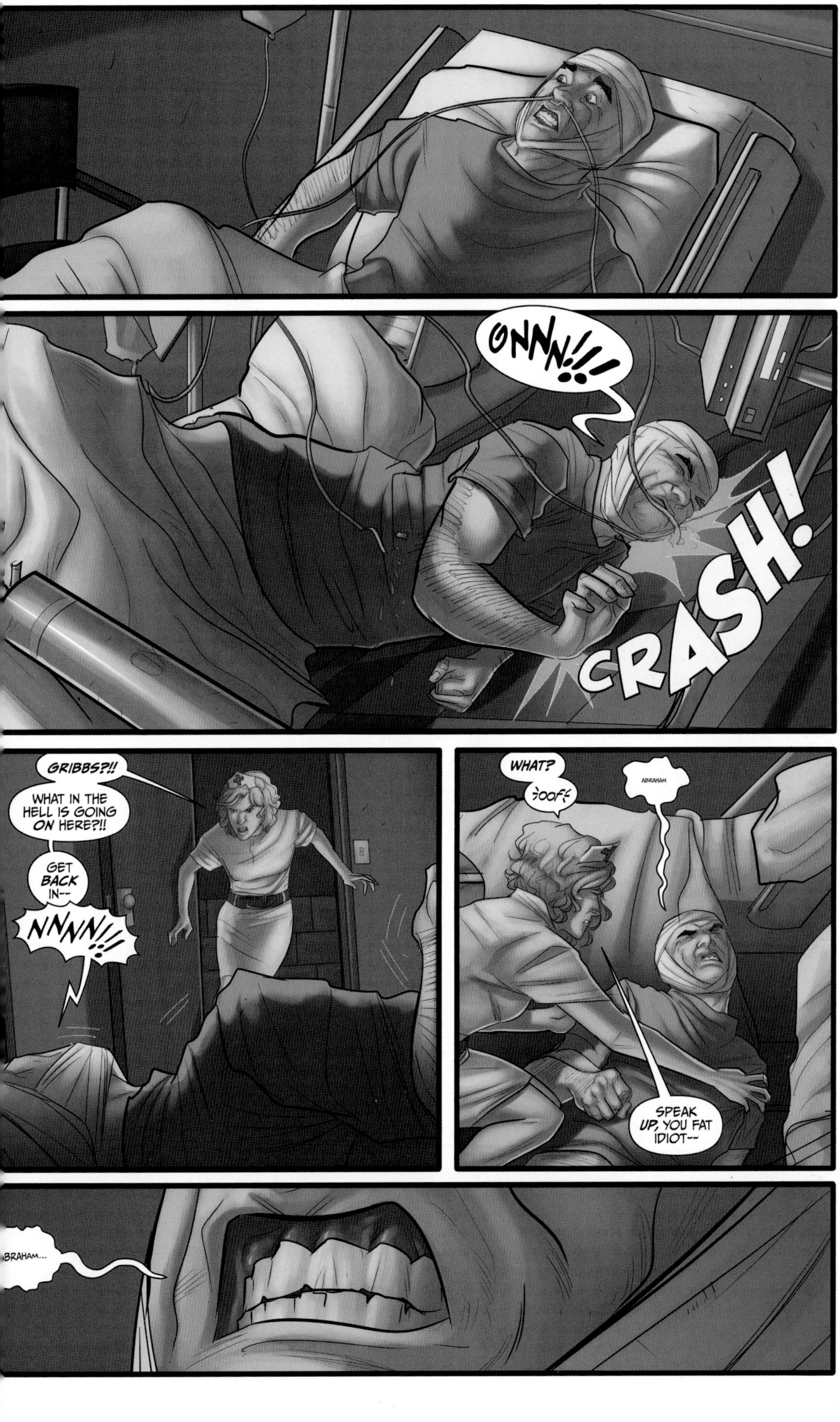
GNNN!!!
CRASH!
GRIBBS?!!
WHAT IN THE HELL IS GOING ON HERE?!!
GET BACK IN--
NNNN!!!
WHAT?
oof
ABRAHAM
SPEAK UP, YOU FAT IDIOT--
BRAHAM...

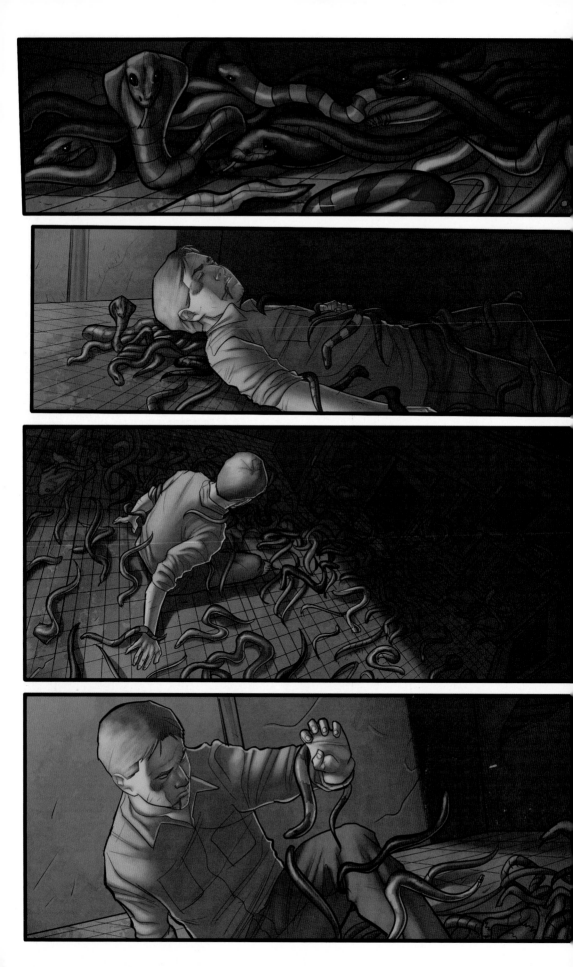

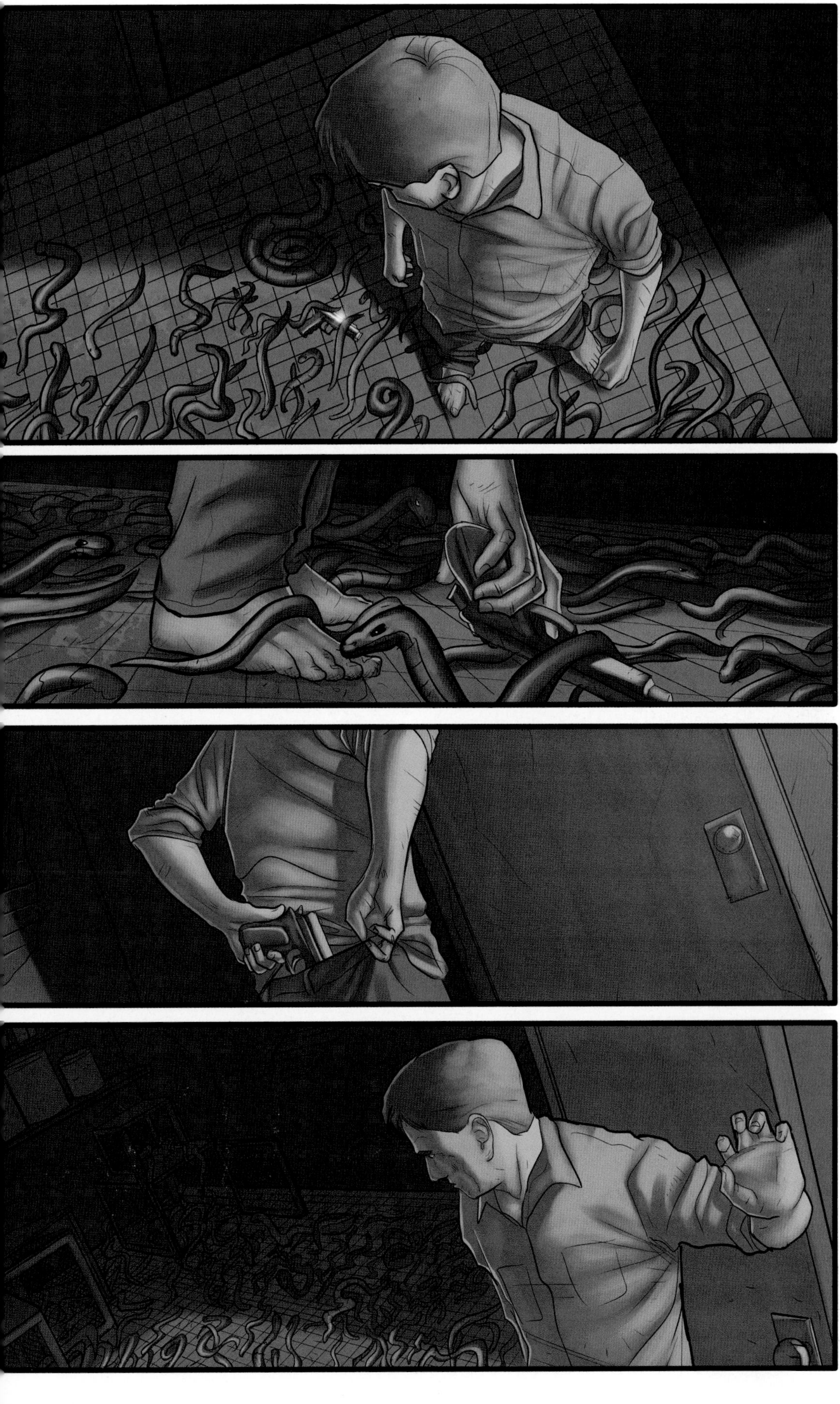

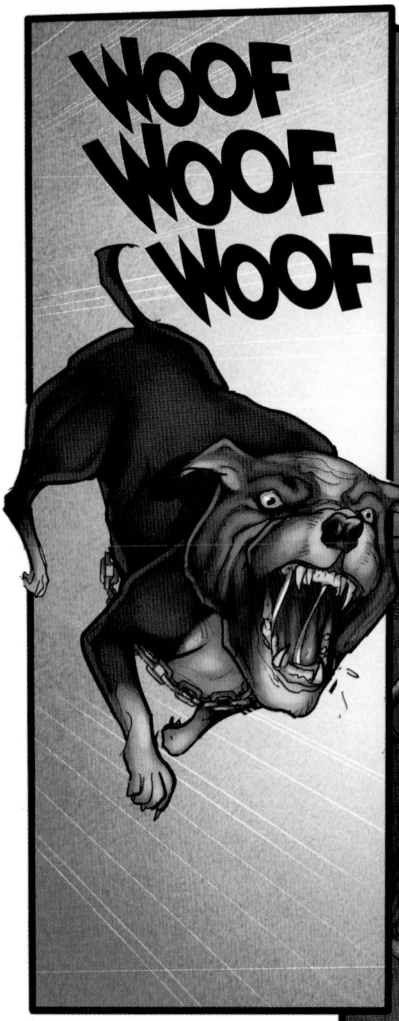
WOOF
WOOF
WOOF

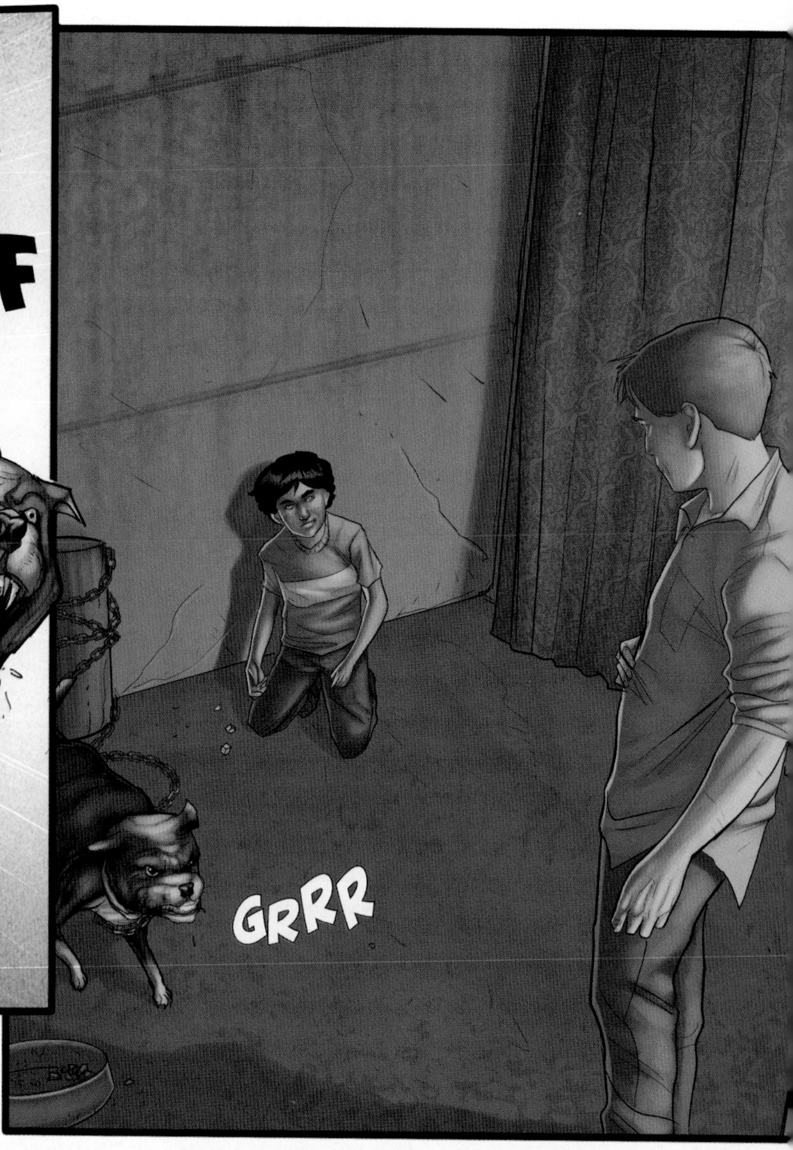
GRRR

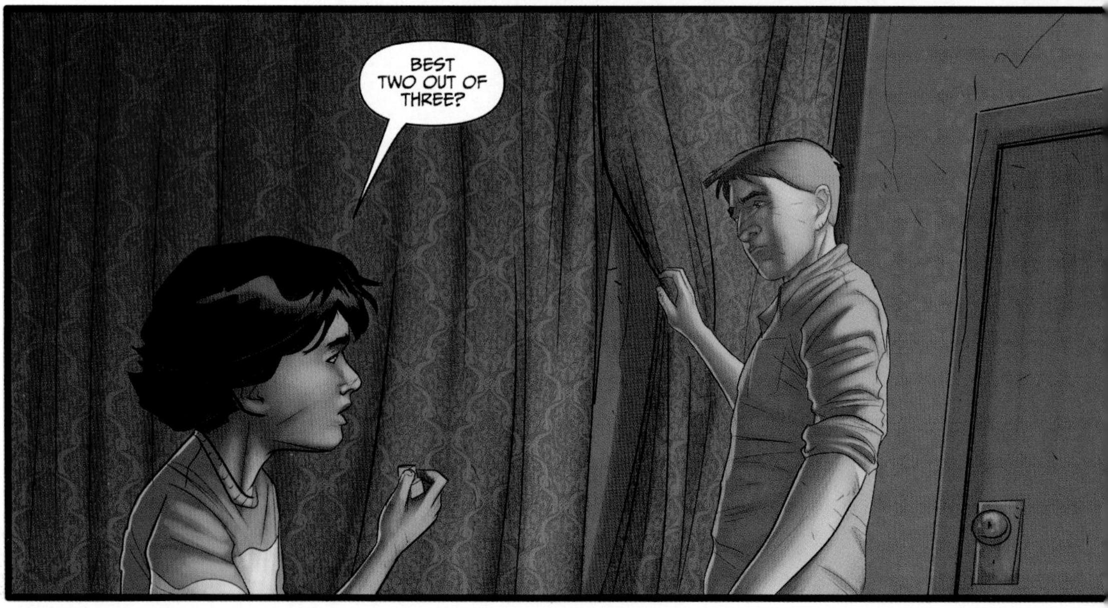
BEST TWO OUT OF THREE?

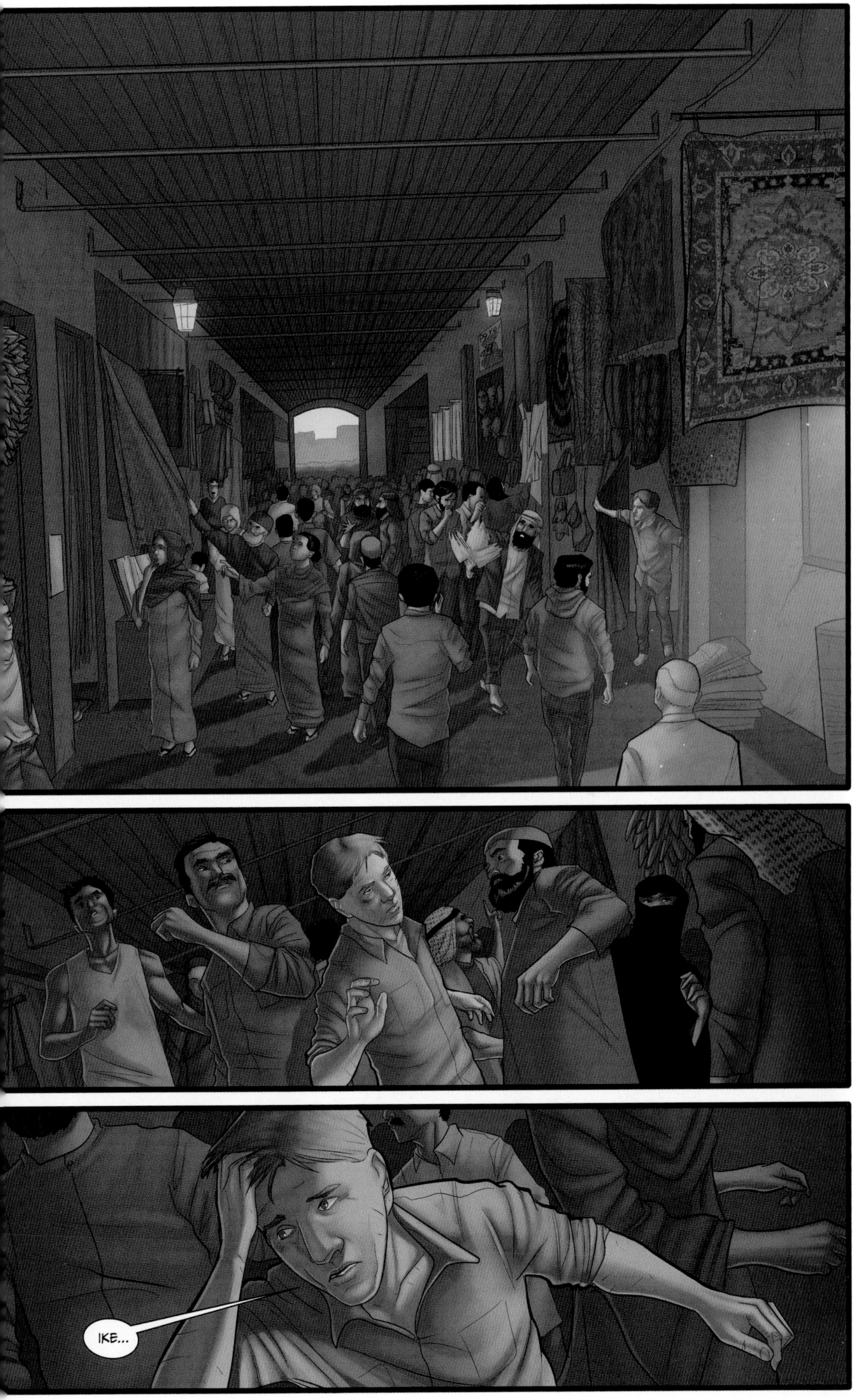
IKE...

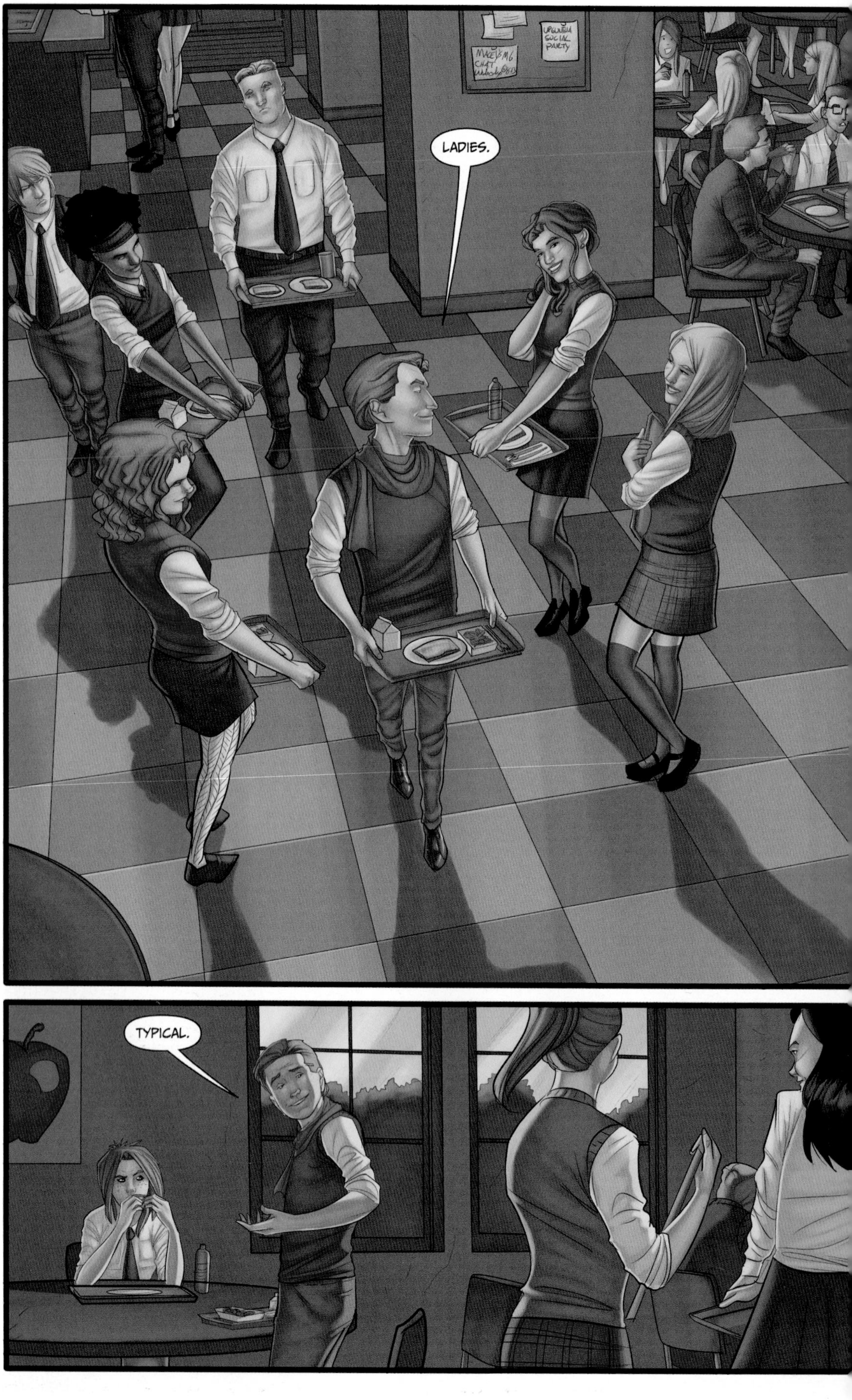
LADIES.
TYPICAL.

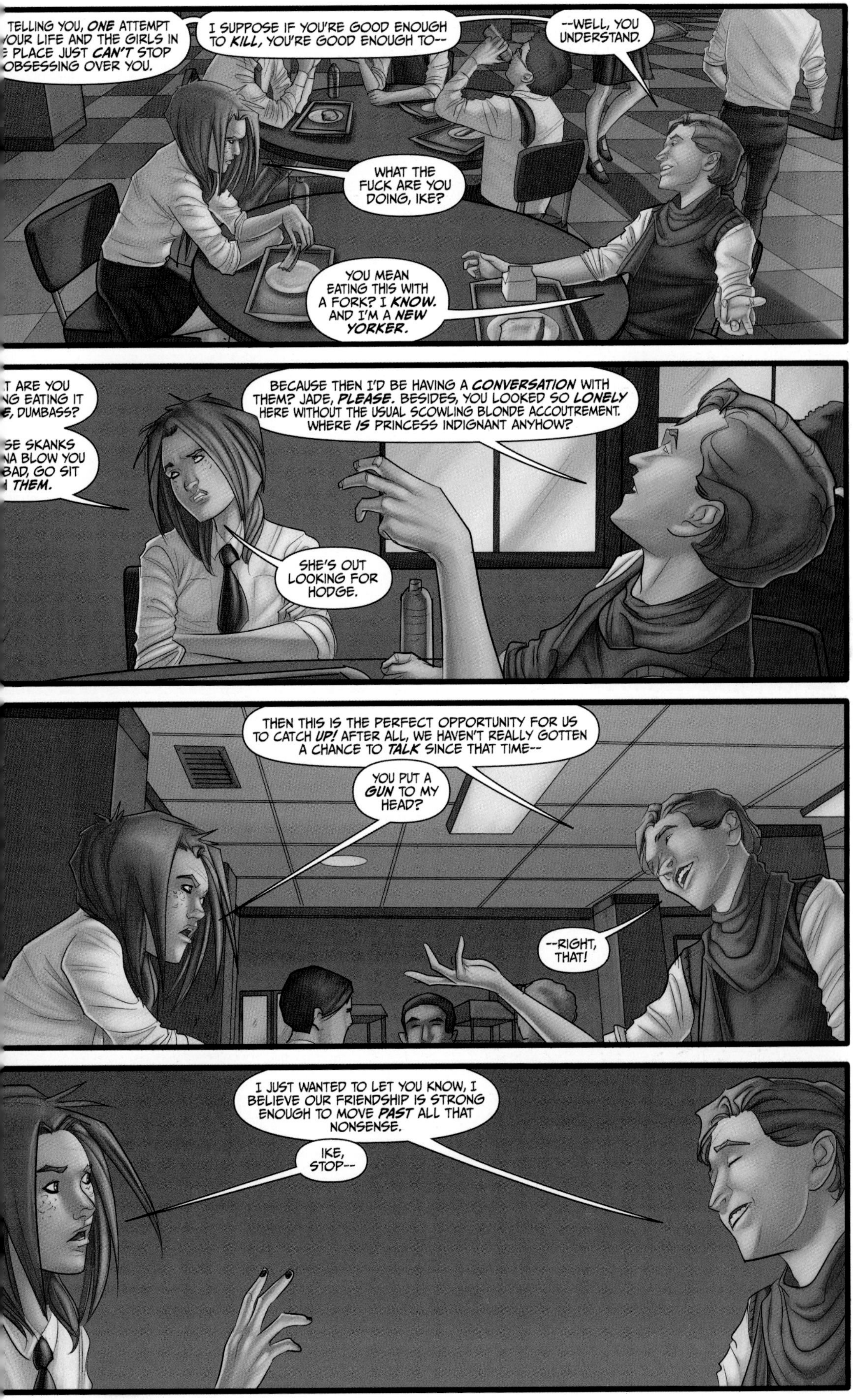
TELLING YOU, ONE ATTEMPT OUR LIFE AND THE GIRLS IN PLACE JUST CAN'T STOP OBSESSING OVER YOU.
I SUPPOSE IF YOU'RE GOOD ENOUGH TO KILL, YOU'RE GOOD ENOUGH TO--
--WELL, YOU UNDERSTAND.
WHAT THE FUCK ARE YOU DOING, IKE?
YOU MEAN EATING THIS WITH A FORK? I KNOW. AND I'M A NEW YORKER.
T ARE YOU G EATING IT E, DUMBASS?
SE SKANKS NA BLOW YOU BAD, GO SIT THEM.
BECAUSE THEN I'D BE HAVING A CONVERSATION WITH THEM? JADE, PLEASE. BESIDES, YOU LOOKED SO LONELY HERE WITHOUT THE USUAL SCOWLING BLONDE ACCOUTREMENT. WHERE IS PRINCESS INDIGNANT ANYHOW?
SHE'S OUT LOOKING FOR HODGE.
THEN THIS IS THE PERFECT OPPORTUNITY FOR US TO CATCH UP! AFTER ALL, WE HAVEN'T REALLY GOTTEN A CHANCE TO TALK SINCE THAT TIME--
YOU PUT A GUN TO MY HEAD?
--RIGHT, THAT!
I JUST WANTED TO LET YOU KNOW, I BELIEVE OUR FRIENDSHIP IS STRONG ENOUGH TO MOVE PAST ALL THAT NONSENSE.
IKE, STOP--

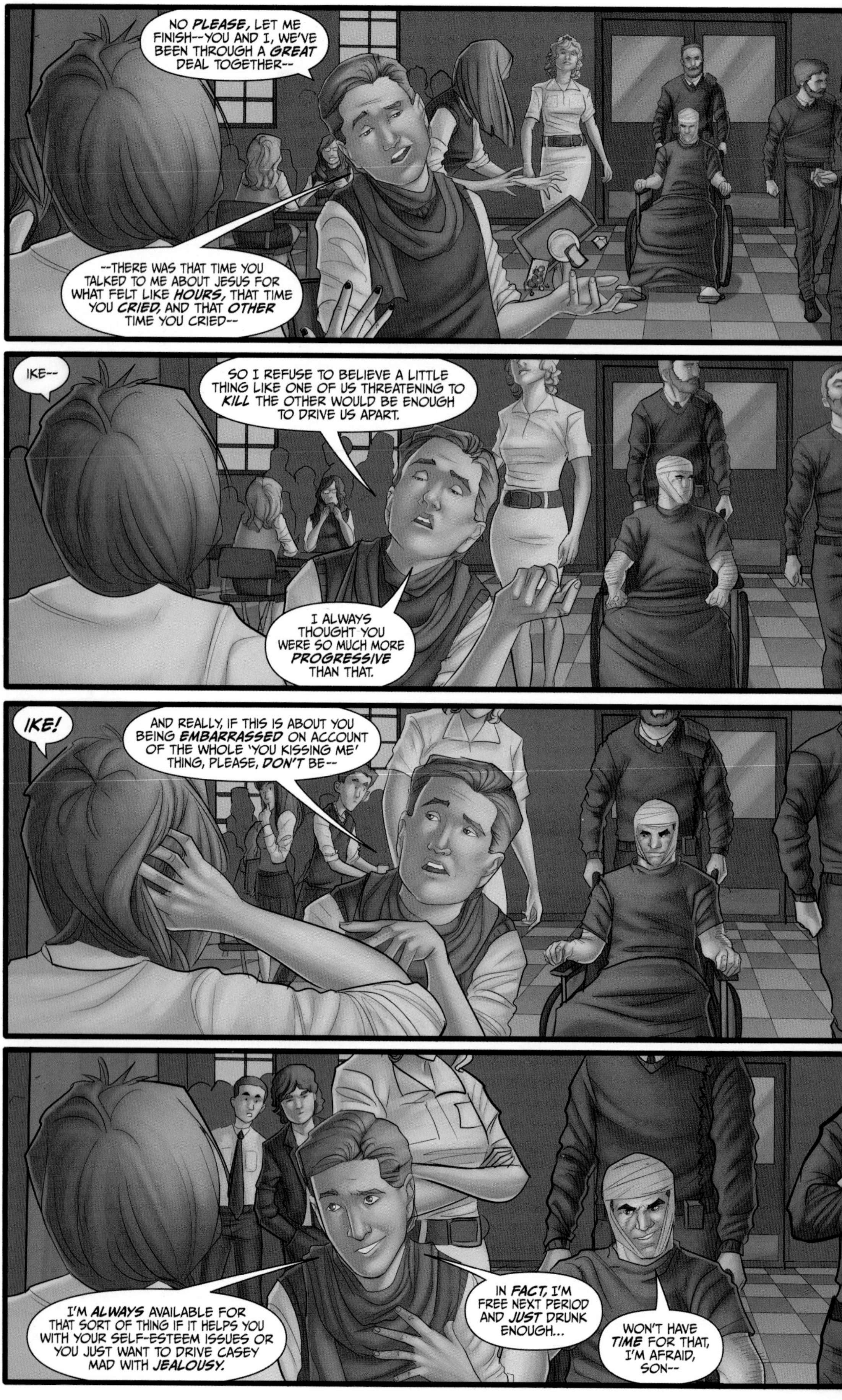
NO PLEASE, LET ME FINISH--YOU AND I, WE'VE BEEN THROUGH A GREAT DEAL TOGETHER--
--THERE WAS THAT TIME YOU TALKED TO ME ABOUT JESUS FOR WHAT FELT LIKE HOURS, THAT TIME YOU CRIED, AND THAT OTHER TIME YOU CRIED--
IKE--
SO I REFUSE TO BELIEVE A LITTLE THING LIKE ONE OF US THREATENING TO KILL THE OTHER WOULD BE ENOUGH TO DRIVE US APART.
I ALWAYS THOUGHT YOU WERE SO MUCH MORE PROGRESSIVE THAN THAT.
IKE!
AND REALLY, IF THIS IS ABOUT YOU BEING EMBARRASSED ON ACCOUNT OF THE WHOLE 'YOU KISSING ME' THING, PLEASE, DON'T BE--
I'M ALWAYS AVAILABLE FOR THAT SORT OF THING IF IT HELPS YOU WITH YOUR SELF-ESTEEM ISSUES OR YOU JUST WANT TO DRIVE CASEY MAD WITH JEALOUSY.
IN FACT, I'M FREE NEXT PERIOD AND JUST DRUNK ENOUGH...
WON'T HAVE TIME FOR THAT, I'M AFRAID, SON--

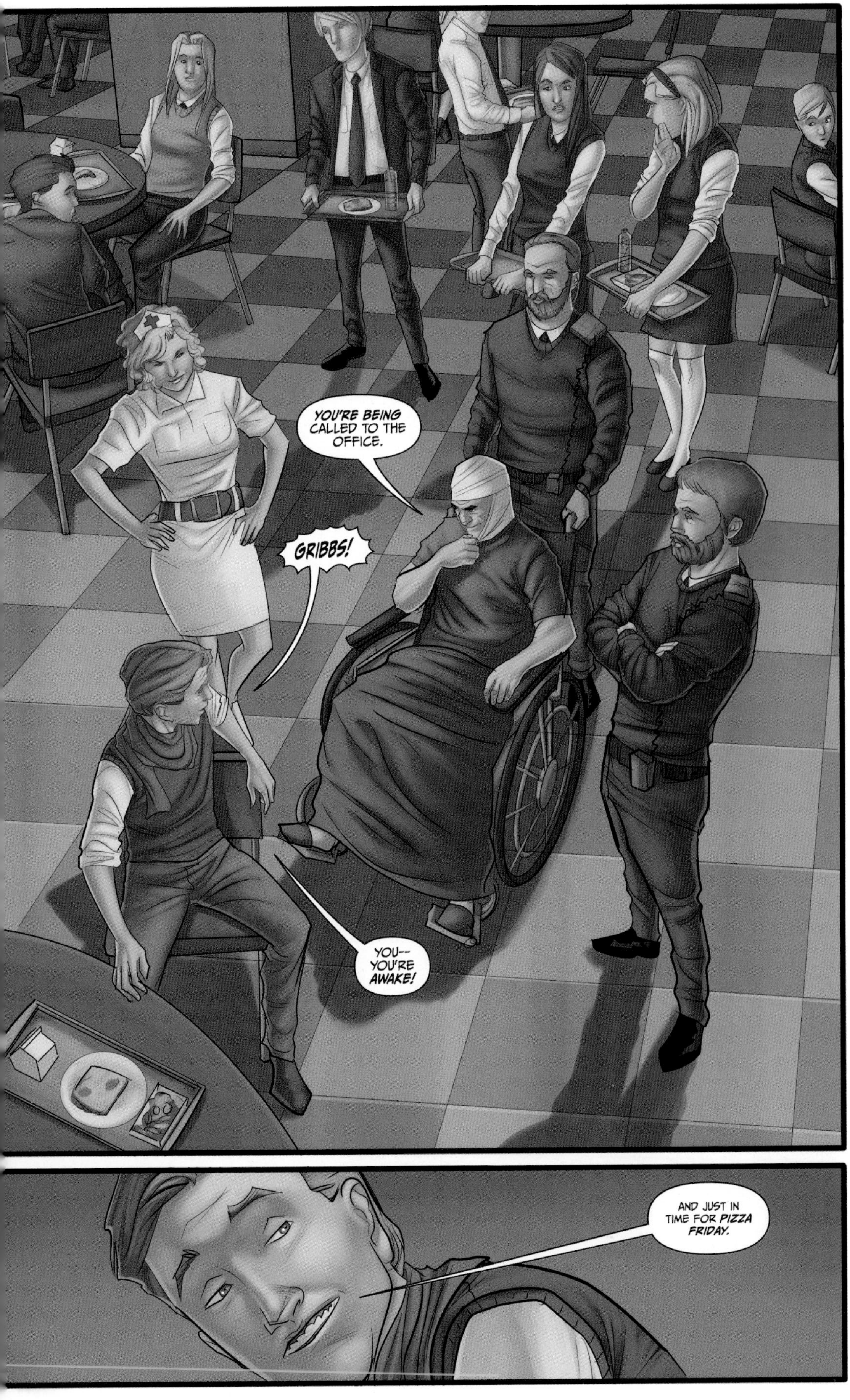
YOU'RE BEING CALLED TO THE OFFICE.
GRIBBS!
YOU-- YOU'RE AWAKE!
AND JUST IN TIME FOR PIZZA FRIDAY.

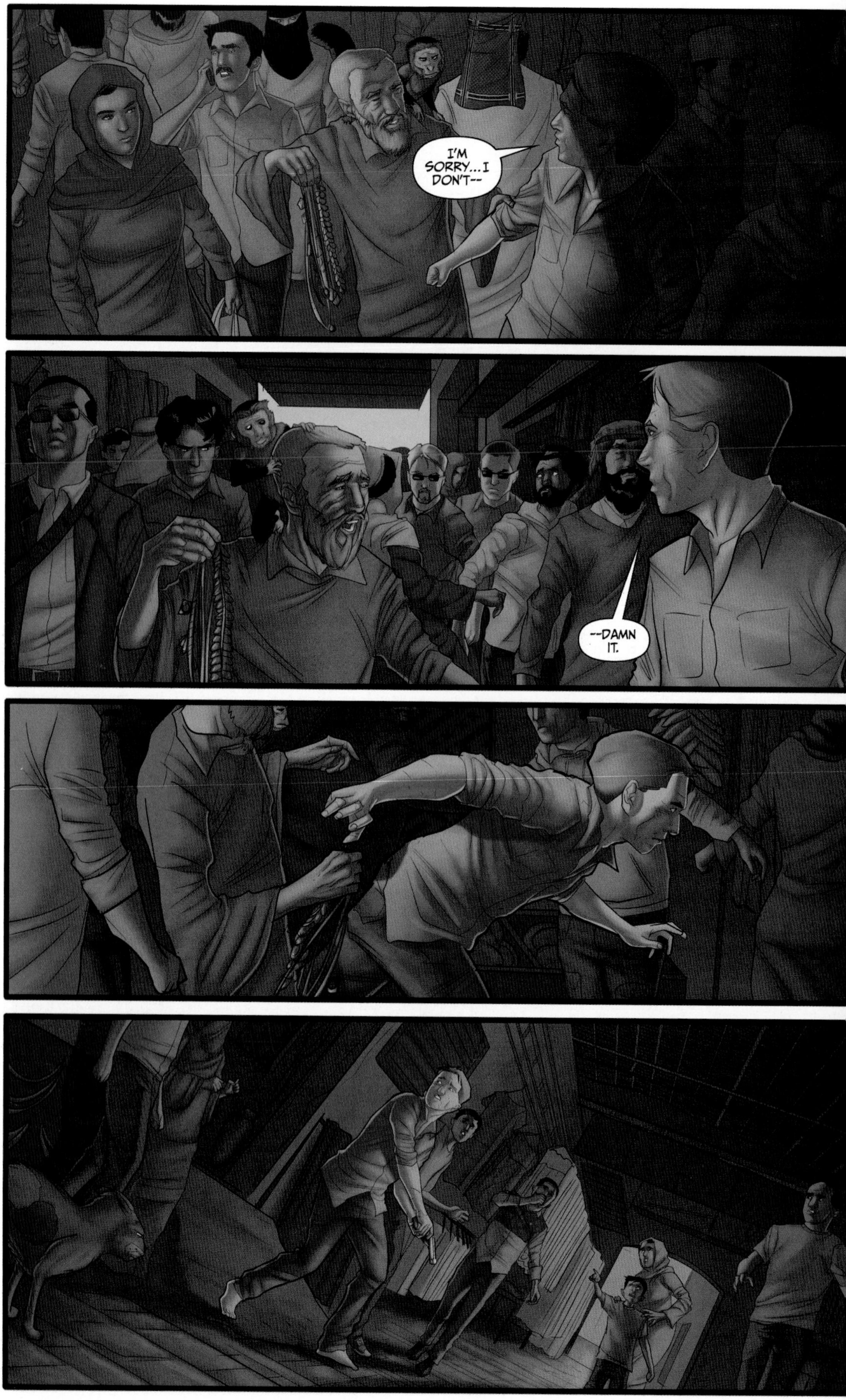
I'M SORRY...I DON'T--
--DAMN IT.

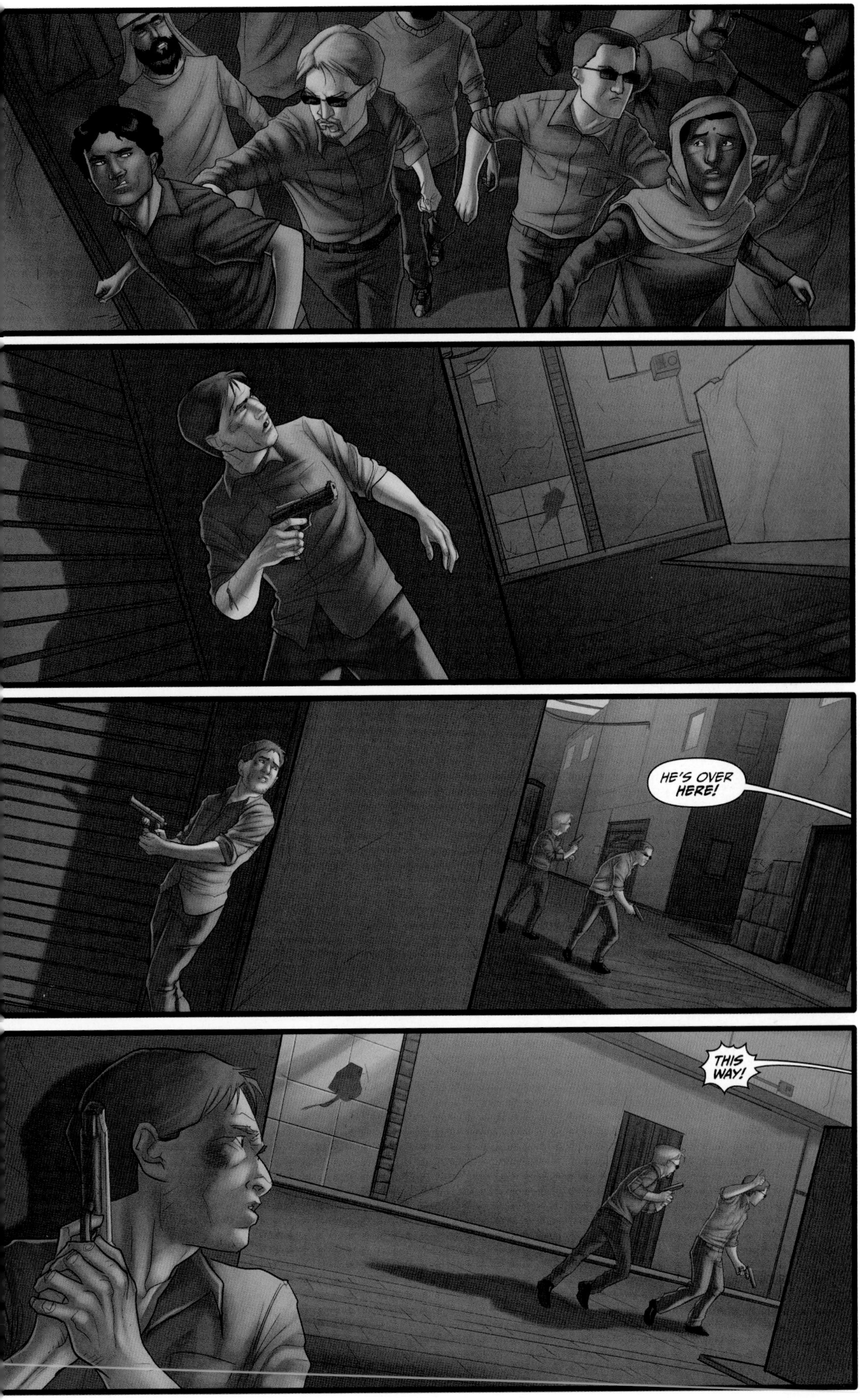
HE'S OVER HERE!
THIS WAY!

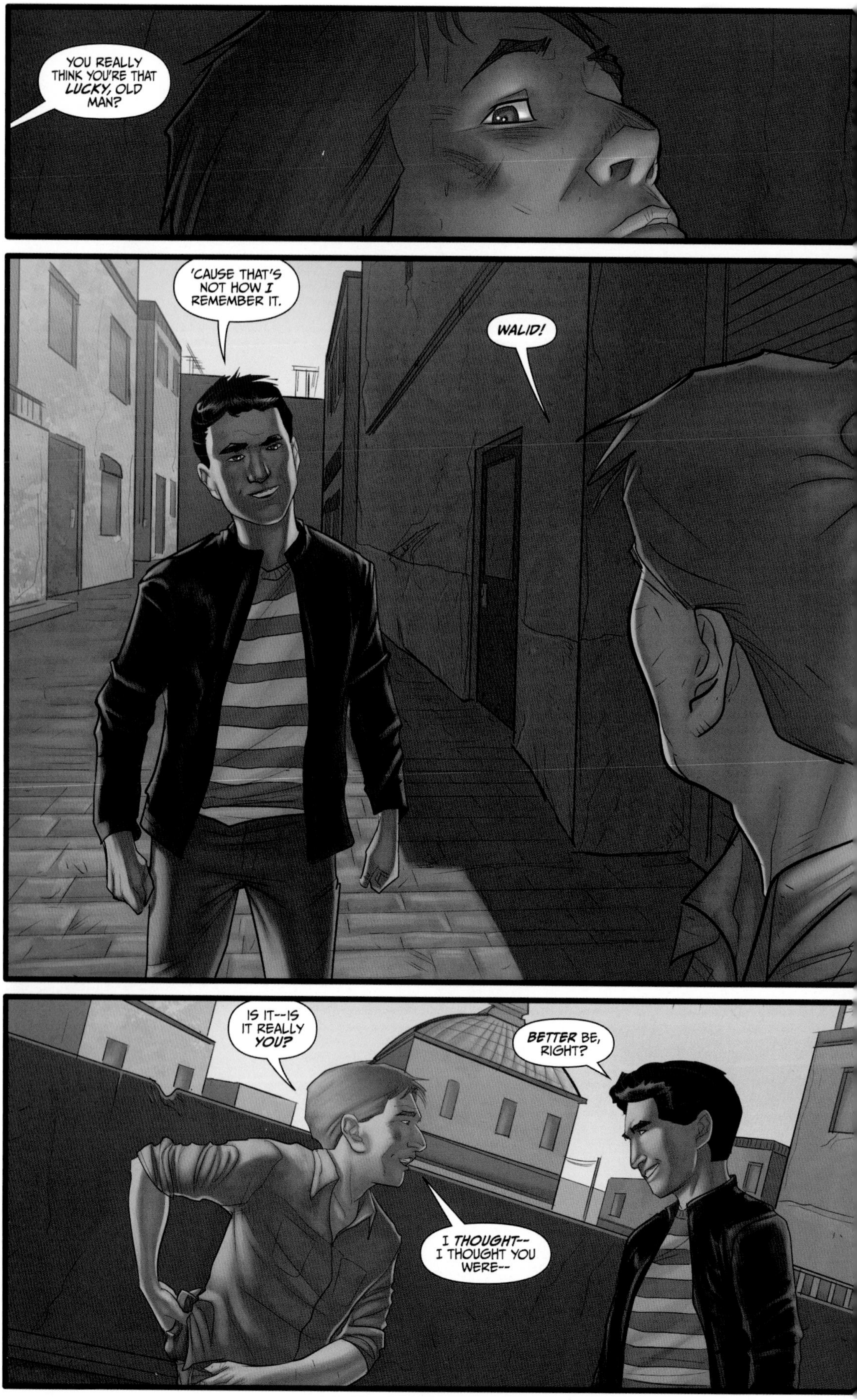
YOU REALLY THINK YOU'RE THAT LUCKY, OLD MAN?
'CAUSE THAT'S NOT HOW I REMEMBER IT.
WALID!
IS IT--IS IT REALLY YOU?
BETTER BE, RIGHT?
I THOUGHT-- I THOUGHT YOU WERE--

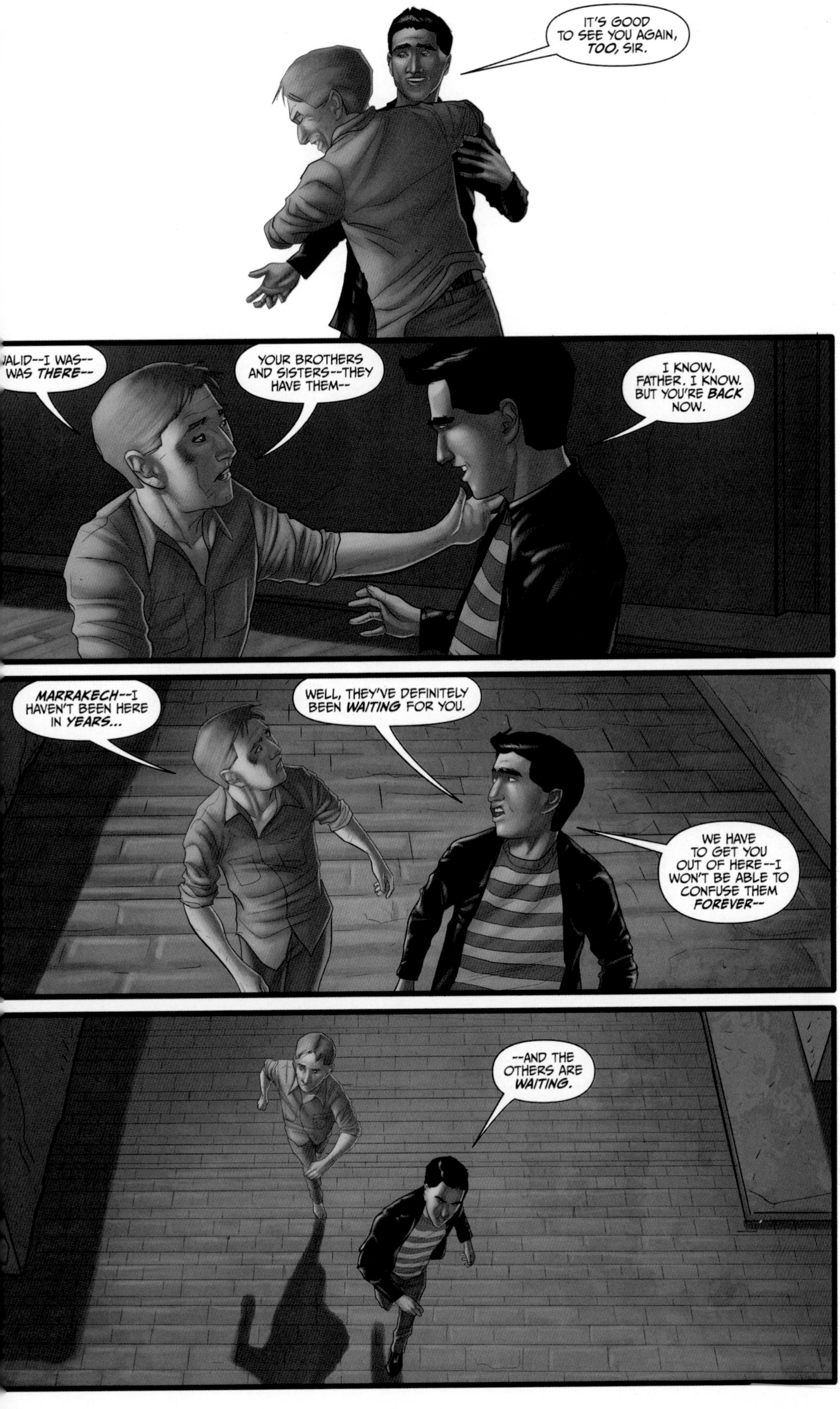
IT'S GOOD TO SEE YOU AGAIN, TOO, SIR.
WALID--I WAS--WAS THERE--
YOUR BROTHERS AND SISTERS--THEY HAVE THEM--
I KNOW, FATHER. I KNOW. BUT YOU'RE BACK NOW.
MARRAKECH--I HAVEN'T BEEN HERE IN YEARS...
WELL, THEY'VE DEFINITELY BEEN WAITING FOR YOU.
WE HAVE TO GET YOU OUT OF HERE--I WON'T BE ABLE TO CONFUSE THEM FOREVER--
--AND THE OTHERS ARE WAITING.

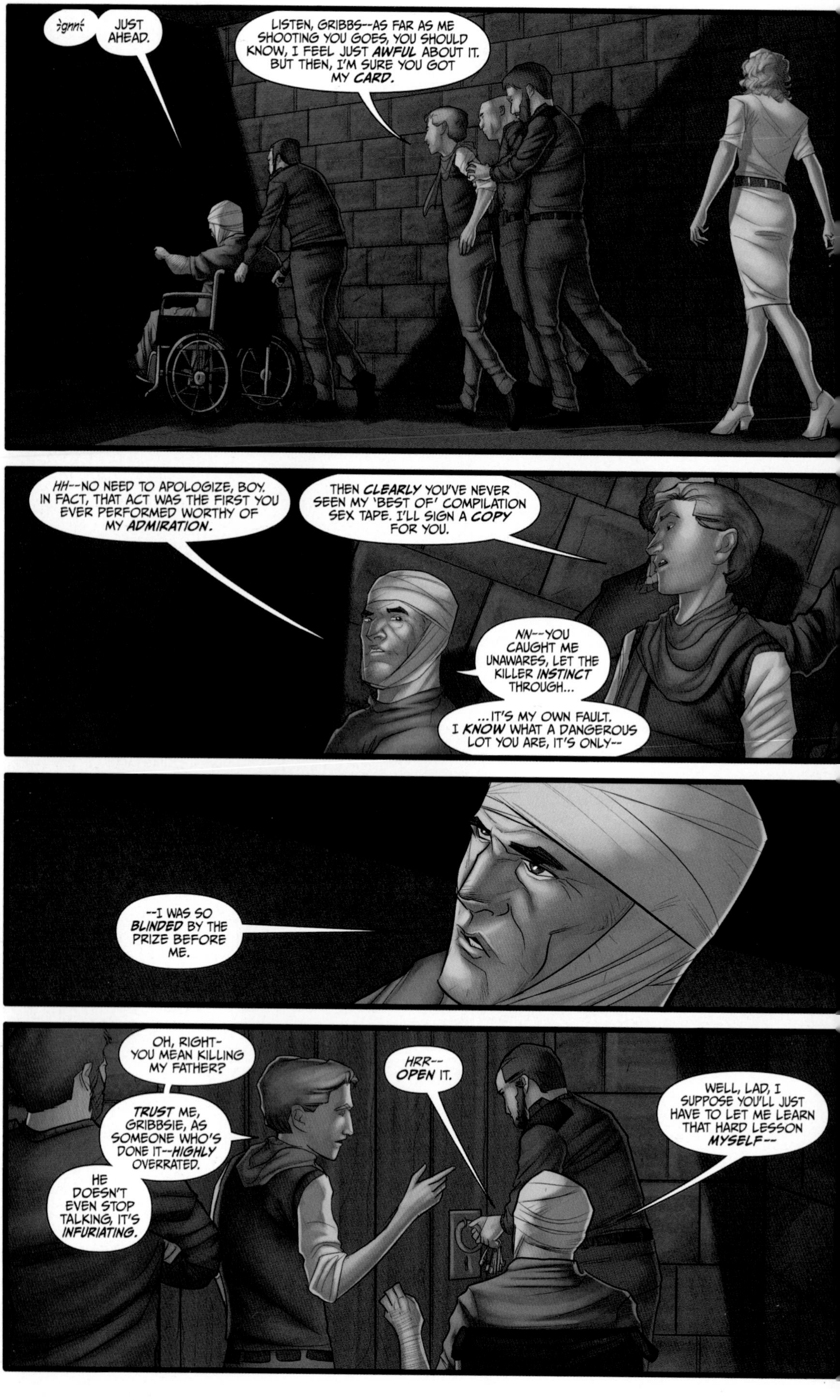

‡gnn‡
JUST AHEAD.
LISTEN, GRIBBS--AS FAR AS ME SHOOTING YOU GOES, YOU SHOULD KNOW, I FEEL JUST AWFUL ABOUT IT. BUT THEN, I'M SURE YOU GOT MY CARD.
HH--NO NEED TO APOLOGIZE, BOY. IN FACT, THAT ACT WAS THE FIRST YOU EVER PERFORMED WORTHY OF MY ADMIRATION.
THEN CLEARLY YOU'VE NEVER SEEN MY 'BEST OF' COMPILATION SEX TAPE. I'LL SIGN A COPY FOR YOU.
NN--YOU CAUGHT ME UNAWARES, LET THE KILLER INSTINCT THROUGH...
...IT'S MY OWN FAULT. I KNOW WHAT A DANGEROUS LOT YOU ARE, IT'S ONLY--
--I WAS SO BLINDED BY THE PRIZE BEFORE ME.
OH, RIGHT- YOU MEAN KILLING MY FATHER?
TRUST ME, GRIBBSIE, AS SOMEONE WHO'S DONE IT--HIGHLY OVERRATED.
HE DOESN'T EVEN STOP TALKING, IT'S INFURIATING.
HRR-- OPEN IT.
WELL, LAD, I SUPPOSE YOU'LL JUST HAVE TO LET ME LEARN THAT HARD LESSON MYSELF--

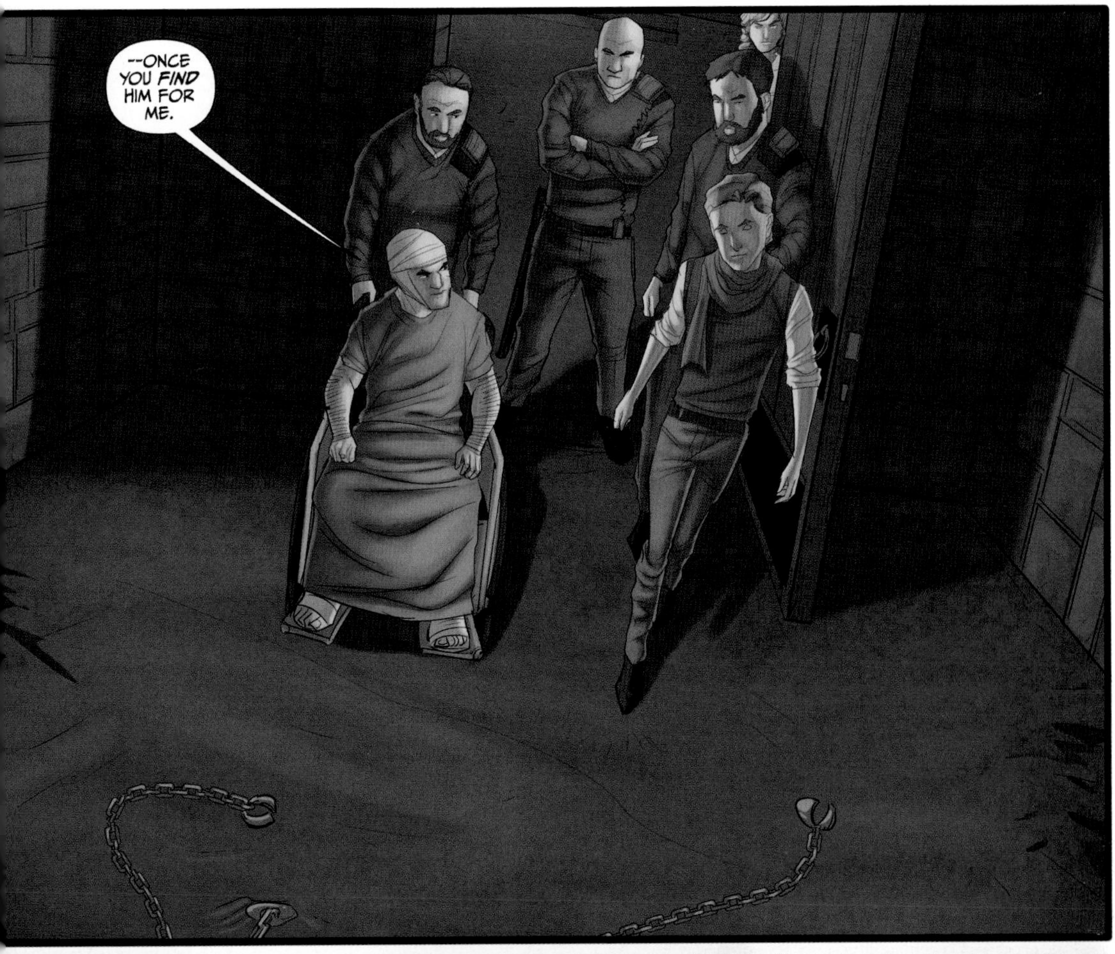
--ONCE YOU *FIND* HIM FOR ME.

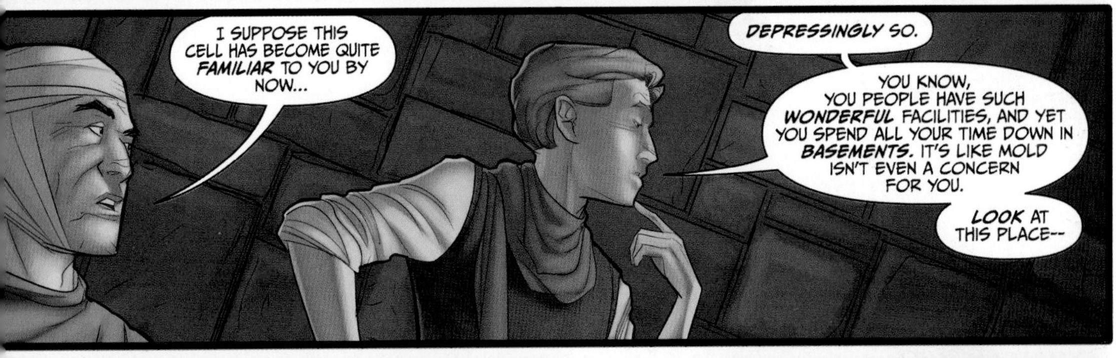
I SUPPOSE THIS CELL HAS BECOME QUITE *FAMILIAR* TO YOU BY NOW...
DEPRESSINGLY SO.
YOU KNOW, YOU PEOPLE HAVE SUCH *WONDERFUL* FACILITIES, AND YET YOU SPEND ALL YOUR TIME DOWN IN *BASEMENTS*. IT'S LIKE MOLD ISN'T EVEN A CONCERN FOR YOU.
LOOK AT THIS PLACE--

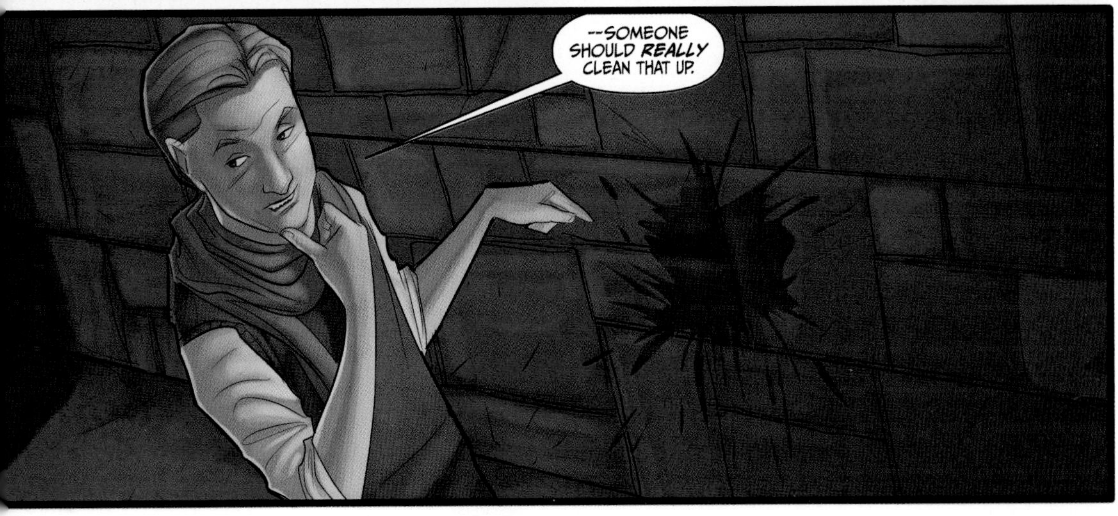
--SOMEONE SHOULD *REALLY* CLEAN THAT UP.

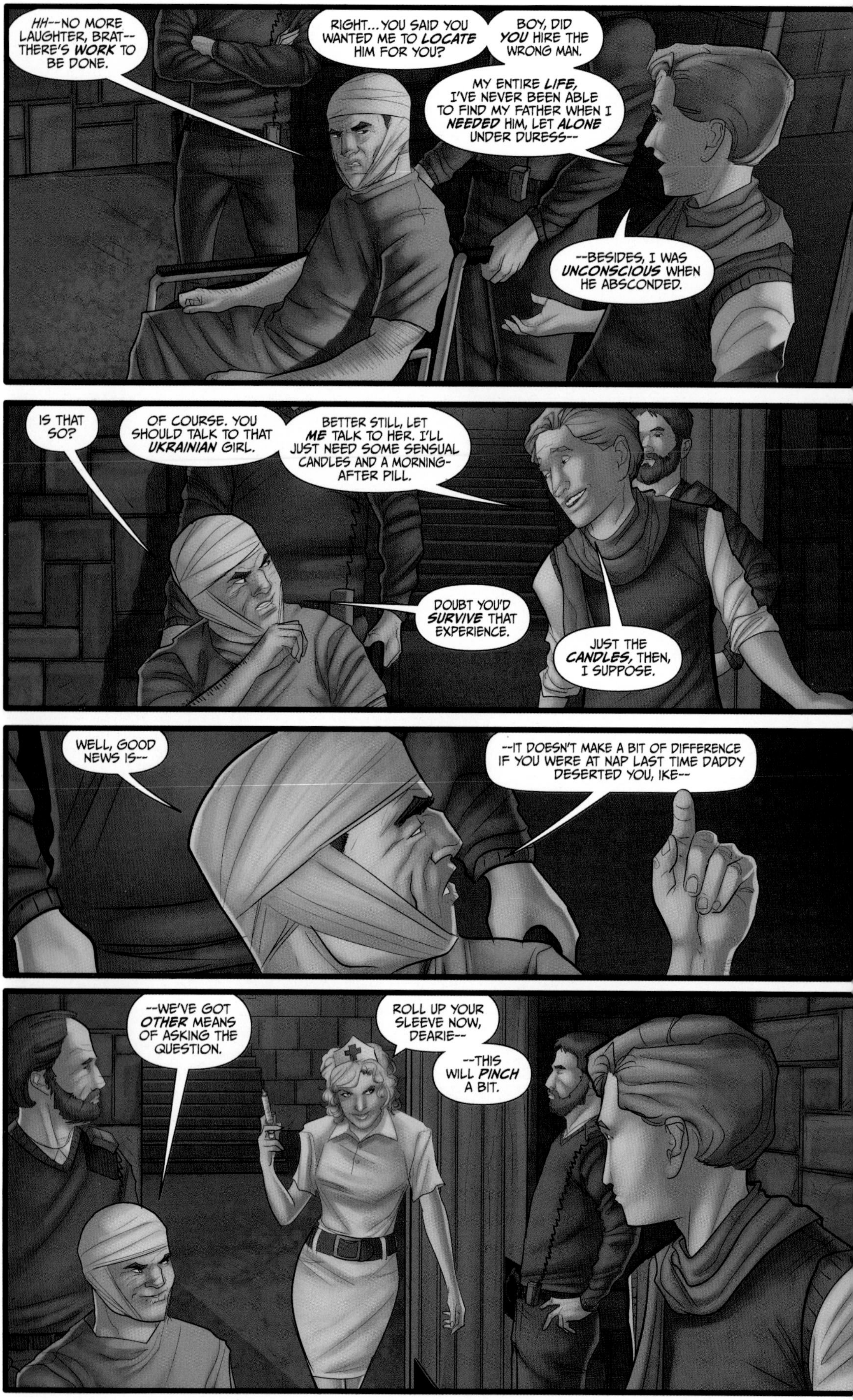
HH--NO MORE LAUGHTER, BRAT-- THERE'S WORK TO BE DONE.
RIGHT... YOU SAID YOU WANTED ME TO LOCATE HIM FOR YOU?
BOY, DID YOU HIRE THE WRONG MAN.
MY ENTIRE LIFE, I'VE NEVER BEEN ABLE TO FIND MY FATHER WHEN I NEEDED HIM, LET ALONE UNDER DURESS--
--BESIDES, I WAS UNCONSCIOUS WHEN HE ABSCONDED.
IS THAT SO?
OF COURSE. YOU SHOULD TALK TO THAT UKRAINIAN GIRL.
BETTER STILL, LET ME TALK TO HER. I'LL JUST NEED SOME SENSUAL CANDLES AND A MORNING-AFTER PILL.
DOUBT YOU'D SURVIVE THAT EXPERIENCE.
JUST THE CANDLES, THEN, I SUPPOSE.
WELL, GOOD NEWS IS--
--IT DOESN'T MAKE A BIT OF DIFFERENCE IF YOU WERE AT NAP LAST TIME DADDY DESERTED YOU, IKE--
--WE'VE GOT OTHER MEANS OF ASKING THE QUESTION.
ROLL UP YOUR SLEEVE NOW, DEARIE--
--THIS WILL PINCH A BIT.

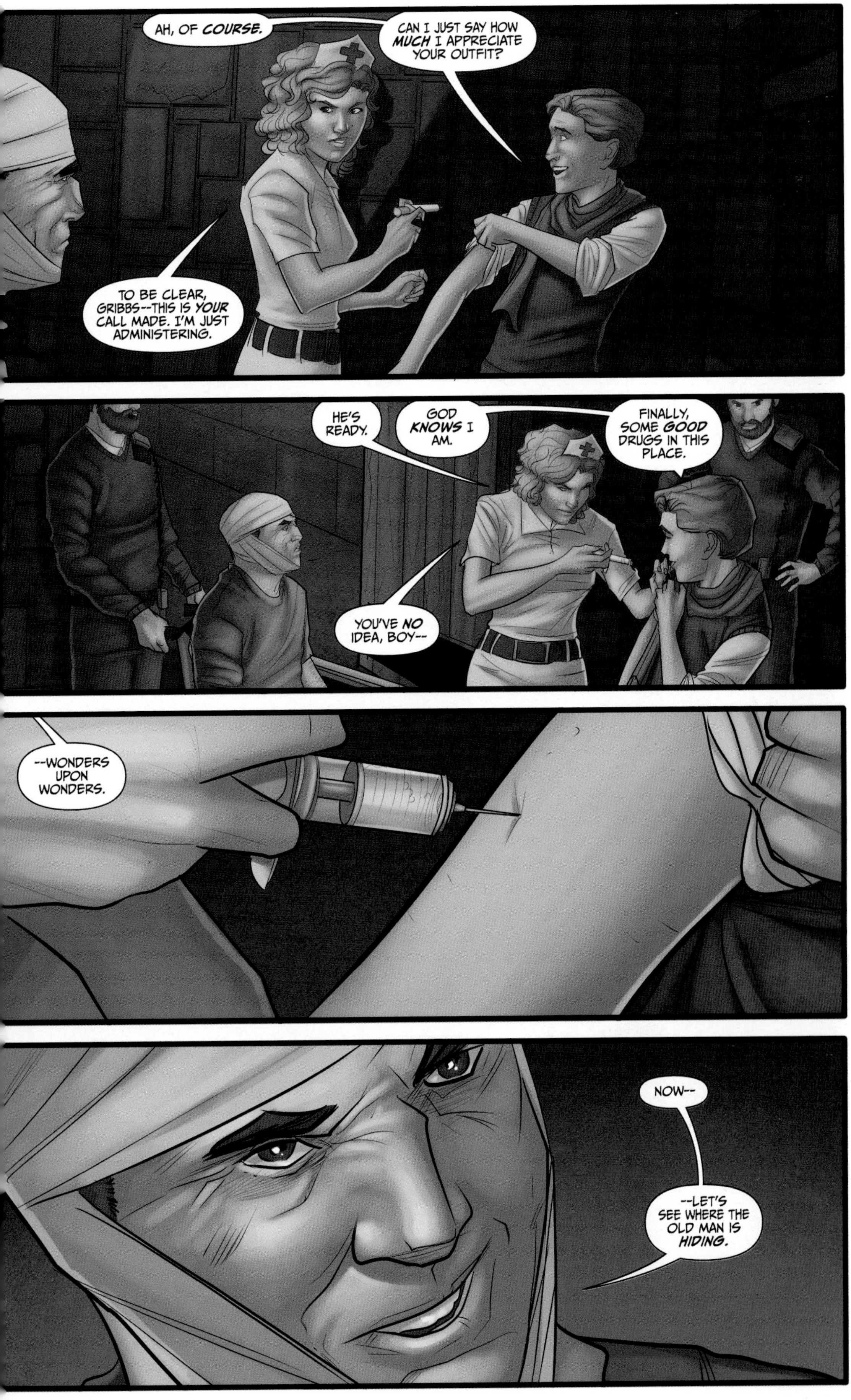
AH, OF COURSE.
CAN I JUST SAY HOW MUCH I APPRECIATE YOUR OUTFIT?
TO BE CLEAR, GRIBBS--THIS IS YOUR CALL MADE. I'M JUST ADMINISTERING.
HE'S READY.
GOD KNOWS I AM.
FINALLY, SOME GOOD DRUGS IN THIS PLACE.
YOU'VE NO IDEA, BOY--
--WONDERS UPON WONDERS.
NOW--
--LET'S SEE WHERE THE OLD MAN IS HIDING.

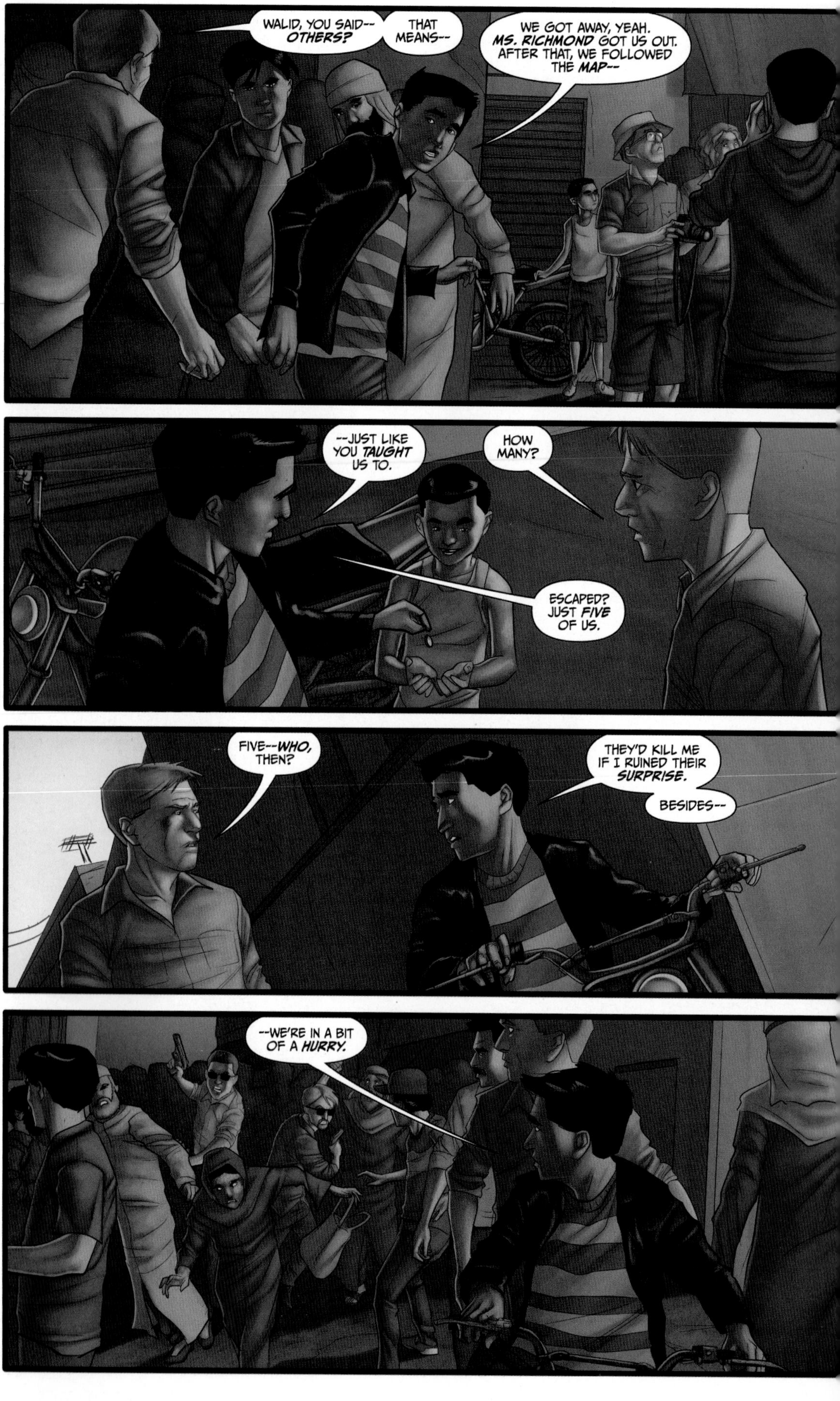
WALID, YOU SAID-- OTHERS?
THAT MEANS--
WE GOT AWAY, YEAH. MS. RICHMOND GOT US OUT. AFTER THAT, WE FOLLOWED THE MAP--
--JUST LIKE YOU TAUGHT US TO.
HOW MANY?
ESCAPED? JUST FIVE OF US.
FIVE--WHO, THEN?
THEY'D KILL ME IF I RUINED THEIR SURPRISE.
BESIDES--
--WE'RE IN A BIT OF A HURRY.

YOU *FEEL* IT NOW, BOY, DON'T YOU?

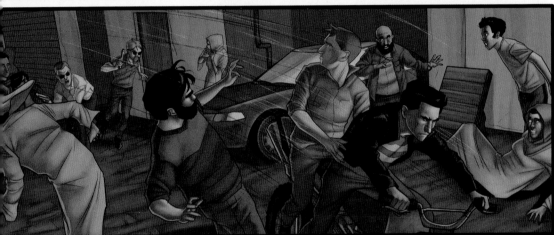

THIS PLACE, THERE'S A WAY MOMMY AND DADDY NEVER LEAVE YOU.

HODGE'LL TELL YOU ALL ABOUT IT IF I LET HER KEEP BREATHING MUCH LONGER.

POINT BEING, A CELL YOU ONCE SHARED-- THE CELL YOUR PA VANISHED FROM--I'D VENTURE A *CONNECTION* IS MADE.

NO *MATTER* THE SUPPOSED DISTANCE.

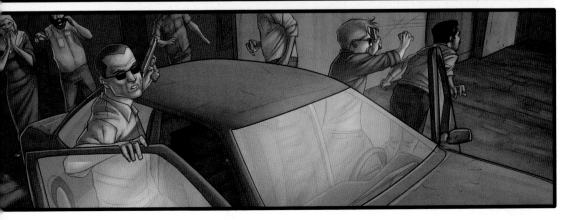

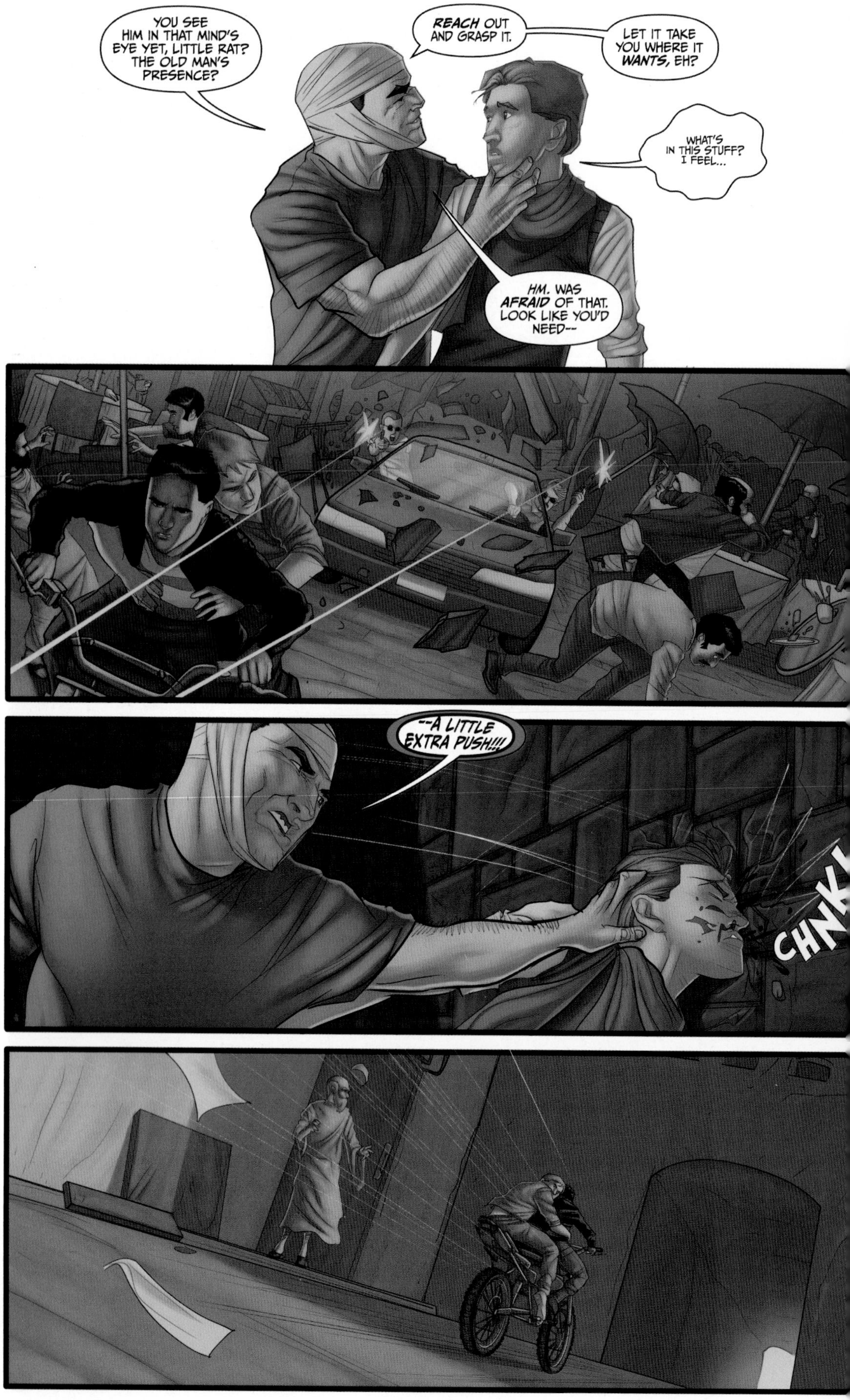
YOU SEE HIM IN THAT MIND'S EYE YET, LITTLE RAT? THE OLD MAN'S PRESENCE?
REACH OUT AND GRASP IT.
LET IT TAKE YOU WHERE IT WANTS, EH?
WHAT'S IN THIS STUFF? I FEEL...
HM. WAS AFRAID OF THAT. LOOK LIKE YOU'D NEED--
--A LITTLE EXTRA PUSH!!!
CHNK

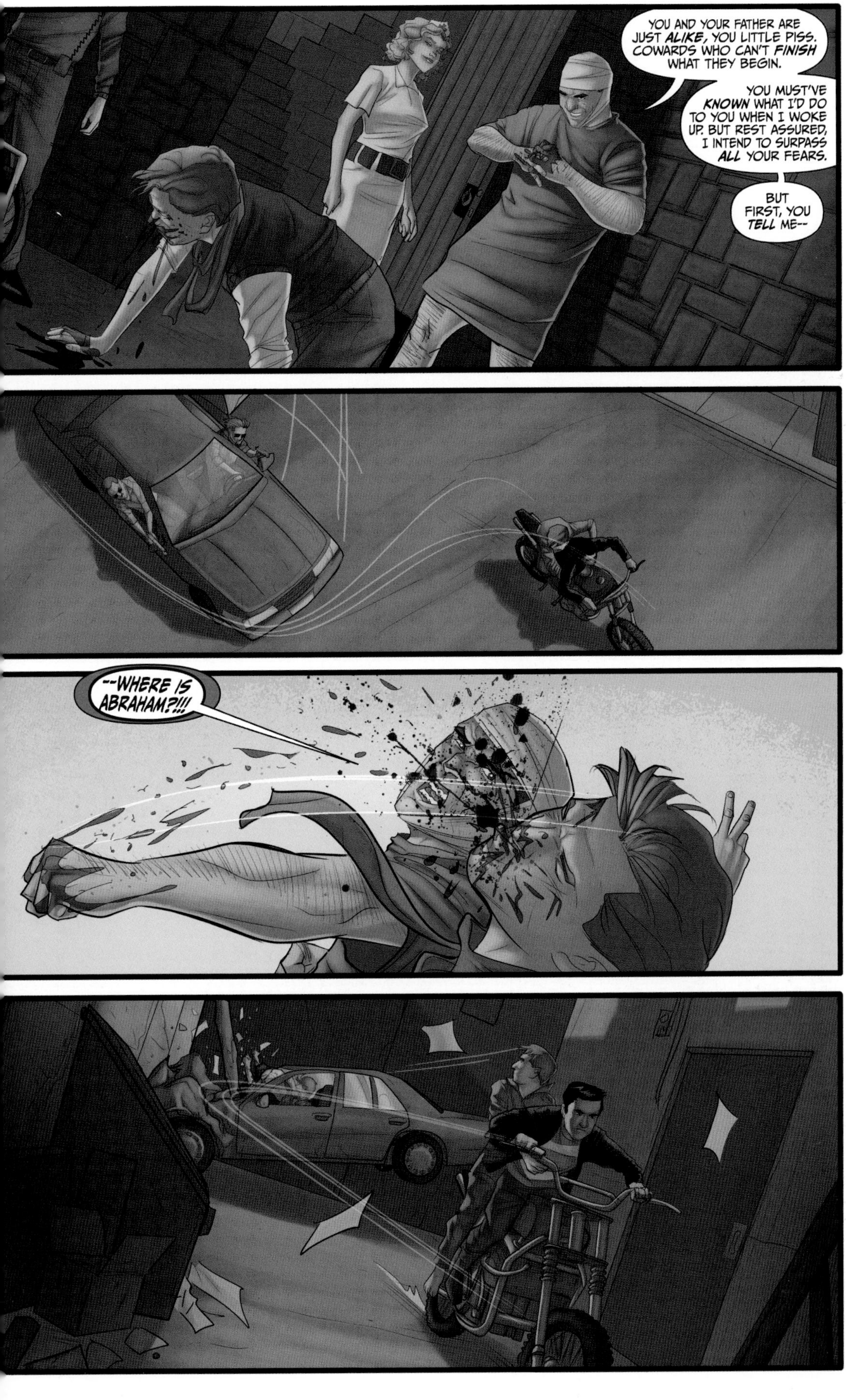
YOU AND YOUR FATHER ARE JUST ALIKE, YOU LITTLE PISS. COWARDS WHO CAN'T FINISH WHAT THEY BEGIN.
YOU MUST'VE KNOWN WHAT I'D DO TO YOU WHEN I WOKE UP. BUT REST ASSURED, I INTEND TO SURPASS ALL YOUR FEARS.
BUT FIRST, YOU TELL ME--
--WHERE IS ABRAHAM?!!!

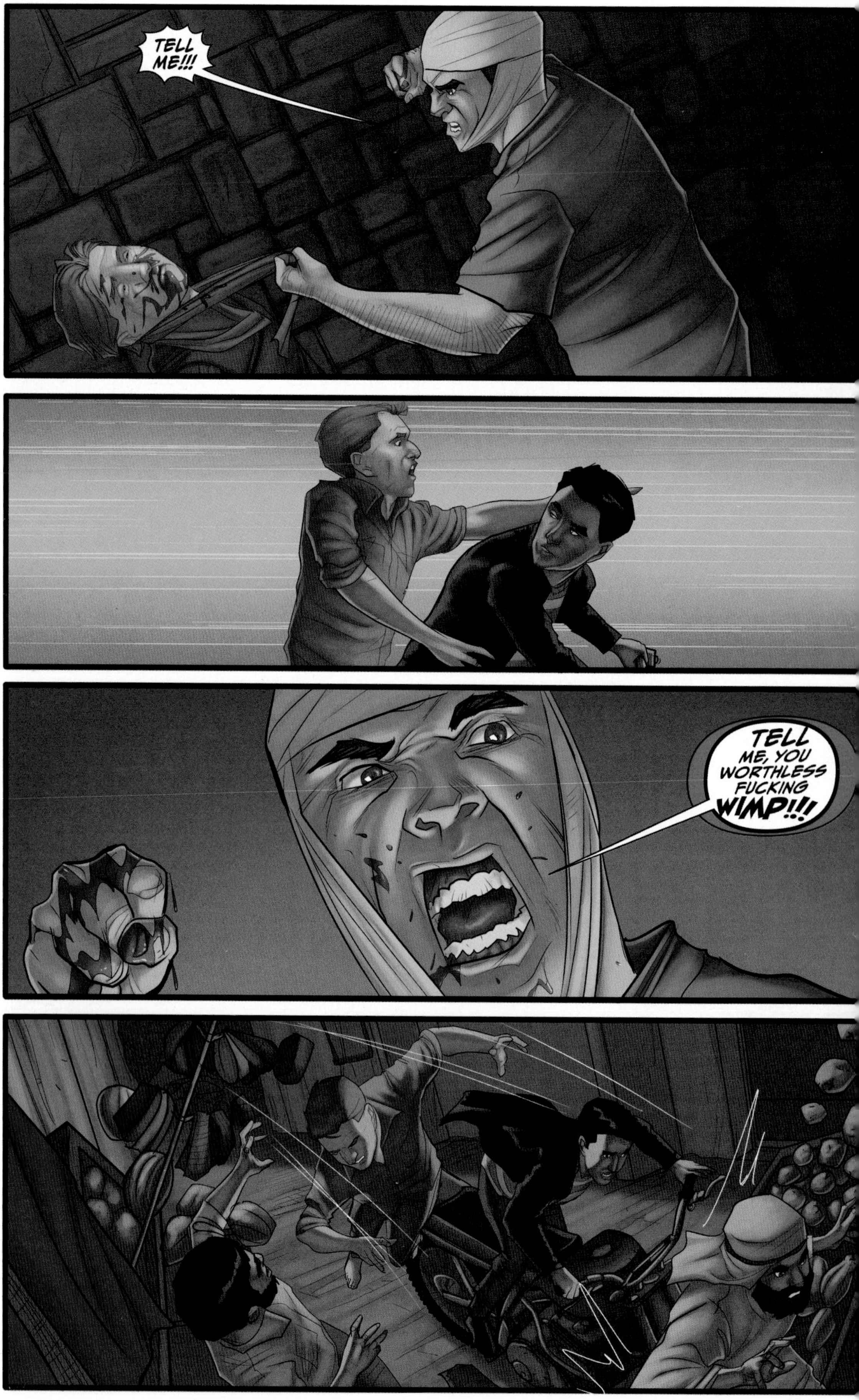
TELL ME!!!
TELL ME, YOU WORTHLESS FUCKING WIMP!!!

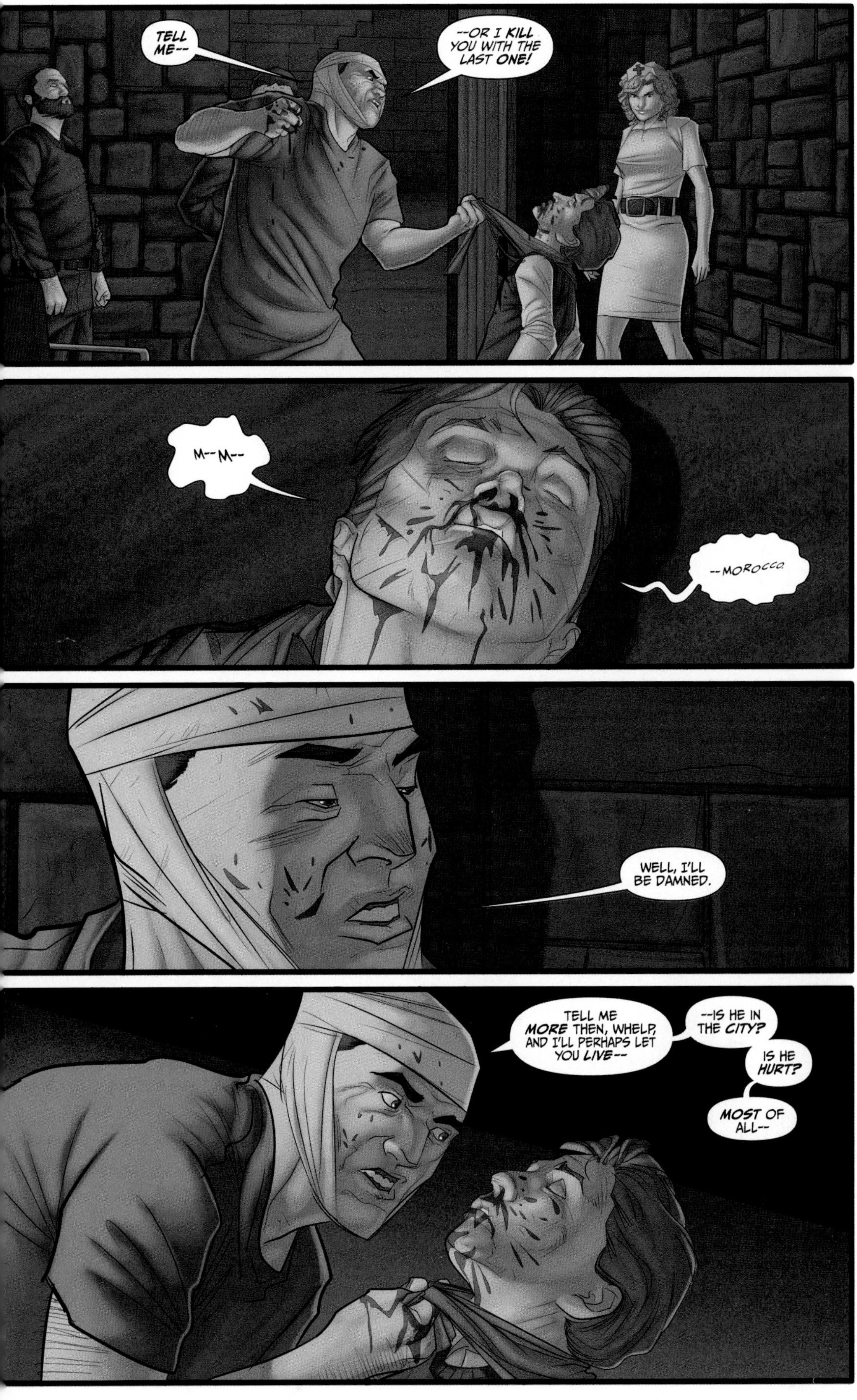
TELL ME--
--OR I KILL YOU WITH THE LAST ONE!
M--M--
--MOROCCO.
WELL, I'LL BE DAMNED.
TELL ME MORE THEN, WHELP, AND I'LL PERHAPS LET YOU LIVE--
--IS HE IN THE CITY?
IS HE HURT?
MOST OF ALL--

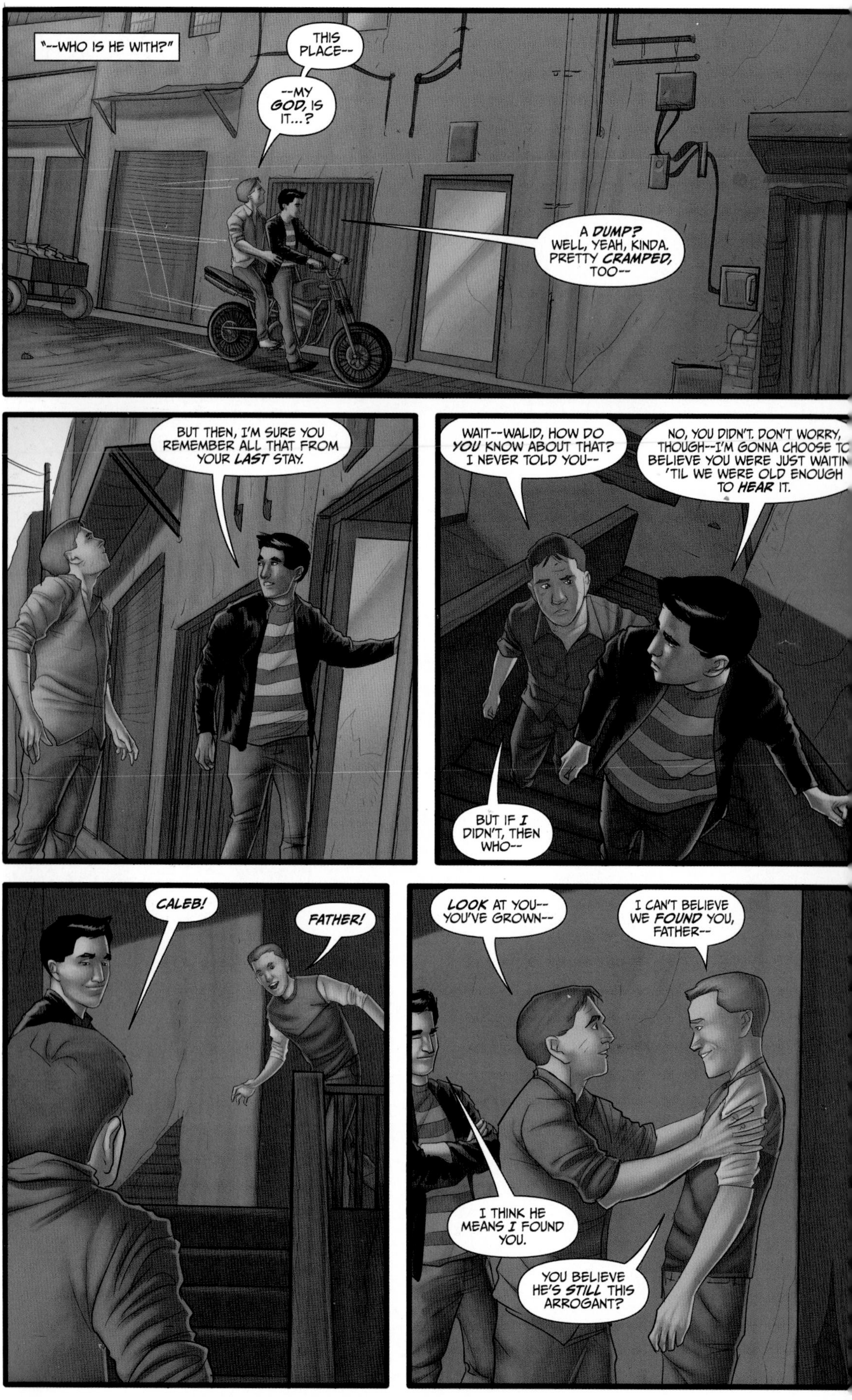
"--WHO IS HE WITH?"
THIS PLACE--
--MY GOD, IS IT...?
A DUMP? WELL, YEAH, KINDA. PRETTY CRAMPED, TOO--
BUT THEN, I'M SURE YOU REMEMBER ALL THAT FROM YOUR LAST STAY.
WAIT--WALID, HOW DO YOU KNOW ABOUT THAT? I NEVER TOLD YOU--
NO, YOU DIDN'T. DON'T WORRY, THOUGH--I'M GONNA CHOOSE TO BELIEVE YOU WERE JUST WAITIN 'TIL WE WERE OLD ENOUGH TO HEAR IT.
BUT IF I DIDN'T, THEN WHO--
CALEB!
FATHER!
LOOK AT YOU-- YOU'VE GROWN--
I CAN'T BELIEVE WE FOUND YOU, FATHER--
I THINK HE MEANS I FOUND YOU.
YOU BELIEVE HE'S STILL THIS ARROGANT?

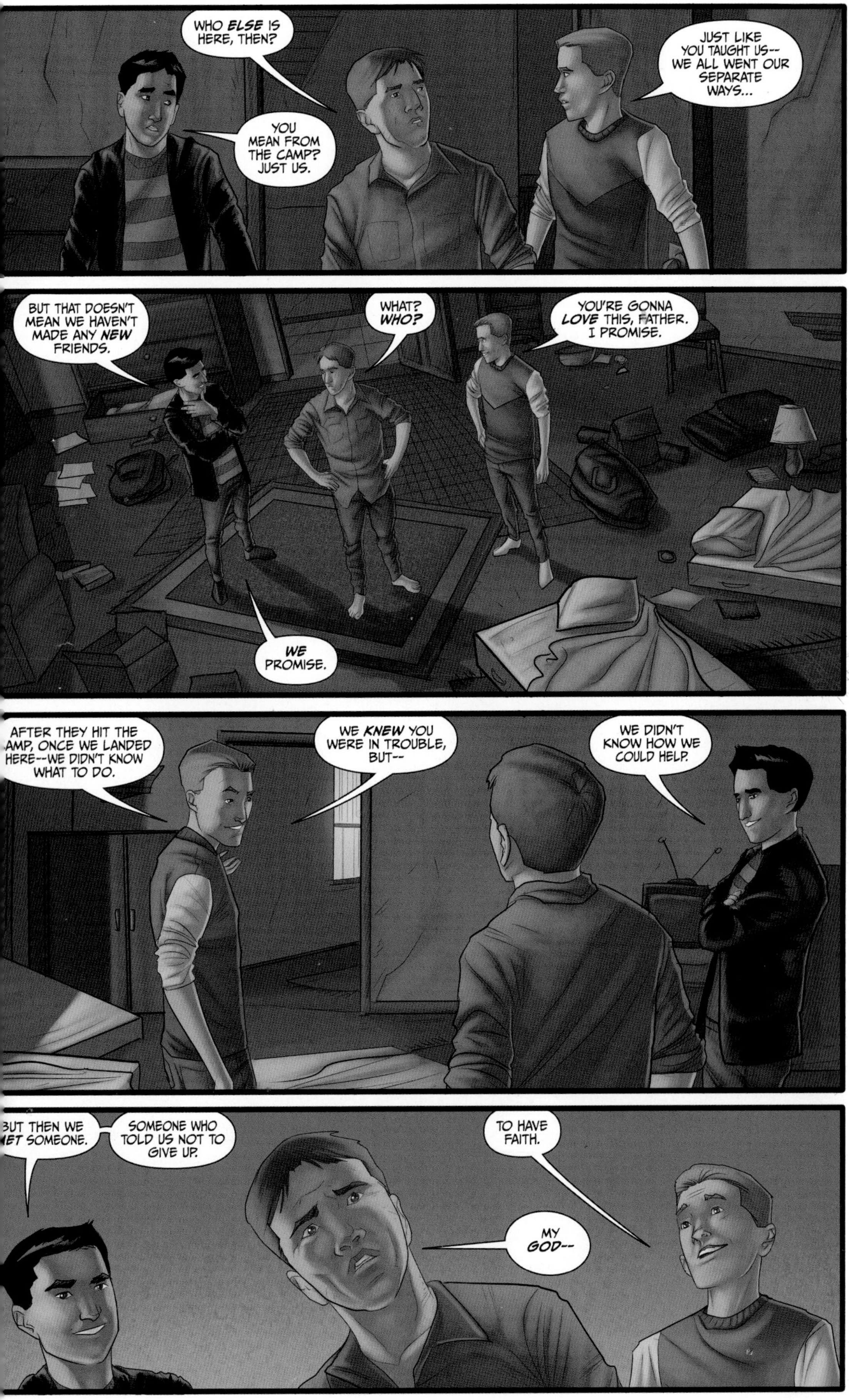
WHO ELSE IS HERE, THEN?
YOU MEAN FROM THE CAMP? JUST US.
JUST LIKE YOU TAUGHT US-- WE ALL WENT OUR SEPARATE WAYS...
BUT THAT DOESN'T MEAN WE HAVEN'T MADE ANY NEW FRIENDS.
WHAT? WHO?
YOU'RE GONNA LOVE THIS, FATHER. I PROMISE.
WE PROMISE.
AFTER THEY HIT THE AMP, ONCE WE LANDED HERE--WE DIDN'T KNOW WHAT TO DO.
WE KNEW YOU WERE IN TROUBLE, BUT--
WE DIDN'T KNOW HOW WE COULD HELP.
BUT THEN WE ET SOMEONE.
SOMEONE WHO TOLD US NOT TO GIVE UP.
TO HAVE FAITH.
MY GOD--

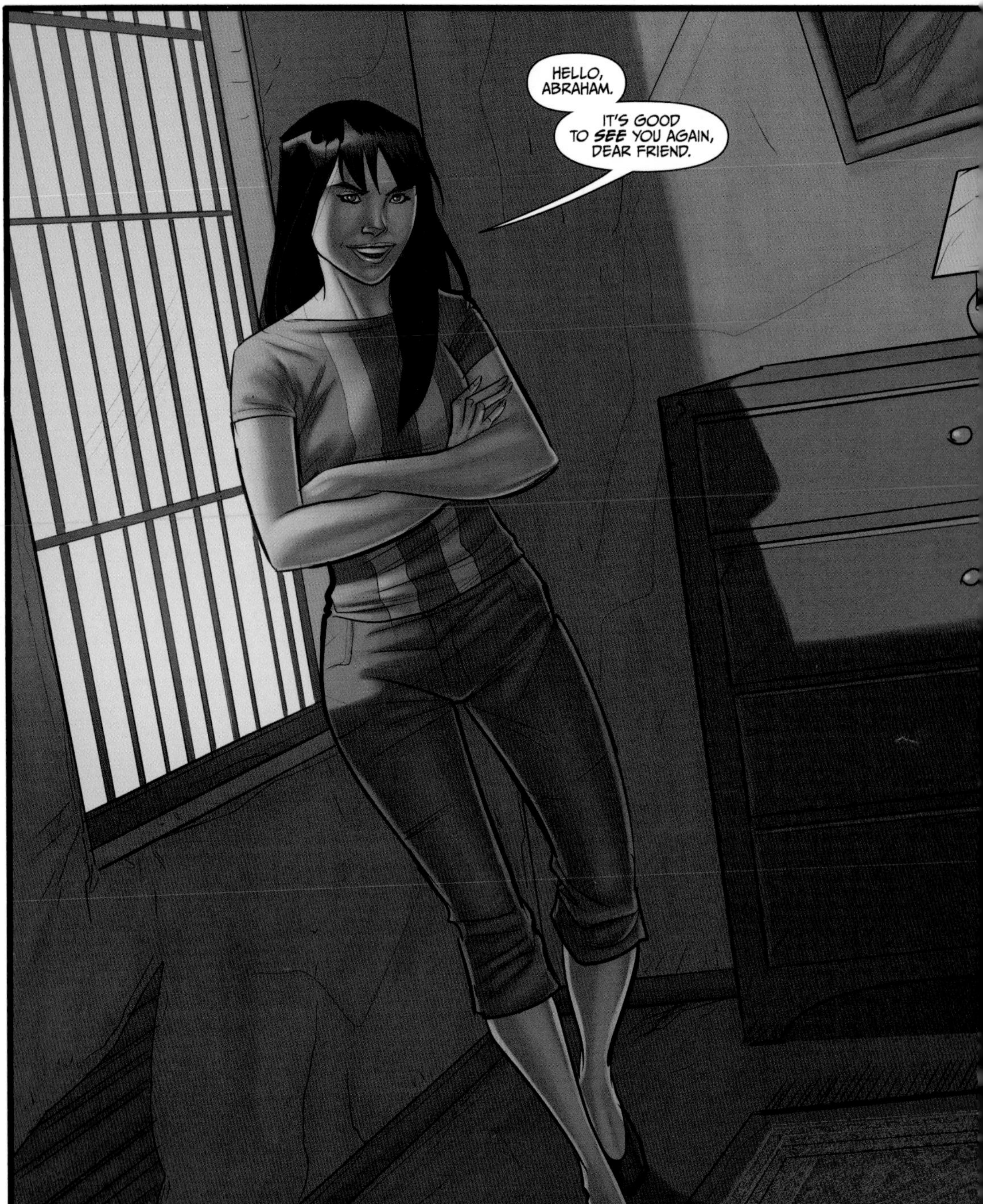
HELLO, ABRAHAM.
IT'S GOOD TO **SEE** YOU AGAIN, DEAR FRIEND.

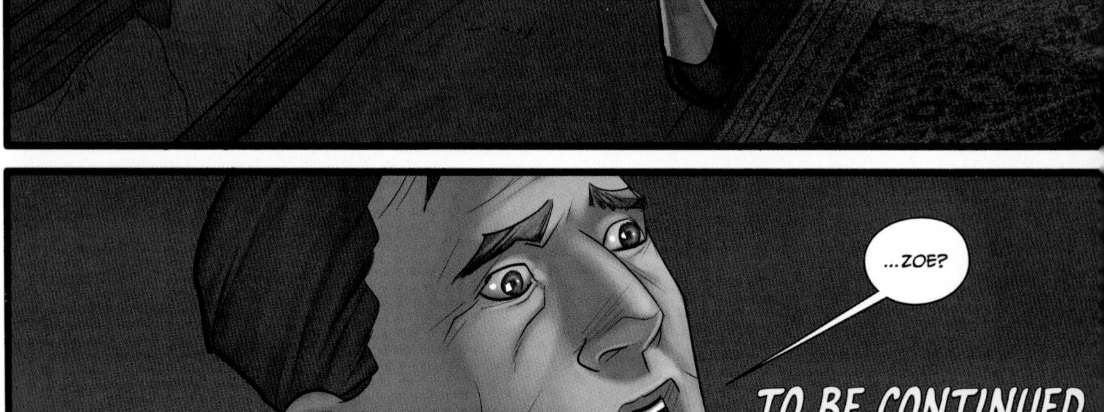
...ZOE?
TO BE CONTINUED...

THE ART OF MORNING GLORIES
FEATURING THE SELECTED WORK OF
JOE EISMA

MGA

Akiko

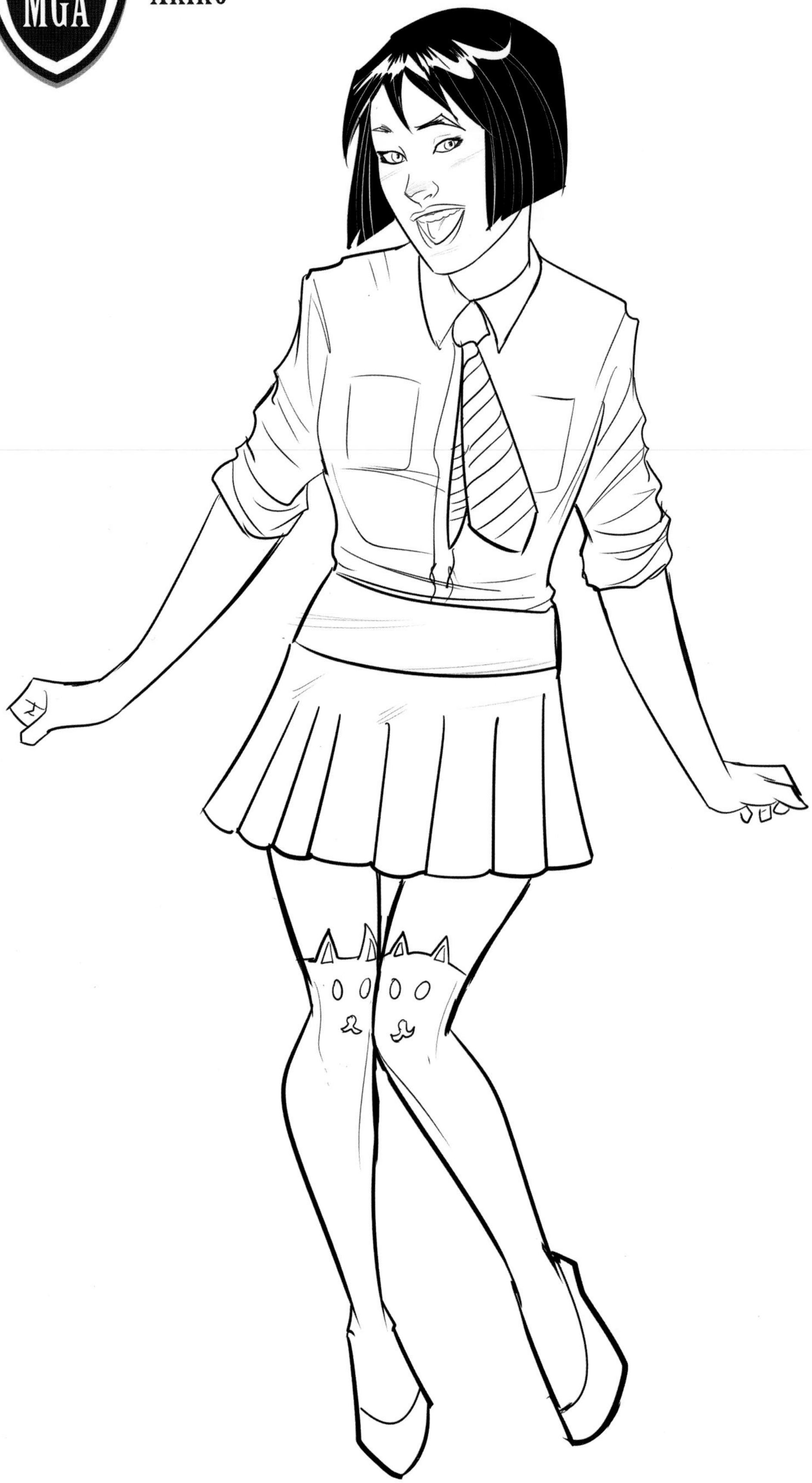

MGA

Jade

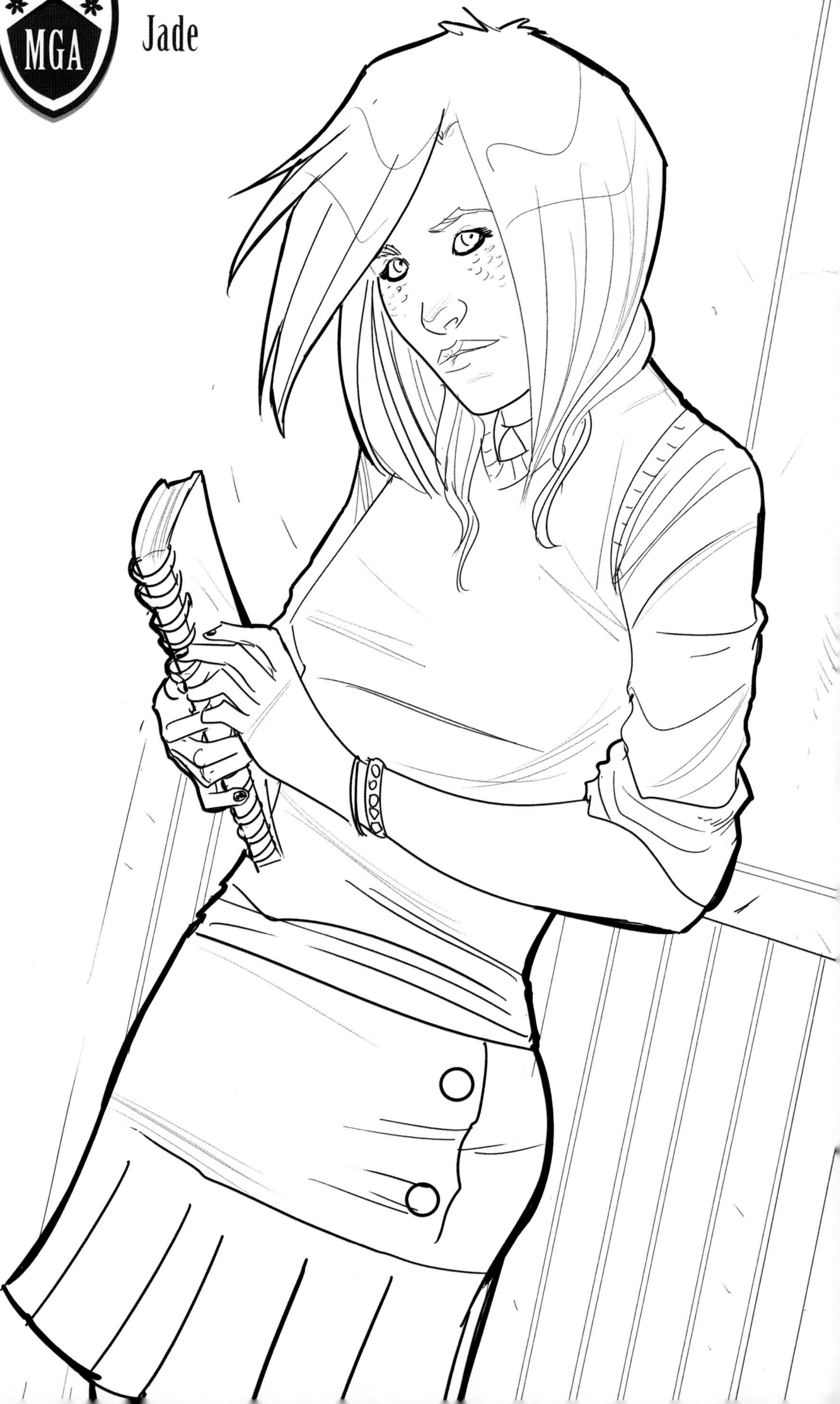

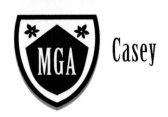

MGA

Casey

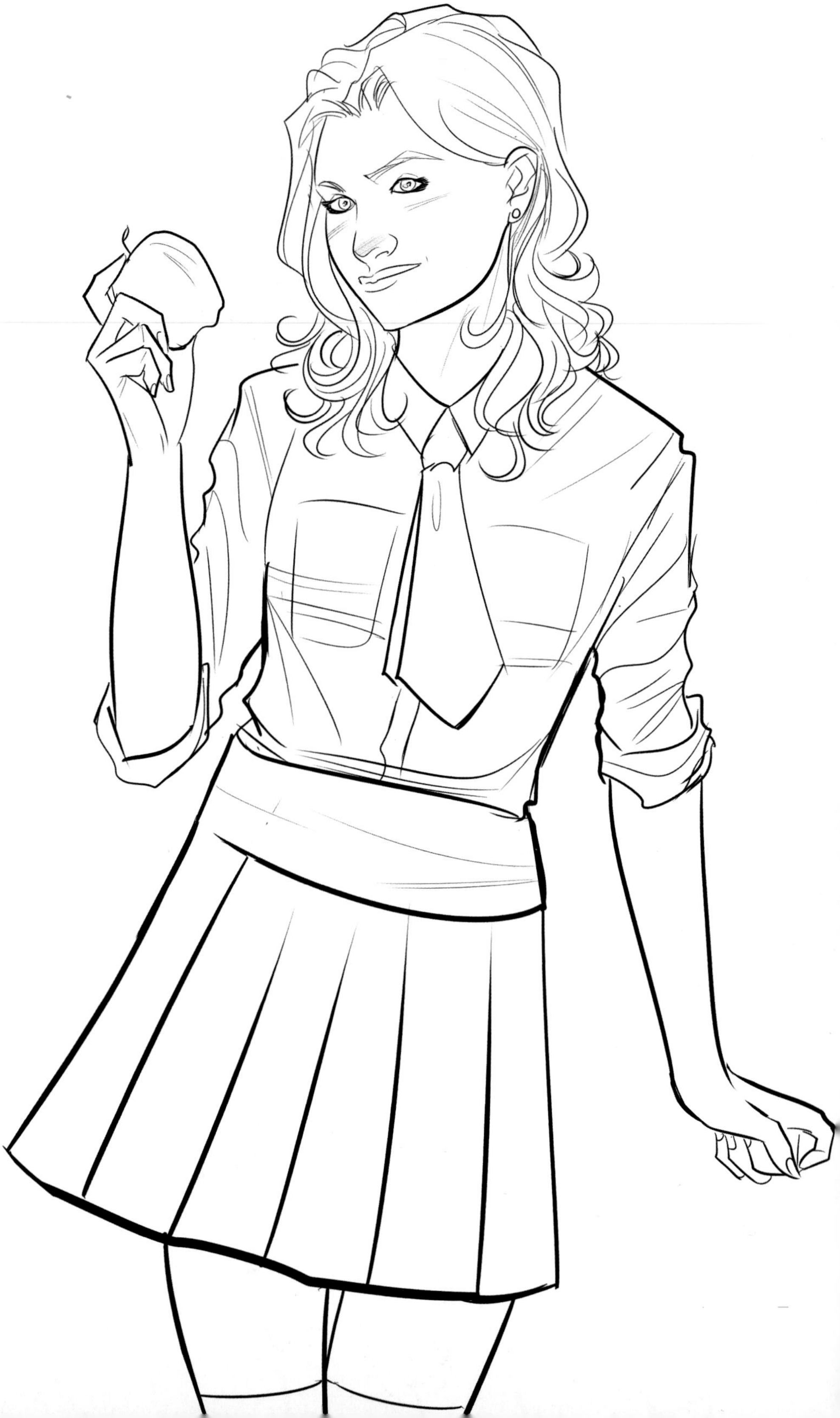

MGA

Casey

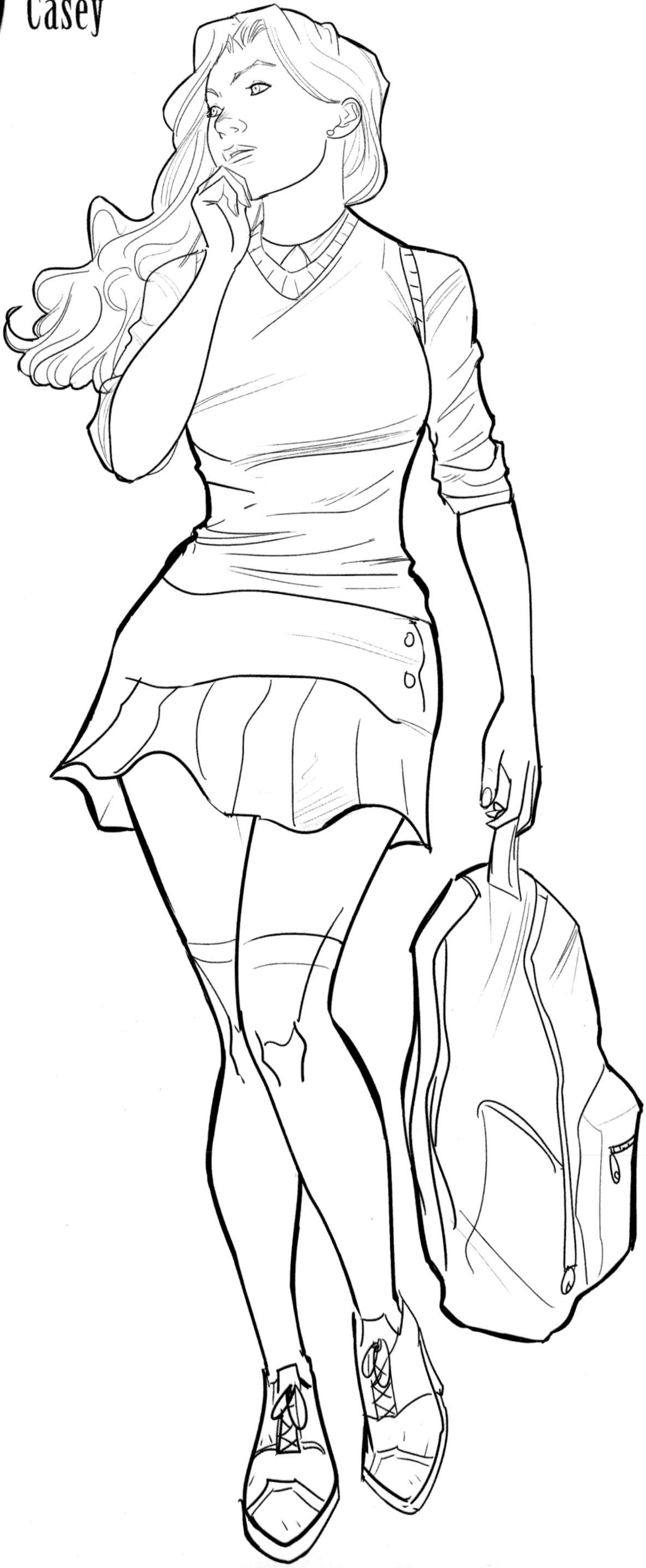

MGA

David

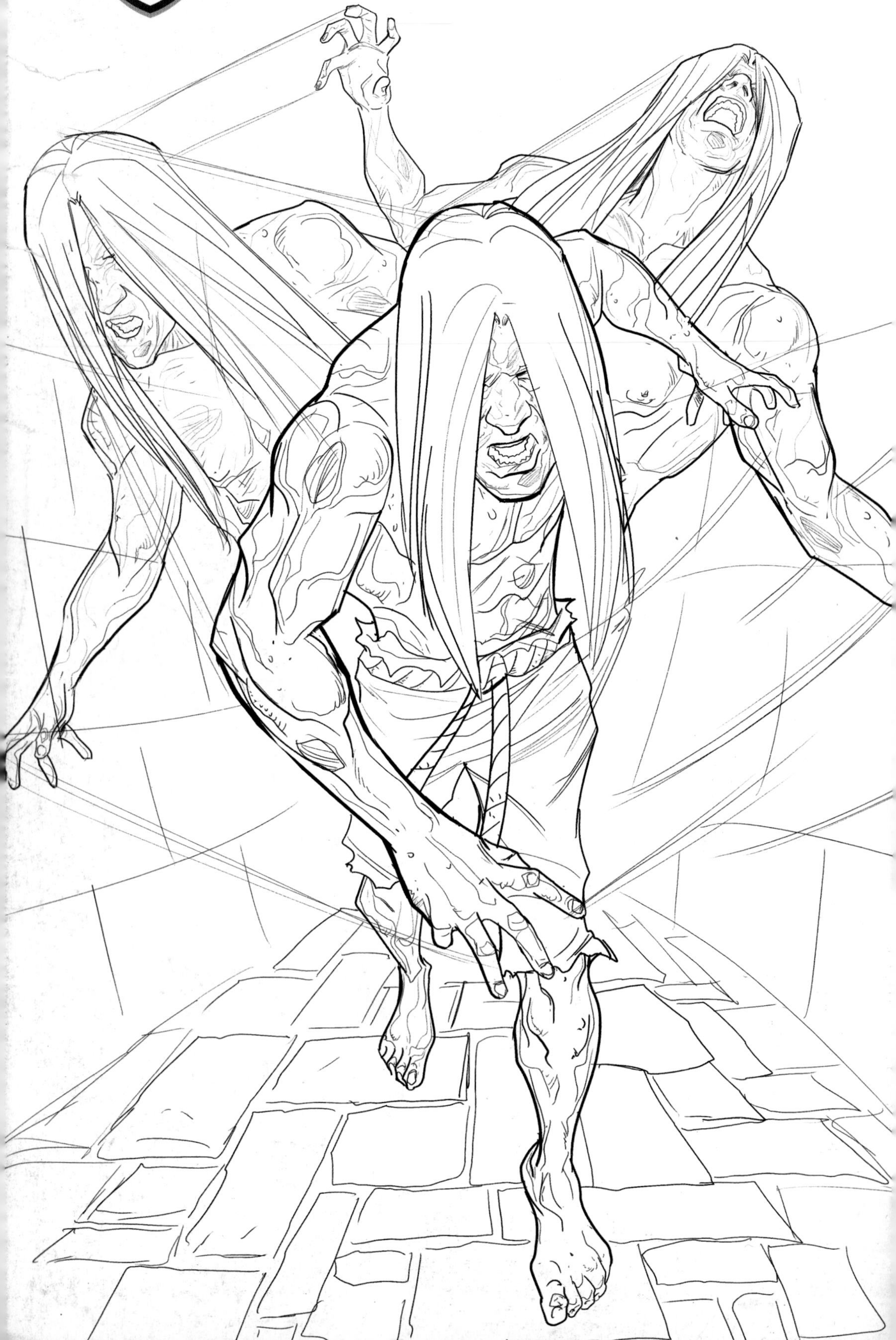